Go Forth, Christian Soul

To my dear wife, Judith

Go Forth, Christian Soul

The Biography of a Prayer

John S. Lampard

WIPF & STOCK · Eugene, Oregon

Wipf and Stock Publishers
199 W 8th Ave, Suite 3
Eugene, OR 97401

Go Forth, Christian Soul
The Biography of a Prayer
By Lampard, John Stuart
Copyright©2005 by Lampard, John Stuart
ISBN 13: 978-1-4982-0758-4
Publication date 1/1/2015
Previously published by Epworth Press, 2005

Contents

Acknowledgements vii
Introduction xi

1 The *Proficiscere*, 'Depart, Christian Soul' 1
2 From Birth to Maturity 30
3 Discovering the Ancestors 52
4 Extinction and New Species 79
5 Victorian Revival 99
6 Old and New Liturgical Uses 117
7 The Liberty to Die 150

Notes 176
Bibliography 194
Index 205

Acknowledgements

In many books the Acknowledgements end with an expression of grateful words to the writer's husband or wife. I want to reverse the order. No words can adequately express my deepest debt of gratitude to my dear wife Judith, who not only inspired, encouraged, offered critical judgements and endlessly proofread, but even funded my work on the dissertation which lies behind this book. Over the last ten years the *Proficiscere* has almost become a (very much loved) third person in our marriage, to the enrichment of us both. Of course our family, Rachel and Steve, Daniel and Anna, have followed the progress of this project (almost from childhood it seems) and supported me with their encouragement, interest and 'Dad, when are you going to finish it?'

This book is based on research I carried out which resulted in a degree of Doctor of Philosophy from Heythrop College, University of London. I have completely rewritten the dissertation, so I hope that the following pages read like the book they are intended to be. I have tried to keep much of the more technical material to the footnotes. However, I am glad to be able to offer words of appreciation to those without whom this book (and the prior dissertation) would not have been possible.

I am grateful to all the following. Because my Latin and French reached the end of their stumbling careers nearly fifty years ago at the O Level grade, I am grateful for advice and assistance with translations to: Fr Michael Cooley, Ms Wendy Cruise, the late Dr Joan Frayn, the late Mr Arthur Hands, the

Revd Ken Howcroft and Ms Jo Maskery. Medieval Latin often expresses itself in terms similar to 'The play what I wrote of', so I hope any classical scholar who reads this will not think that the footnotes are full of misprints. The following all gave generously of their time, wisdom and guidance in my researches either in correspondence, on the telephone or at arranged meetings: the late Mr George Every, the late Revd A. Raymond George, the Revd Bernard Green, the late Fr Pierre-Marie Gy, Dr Bernard Moreton, Dr Tom O'Loughlin, Dr Richard Price, Fr Anastasios Salapatas, the late Br Tristram SSF, Fr Chris Walsh, Dr Benedicta Ward and Prof. John Wells.

Dr James Leachman OSB, formerly of Heythrop College, University of London, and now at the Pontifical Liturgical Institute at St Anselmo's College, Rome, was my knowledgeable supervisor for nearly seven years and constantly sharpened and deepened my thinking. The Rt Revd Dr Kenneth Stevenson, Bishop of Portsmouth, and Dr Graham Gould of Kings College were the examiners of my dissertation and served me refreshing glasses of cold water as they gently grilled me on one of the hottest days of the summer.

No research can be carried out without the help of libraries and their staff. My gratitude to the resources and staff of the following libraries: the Bibliothèque Nationale and the Bibliothèque Mazarine in Paris, the Bibliotheca Vallicelliana in Rome, the Bibliothèque Municipale in Rouen, Cambridge University Library (Rare Books Department), Downside Abbey Library, Heythrop College Library, St Christopher's Hospice Library, St Deiniol's Residential Library, Oscott College Library, Dr Williams's Library, and the University of London Library. The Guardians of the Catacombs of Priscilla, Rome, kindly showed me the wonderful early church wall paintings of scenes from the *Proficiscere*. My thanks also go to fellow members of the Society for Liturgical Study and the *Societas Liturgica*, especially Dr John Baldovin who commented most helpfully on a draft of my work, and to members of the ecumenical Churches' Group for Funerals. In and out of

Acknowledgements

our meetings I have especially enjoyed the stimulating colleagueship of the Rt Revd Dr Geoffrey Rowell, the Revd Dr Peter Jupp, Mr David Hebblethwaite, Monsignor Kevin McGinnell, Fr Alan Morris and the Revd Dr Paul Sheppy. This book and I come out of the Methodist Church 'stable'. I am grateful to Dr Natalie Watson, the commissioning editor of Epworth Press, for her support and encouragement. I also express thanks to the Church for the gift of sabbatical leave and financial assistance for my research. In particular I want to express gratitude to fellow members of the Methodist Church Faith and Order Liturgical Sub-Committee, especially for the friendship and companionship of the Revd Neil Dixon, the Revd Michael Townsend, the Revd Don Pickard, Mr Dudley Coates, the Revd Judy Davies and Mrs Kathryn Schofield. All of these friends, in hours of writing, discussing and arguing over a period of over eight years, helped shape my liturgical awareness and appreciation. I express my thanks to the Revd Peter Francis, Warden of St Deiniol's Library, Hawarden, for granting me a three-month scholarship and chaplaincy, so that I could work at the library during a sabbatical, thus enabling me to write this book in the peaceful atmosphere of the library.

Finally, I want to say how much I owe to the wonderful African and Caribbean members of the three Methodist congregations I have had the privilege to serve in London over the last twelve years, in Southwark at Bermondsey Central Hall, and in Hackney at Dalston (Richmond Road) and Clapton (Downs Road). I thank them for the depth of their Christian devotion, their love and ministry to Judith and me, and most importantly for their assumption that it is right that 'the Reverend' should spend time on studying, as well as being their minister. I hope they will not be disappointed with the results.

John Lampard
23 September 2005
The Feast Day of St Thecla

Introduction

Prologue

I left the hotel where I was staying in Rome on a warm spring morning and took a crowded bus to the Corso Vittorio Emmanuele II, just across the Tiber from the Vatican. I then started to look around in the long street for the Bibliotheca Vallicelliana, a private academic library dating from the seventeenth century. Eventually I found it, set anonymously in a nondescript row of tall, grey-coloured stone buildings, and only indicating its presence by a very small brass plate. I had to climb two flights of wide stone stairs before pushing open a huge wooden door into the library entrance lobby, where a junior librarian was sitting at his desk.

Because I speak no Italian, I had armed myself with my passport, extra passport photographs, and a letter written in Italian and addressed to the 'Most illustrious director'. I was told this was the way the library director would wish to be addressed. The letter requested that I be allowed to see a particular and unique medieval manuscript held by the library. There was no guarantee that this letter would be sufficient to encourage the library to let me handle such a valuable and ancient document. The junior librarian duly read the letter, indicated that I should wait and disappeared out of his office. Shortly afterwards he came back and handed me a form to fill in with name, home address, passport details, my address in Rome and the university where I was studying, together with details of the manuscript I wanted to examine. When this had been completed, and handed back to him together with my passport and spare photograph, he again left me in his office. After a long wait he returned, motioning me to follow him. I was taken into the main part of the library, a large, magnificently decorated room with heavily embossed ceiling and book-lined walls. Sitting at the front, behind an imposing desk set on a stage area above the rest of the library, was the serious and important-looking illustrious director himself.

The junior librarian, in obvious awe of the director, handed my papers to him and crept back. The director took a careful look at me, then at my letter and the form I had completed, and finally at me again. Then, after stamping the form two or three times, he put my passport carefully in his desk, curtly motioning me to sit at a desk below and right in front of his, and wait. Some minutes later the junior librarian returned, carrying a leather-bound volume, and placed it on a stand on the desk in front of me. I took it carefully and started to move to a less conspicuous part of the library to study it, but the director indicated very firmly that I was to sit directly in front of him. I felt as though I was in school detention, but I had in my hands the manuscript I had wanted to see for some five years.

Gingerly opening the volume on its stand, I was able to look at the 1,000-year-old prayer book or Missal known in the library as *Codex* (book) B63. The manuscript was not like the beautifully illuminated manuscripts on display in libraries and museums. In fact there were no illustrations, nor were any of the capital letters illuminated, as it was very much a working book, for use by a monk or priest. As I looked through the pages, it was clear that it was the work of several different monks, each with his own style of handwriting. I was not able to study the binding or the whole of the manuscript in any great detail, but possibly the manuscript was a compilation of a number of orders of service written separately and bound together at a later date. Its lack of illuminations did not in any way detract from the sense of awe and fascination I felt as my trembling hands carefully turned the stiff parchment pages looking for the text of one particular prayer, known as the *Proficiscere*, its opening word, in Latin, meaning 'Depart'.

Introduction

Although my ability to read medieval Latin texts is very weak and self-taught (a crash course in London University Library), I soon found the prayer I was looking for, helpfully guided by the fact that the initial 'P' of the opening word, *Proficiscere*, was enlarged, so it stood out on the page. I had previously received from the Bibliotheca a rather poor quality photocopy of the pages covering the prayer, but to see the actual words and handle the manuscript for the first time for real was awesome. It was the equivalent of seeing and handling an original work of art in a gallery, after having previously possessed only a rather poor postcard copy.

The prayer took on a new life when examined in the original manuscript, revealing signs which were not visible in the photocopy. I could see the clarity of the letters beginning to fade when the ink in the monk's quill had started to run out on the rough surface of the brown parchment pages. Also visible were a regular series of small holes down the sides of each page. The medieval monk used these marks to guide light horizontal indentations between them, made with a sharp object. These, almost invisible, lines indicated the straight line for writing. For a moment I was at one with the medieval Benedictine monk who had in about AD 1000 copied out this prayer, perhaps in a monastery in Nursia in Italy, about seventy miles north of Rome.

Although liturgical scholars had previously noted that this unique prayer book contained a version of the *Proficiscere*, no one had ever before studied it in detail, transcribed its text or made a translation of it. In fact the world-renowned scholar who had collected the most comprehensive list of medieval manuscripts containing this prayer, and published the contents, had inexplicably missed the *Nursia* text. The other reason it excited me so much was that, although it was not the earliest, it was among the fullest and longest versions of this particular prayer, out of more than forty medieval manuscripts which contained it.

Using the original manuscript, my poor quality photocopy, a magnifying glass and a typed draft transcription, I began to work through the prayer, letter by letter and word by word, to check if I had previously transcribed it correctly. I discovered many minor errors I had made and amended these in pencil (no pens are allowed near a manuscript) on my draft transcription. The task of transcribing the medieval Latin was not helped by the fact that the writer had often abbreviated words to save space on the page. '*Anima*' (soul), for example, was '*aa*'; '*dei*' (God) could be '*di*'; and '*Christiana*' (Christian) was '*Xpiana*'. In addition, two or three words were often run together as though they were one, particularly if the scribe was getting near the end of a line. Although the library was cool, compared to the heat outside, after the hours it took me to complete my work I felt mentally drained, and longed for a cold drink at a local bar as soon as I could leave.

In return for handing back the *Nursia* manuscript, I received my passport from the director, and I eventually found my way back to my hotel for a rest, clutching my valuable day's work. I set out on my bed the pages of text, covered with the pencil corrections I had made to my very inadequate first draft. In that one, uniquely important, day I had made a major advance in the research I had been doing for five years. It was the holy grail of my research in studying a prayer that had increasingly dominated my life. In that high moment I knew that no one else but I could tell the world (or all who wanted to know) just what was contained in that unique manuscript.

Two days later I packed my bags and, not risking the precious pencil-amended *Nursia* transcription to the mercy of the airline by putting it in my suitcase, I carefully placed it in my small backpack, with my passport and currency etc., and set off for the airport. On returning late in the evening to Stansted, I caught the train and then a late bus to Hackney, where I lived. As I looked around for my possessions on leaving the bus I discovered that I had my suitcase but not my backpack. Within a sickening second I realized I had left it in the luggage rack of the Stansted train, for anyone to steal. The fact that it also contained my passport, travellers' cheques, credit cards and currency was, at that moment, a matter of

Introduction

secondary importance. The prospect of the cost, time and effort of needing to repeat the exercise, and further dealings with the illustrious director, was overwhelmingly awful.

Furious with myself for my utter stupidity, and with a sense of helpless desperation in the pit of my stomach, I tried to ring the railway company to report my loss. No one answered the phone, which was not surprising as it was nearly midnight and a bank holiday weekend. So I rushed back to the station to discover from a very helpful platform supervisor that the train on which I had left my backpack had returned to Stansted to pick up the last passengers of the night to bring them back to London. I will always be eternally grateful to her that she rang a colleague at Stansted station to report my loss.

After an agonizing period of waiting, the supervisor's colleague there eventually reported back to her that they had found the backpack still on the train. She said it would be given to the driver to bring back when he made his final return trip. Nearly two hours later, in the early hours of the morning, the most wonderful driver in the entire railway system walked down the platform waving my backpack and thrust it into my hands. I quickly checked to see that the precious *Nursia* transcription was there. It was only when I got home that I remembered to check that my backpack also still contained my passport, travellers' cheques, credit cards and currency. All were safe. Fortunately, the course of scholarship and my study of the life of the *Proficiscere* prayer had not been frustrated.

A life in brief

This book tells the story of the life of the *Proficiscere*, one version of which is contained in the *Nursia* text. It also asks the questions, 'What do you want to hear said when you are in the final moments of your life?' and, 'What words of prayer would help you to have a "good death"?' The prayer's traditional place in the liturgy of the Church is as a prayer to be said when a person is approaching death. It is best known either by its first words in Latin, *Proficiscere, anima*

Christiana, de hoc mundo, or by the opening words of its most famous translation, by Cardinal John Henry Newman, 'Go forth, Christian soul, on thy journey from this world.' The words 'on thy journey' are not supported by the Latin, but they were an inspirational addition by Newman. Because this book is the story of the life of a prayer rather than a person, it may seem strange to think of it as the subject of a biography. I have found it helpful and revealing to think of it having a life of its own. As the prayer is some 1,200 years old, and still very much alive and active, it must be one of the longest-living subjects of any biography.

This Introduction will focus on four of the events in the life of the prayer, and suggest why it is worthy of a biographical treatment. Many biographies carry photographs of the subject of the biography, so that the progress of the subject from youth to old age can be illustrated. As this is not possible with the *Proficiscere*, most chapters will present a version of the prayer to show how it has developed and changed to meet the circumstances of the age in which it was living. One of the themes that constantly runs through this biography is the way in which the *Proficiscere* has been able to adapt and change itself to speak to the differing needs of people in different ages. It carries within itself an 'excess of meaning', with the result that people of different generations have turned to it and found new significance in it in varying circumstances. It constantly re-adapts itself for a new age. Rather like a Shakespearean play (which does not change its actual words) it has been able to survive to speak afresh to new generations.

Medieval birth

The prayer known as the *Proficiscere* had its liturgical origins probably in a monastery in Northern France or Germany towards the end of the eighth century (760–800) so, inevitably, details of its birth are lost in the mists of history. There must, however, have been an occasion when it was first used, and thus came to birth. Some time towards the latter part of the eighth century, a monk lay dying in a Benedictine monastery in the Frankish Church (the description for the Church in that part of Northern Europe). The monastery would probably not have been a massive stone building, as were later monasteries, but one built of wood, cut out of a clearing in the forests which covered this part of Europe over a thousand years ago.

The monk may well have been dressed in a simple sackcloth tunic, and his body laid out on the chapel floor, on a bed of ashes, a symbol of penitence. The new prayer would have been written on a scrap of parchment, or perhaps in a little book of prayer material (a *libellus*), before it ever became part of a sacramentary. A sacramentary was a prayer book used by a priest. In a society which was mainly illiterate, and in which there were no printed books, he alone would have a copy.

It is perhaps not too dramatic to imagine that it was a dark night, with a cold winter wind whistling through the cracks in the wooden walls of the small chapel, causing the reed lamps to flicker and smoke. In the middle of the dark forest, during a long winter's night, it was easy to believe in the continuing power and presence of pagan gods and evil spirits, in spite of generations of Christian teaching about the power of Christ. The soul of the monk who was dying was about to leave the security of his body and, as a new and vulnerable entity, would face the perils of a journey before it reached the safety of heaven. As the monk lay dying, perhaps racked in pain (a sure sign that his soul was trying to wrench itself away from the dying body), his soul needed the assistance of powerful prayers, offered by the community, to enable it to leave the body and journey safely to heaven.

A prayer was needed to commend the soul of the monk to God, as a reminder of what God had done in the past in saving his people, and to ask for assistance from all possible sources. His brother monks may well have surrounded the prostrate man, reciting or chanting the words of this new prayer to aid the passage of his soul in his dying moments, as it made the fear-filled journey from this life to the next. One of the monks, or perhaps a group of them, reflecting on the spiritual needs of a dying monk, had composed this new prayer of assistance. The prayer met a newly felt need in the liturgical and spiritual life of the community, and thus a new liturgy started to come into being. Its purpose was to commend to God the soul of the dying monk and to ensure that his soul was assisted in its journey to heaven. In a sense it helped him have a 'good death', it offered him the liberty to die, because his soul would be protected by heavenly powers as it went forth from his body.

It is apparent that the prayer met with the approval of the other Benedictine monks and was added in due course to the sacramentary used in the monastery, being further copied and distributed within Benedictine monasteries. The earliest prayer book in which it is found, the Sacramentary of Gellone, was later taken from the north to Gellone in southern France before eventually ending up in the Bibliothèque Nationale in Paris, where it can be seen today.

This prayer, to be said when someone was dying, thus became part of the liturgical prayers of the Benedictine Order and of the Catholic Church. From this moment in history, when the prayer was first born, it began to develop a life of its own. It became a standard prayer in the liturgical books of the Western Church (but not in the Orthodox East) as part of a developing funerary liturgy entitled 'The Commendation of the Soul'. Its use spread to England, and a version is found in the prayer books used at Salisbury Cathedral (the Sarum Missals). It was in continual use in this country for the spiritual benefit of the souls of clergy and lay people for some 700 years. But then attitudes changed.

Extinction

In England, after the Reformation and the publication in 1549 of the first Prayer Book (the best known and longer version was published in 1662), dying members of the new Church of England were no longer allowed, after 700 years, to hear and be comforted by the familiar words of this prayer. In the reshaped and reduced funerary material in the Prayer Book (continued through into the 1662 version) the commendation contained in the *Proficiscere* was omitted, being judged no longer necessary, theologically unsound and of no spiritual value. Although there was material for the 'Visitation of the Sick', it was decided that no prayerful assistance was needed when dying as the person's ultimate destiny lay solely with God. This was the result of a new interpretation of the meaning of death. To oversimplify the new approach, the dying were left on their own with God and no prayers of commendation to God on their behalf would help them.

The *Proficiscere* was, however, retained in many private prayer books in which those who continued to espouse the Catholic faith (and those members of the new Church of England who did so in secret) could read and be comforted by it. On a visit to Oscott College, outside Birmingham, I was able to examine a rare example of such a prayer book, printed secretly abroad in 1614. It was immediately noticeable that, for a reason I cannot explain, of all the prayers in the book just one had been set in italic typeface. It was the text in English of a version of the *Proficiscere*.

Thus, during a period of religious persecution, the prayer went underground, and was used mainly in secret. The Elizabethan period was a time of Catholic persecution, which became heightened under James I. There was an unsuccessful attempt in 1605 by a group of Roman Catholics, whom we would describe today as 'terrorists', to kill the king, his family and members of Parliament by means of an explosion. The exposure of the Gunpowder Plot led to years of terrible persecution of Catholics and death for priests. Again, using one's imagination, it is possible to picture a family, still loyal to the Catholic faith, gathering around the bedside of one of its members as she lay dying. At times of extreme persecution no priest would have been available to offer a prayer, but perhaps the family had one of the private devotional books, such as the one held at Oscott, which contained a version of the prayer.

Or, perhaps, an older member of the family might have known the Latin version by heart, having heard it many times before. In a time of profound religious change, when so many of the familiar spiritual anchors had been torn adrift, the dying woman would still have been comforted by a prayer which fewer and fewer people would hear and know. The *Proficiscere* itself had entered the time when its life almost came to an end. But, it managed to survive.

New respectability

Moving on again through history, the third snapshot comes some 350 years later, on 3 October 1900, in the magnificent Birmingham Town Hall, to all intents and purposes a secular setting. There the English public heard for the first time a performance of Edward Elgar's oratorio version of John Henry Newman's *The Dream of Gerontius*, sung by a choir of 350 singers. The oratorio included a musical setting of some of the words of the *Proficiscere*, which in 1865 Newman had incorporated into his popular and influential poem *The Dream of Gerontius*. The words were sung in a particularly dramatic scene by a 'priest' and then by a massed chorus as the old man Gerontius lay dying. For the first time ever, the prayer had been taken out of its liturgical setting or its use in a book of devotions for a dying person. Now it had been included in an oratorio which could be performed at any time in any secular place. It had thus changed its nature and purpose to meet a new need, that of entertaining the paying public, who ever since have come in their thousands to listen to *The Dream of Gerontius*.

Although the first performance was not well received, the work has regularly been recorded and performed around the world, introducing many people for the first time to the words of the prayer, 'Go forth, upon thy journey, Christian soul! Go from this world!' Through Newman's popular poem and Elgar's oratorio its words were now being inserted ever more widely into the popular conscience. In fact, frequently, when I have talked to people about the subject of my research and this book, they have said, 'Ah yes, that was by Newman and Elgar.' As so often happens in life, their response was both right and wrong.

Worldwide audience

Our last scene illustrating the changes in the life of the *Proficiscere* is an event as recent as 1997. On the night of Saturday 30 August that year, as the clergy of Westminster Abbey retired safely to their beds, they would have had no idea of the maelstrom into which they would be cast during the next seven days. That night Diana, Princess of Wales, divorced wife of Prince Charles, died in a tragic car crash in Paris. After her body had been returned to this country, the decision was made that her funeral service should be held in Westminster Abbey. It was necessary to construct a service which would be suitable for such a difficult occasion, bearing in mind Diana's ambiguous role as the divorced wife of the heir to the throne, uncertainty about the nature of her faith, and the conflicting requirements of the Church of England, the Spencer family, the Government and the various, not wholly united, members of the Royal Family.

As Diana was one of the world's most famous women, the service was televised. It was watched by nearly three-quarters of the adult population of the United Kingdom, and by a worldwide audience estimated to be in the region of 2.5 billion. All those who listened to more than the startling eulogy given by Earl Spencer, Diana's brother, or the moving version of 'Candle in the Wind' sung by Elton John, will have heard an original modern English version (based on a New Zealand adaptation) of part of the *Proficiscere*. The decision was made that the Dean of Westminster, Dr Wesley Carr, standing by the catafalque, would speak the words, not as a prayer for the dying, as they had originally been intended, but as a

Commendation for the Dead. A new chapter had been written in the biography of the *Proficiscere*. It had returned to English liturgy in triumph.

Biographies and biographers

Before going any further with this story, I want to say something about biography, particularly if it is used as a means of studying a prayer, and a word about the role of the biographer. As I have indicated, the best and most appropriate way to handle the story of this prayer is to treat it as if it were a living being, which was born, grew and changed as the years went by. In other words, the approach taken to it should be that of a biographer. In recent years a biographical approach has been extended to the life of at least two cities (*London*, by Peter Ackroyd, and *Paris*, by Colin Jones) and the seasons of the year (*Autumn: A Spiritual Biography*, by Gary Schmidt). To these can now be added a prayer.

The role of biographers is usually to chart the background and birth of their chosen subjects, their development in life, the influences that shaped them, their career and achievements, aspects of their personal life, and a critical assessment of the value and importance of their lives. All these aspects of biography are relevant to a study of the life of this prayer, but there are two additional matters that always concern, or should concern, biographers.

The first is the relationship between the subject and the context in which they lived. Subject and context should always interact. It is possible to write a detailed account of a person's life, setting out what they did and where they went, but without ever providing the context that influenced that person's thoughts and actions. You can write about a missionary who went to Africa in the nineteenth century and of his or her adventures and work. But if the biography does not attempt to put the life in the context of the political, social and religious attitudes in Africa and Britain, it remains an isolated life, which cries out to be set in a wider context. Context is always

Introduction xxiii

important to make sense of the person's life and to give their biography a breadth of meaning. In order to write a biography of the prayer *Proficiscere*, which spans over 1,200 years, rather than a more normal three score years and ten, it will be necessary to sketch (all too often very briefly and inadequately) the historical contexts to which the *Proficiscere* responded and which shaped its life. Getting the balance right between a life and its context is a task that strains the skills of any biographer (and the length of the biography).

The second matter, which concerns a biographer, is the extent to which the biographer stands or attempts to stand at an objective distance from the subject of the book. Some biographers (such as Martin Gilbert on Winston Churchill or Roy Jenkins on William Gladstone) give a great impression of objectivity, standing back from their subject and in no way intruding themselves into the exploration of the life described. Other biographers (such as Boswell on Samuel Johnson, or more recently Humphrey Carpenter on Robert Runcie) recognize that they cannot be as objective as other biographers aim to be. They see their biographical explorations, and their involvement with their subject, as an essential part of the process. This approach inevitably seems more subjective, indeed Boswell and Carpenter entered into dialogues with their subjects and became characters in what they were writing. It will already be apparent that my own involvement in discovering the life of the *Proficiscere* forms an integral part of the biography, so I invite you to come on the journey of exploration with me. This also enables me, as I hope I have already shown, to communicate something of the excitement of sharing in original historical and biographical research. Of course it is not a wholly original journey. Parts of the path have already been explored by others, through their own researches and in books they have written. But no one else has joined the different parts together to make a consecutive biographical narrative of the life of the *Proficiscere*.

The choice of the *Proficiscere* as the subject of this biography is inevitably a personal one, but its study crystallized out of a wider interest in funerary prayers. When in 1990 the Methodist Church decided to produce a new service book, the *Methodist Worship Book*, I was invited to join the Liturgical Sub-Committee of the Faith and Order Committee, which had been given responsibility for this task. I was a member of a small sub-group, responsible for working on the initial drafts of the funerary material. An invaluable sabbatical enabled me to study the history of funeral services, ancient and modern, and the extensive liturgies associated with dying and death. One of the prayers in these liturgies which caught my eye once again was the *Proficiscere*.

I cannot say when I first met the *Proficiscere*. I know I heard a performance of Elgar's *The Dream of Gerontius* more than half a lifetime ago, but cannot say its words registered with me then. I think the words slowly entered my consciousness over the years, but they certainly registered sharply when I started to research funeral liturgies in a serious way. No other prayer associated with death has gripped hold of me in the way this prayer did. I purchased first a tape and later a CD of Elgar's work, and I started using the prayer in services associated with dying and death. Thus began a relationship that has now consciously lasted over ten years. I think I can claim to know the life and history of the *Proficiscere* more fully than anyone else. I certainly believe it has something to say to people who are dying in the twenty-first century, as it did at its birth in the eighth century. So I am delighted that I am its first biographer.

An outline of the biography

The four examples of the use of the prayer illustrate highlights in its life. This biography of the *Proficiscere* will show how it first came into written form and then subsequently changed and developed itself to express, liturgically and pastorally, appropriate ways in which dying could be interpreted and facilitated in a Christian context. In each selected period of history, a prevailing attitude to dying and death was 'matched'

Introduction

by the *Proficiscere* adapting itself to speak in new and appropriate ways. Today, in particular, it offers a new aid to 'letting-go', offering people the dignity of the liberty to die at a time when medicine and society often look on death as 'failure'.

Chapter 1 introduces the full text of the prayer, as set out in the *Nursia* manuscript, and provides a commentary and explanation of the contents of the prayer. It explores the wide variety of images and figures used in it. Chapter 2 explores the circumstances of the birth of the *Proficiscere* in the early medieval world. In particular it will answer the question, why was there a change in attitudes to death, which necessitated the birth of the prayer?

Many biographies, having recounted the subject's birth, say something about the forebears. The same pattern will be followed in Chapter 3, which looks at earlier liturgies, prayers and archaeological remains, which, as its possible ancestors, may have influenced the earliest form of the *Proficiscere*. Every new birth carries within it the genes of its forebears, and this chapter looks at what might be called the possible ancestors of the medieval prayer.

Chapter 4 deals with the most difficult years in the life of the *Proficiscere*, when it almost died. As has already been mentioned, at the time of the Reformation it fell out of favour, disappearing from the English liturgies because of another change in the way death was interpreted. The chapter explains how this happened and then shows how the prayer survived in a variety of books of personal devotion. Chapter 5 recounts its revival in the later Victorian era, as it found new life and significance in Newman's *The Dream of Gerontius*, and through the musical setting of Edward Elgar. They brought it to a new prominence. Then the social changes brought about by the First World War led to the prayer no longer being shunned, as it found a new respectability again.

Chapter 6 shows how the *Proficiscere* was able to find not only new places but also new purposes in English liturgical books at the end of the twentieth century. As the *Proficiscere* has grown older, it has changed its wording (both in Latin and in English), altered its use, context and role, both liturgical and non-liturgical, in order to continue to express a Christian hope in changing pastoral contexts.

The last chapter explores the significance of the life of the *Proficiscere* today. It discusses how death is seen in new ways in modern times, and the role that the use of the *Proficiscere* can play in this further reinterpretation of death. To assist this understanding it also looks at how the power or 'efficacy' of the words of a prayer can be seen to be effective.

The *Proficiscere* still expresses Christian hope in the face of death, offering people the liberty to die when many of the traditional certainties of heaven are less clear in a so-called secular society. In particular, the prayer offers itself as a new pastoral aid to 'letting-go' when medicine and society often look on death as 'failure'. This is the reason I call it a 'euthanastic' prayer, as it is a means through which a person can have a good death as they are helped to be released from holding on to life. It is the means by which a person can find the strength to let go of this life and find the liberty to die.

Although it is 1,200 years old, 'Go forth, Christian soul, on your journey from this world', reveals itself to be a prayer which has been a blessing to Christians ever since its birth, as it still is today. As a venerable, but still lively, contributor to the spiritual life of Christians, it is a worthy subject of a biography.

I
The *Proficiscere*, 'Depart, Christian Soul'

The Introduction has said much *about* the *Proficiscere*, but has not said *what it is*. We can therefore turn to the first full 'picture' of the prayer, not as it was at birth, but in its full maturity, at the moment of its most glorious development. It is like the 'best' photograph of someone on the front cover of his or her biography, in this case it is the one from the late eleventh- or early twelfth-century sacramentary, which originated in Nursia in Italy. I have already described my examination of the text in the Bibliotheca Vallicelliana in Rome. As it is, in a sense, a 'photograph I took', it is of particular significance to me, revealing as it does the full splendour of the prayer. So let me introduce you to the full *Nursia* text.

The *Nursia* text

Although the rubric refers to two prayers, you will notice that the prayer falls into three sections. The first begins, 'Set out, Christian soul'; the second, 'May the holy angel Michael'; and the third, and longest section, begins 'Set free, Lord, the soul of your servant'. The third part is known as the *Libera* (set free). The first two were sometimes joined together as one. The following is my translation of the Latin text.

Rubric. Here the commendation of the soul begins with two prayers.

Set out, Christian soul, from this world.
In the name of God the Father Almighty who created you.
In the name of Jesus Christ, Son of the living God, who suffered for you.
In the name of the Holy Spirit, who was poured out upon you.
In the name of angels and archangels.
In the name of thrones and dominions.
In the name of principalities and powers and of all the heavenly authorities.
In the name of cherubim and seraphim.
In the name of all the human race which is sustained by God.
In the name of patriarchs and prophets.
In the name of apostles and martyrs.
In the name of confessors and bishops.
In the name of priests and deacons and of every rank of the catholic church.
In the name of monks and anchorites.
In the name of virgins and faithful widows.
Today his place is made in peace and his dwelling in heavenly Jerusalem.

May the holy angel Michael, who won the leadership of the heavenly army, uphold you.
May the holy angels of God come to meet you, and may they lead you into the holy city Jerusalem.
May the blessed apostle Peter, to whom the keys of the kingdom of heaven were given by the Lord, receive you.
May Saint Paul, who was worthy to be a vessel of God's choice, help you.
May Saint John, elected to be the apostle of the Lord, to whom were revealed the secrets of heaven, intercede for you.
May the saints, chosen apostles of the Lord, to whom have been given the power of binding and loosing, pray for you.
Go in peace, in the name of the Father, and of the Son, and

The Proficiscere, 'Depart, Christian Soul'

of the Holy Spirit, who is to lighten your way into eternal life. (Amen. Pray for us.)

Lord, Holy Father of Jesus Christ, receive the soul of your servant in peace and forgive all his sins.

Saviour of the world, with the Father and the Holy Spirit, receive, Lord, the soul of your servant into your blessed abode.

Set free, Lord, the soul of your servant from all the dangers of hell and from all evil tribulations.

Set free, Lord, the soul of your servant, as you set free Noah from the flood.

Set free, Lord, the soul of your servant, as you set free Elijah and Enoch from the common death of the world.

Set free, Lord, the soul of your servant, as you set free Abraham through faith and trustfulness.

Set free, Lord, the soul of your servant, as you set free Lot from Sodom and from the flames of fire.

Set free, Lord, the soul of your servant, as you set free Isaac from the sacrifice and from the hand of his father Abraham.

Set free, Lord, the soul of your servant, as you set free Jacob by the blessing of your majesty.

Set free, Lord, the soul of your servant, as you set free Moses from the hand of Pharaoh, king of the Egyptians.

Set free, Lord, the soul of your servant, as you set free Jonah from the belly of the whale.

Set free, Lord, the soul of your servant, as you set free David from the hand of King Saul and from Goliath and from all his bonds.

Set free, Lord, the soul of your servant, as you set free Daniel from the lion's den.

Set free, Lord, the soul of your servant, as you set free the three young men from the furnace of blazing fire and from the hands of an evil king.

Set free, Lord, the soul of your servant, as you set free Susanna from false witness.

> Set free, Lord, the soul of your servant, as you set free the human race through the passion of our Lord, Jesus Christ.
>
> Set free, Lord, the soul of your servant, as you set free Peter and Paul from prisons.
>
> Set free, Lord, the soul of your servant, as you set free Thecla from the midst of the spectacle.
>
> So deign to set free the soul of this man and allow him to dwell with you in the blessings of heaven. Through [Jesus Christ our Lord. Amen.]

Whenever I read through this prayer and think of it being said to a dying person, my first reaction is, perhaps like yours, what a way to go! I hope you feel something of its pastoral power and strength, as a person slips into death. But it is also likely that there are some words, names and references, together with theological and historical issues, which are not clear. Who were all the ranks of the Church? Who was Thecla, who is mentioned in the climax of the prayer? Why were the particular biblical figures mentioned included in this prayer? The rest of this chapter will offer an explanation of these and other points.

A commentary on the text of the *Proficiscere*

In this commentary I try to set out what the *Proficiscere* says about life and death. Some of the views and understandings are not those that are commonly held today, but you may wish to consider you own views in the light of them. Some of the references or biblical characters mentioned in the prayer are well known, others less so, but for completeness this commentary does not discriminate. You can also look up the biblical references for further details. In the following commentary some lines are commented on which do not appear in the *Nursia* text. Although it is one of the longest and fullest versions, some other manuscripts include lines or phrases not in it, and they are included here set in square brackets [ ].

'Set out' or 'Depart'

(I have used these words rather than 'Go forth', as they were more usually used in translations, until 'Go forth' was introduced by Newman.) A number of manuscripts do not begin with this word. Before 'Depart' they say words such as, 'Farewell in Christ, peace be with you. Amen.'[1]

I have not discovered any prayer which begins with such a startling or powerful word of command as 'Depart'. The instruction or command to the dying person, or to their soul, is unique in funerary liturgy, or indeed in any other liturgy. The opening line of the *Proficiscere*, 'Depart, Christian soul, from this world', addressed at the moment of death, is an instruction, encouragement, authorization or permission for the soul to set out, to depart, or to journey from this world. It offers to people who are dying the liberty to offer themselves to God in death by giving up their souls. They have come to the end of their struggle in this life and they are told, on the highest authority, that they may go. As they find the liberty to die they can accept death. This is why I call it a euthanastic prayer. The word 'euthanasia' is often misused to mean mercy killing, but the word really means a good death, death at the right time in the right way. The end of the first part of the prayer affirms that the place of the soul will be in peace in the heavenly Jerusalem, so whatever the pain and agony, its destiny is to be with God. In death a Christian hopes for a euthanastic death.

Although a word which can be translated 'journey' does not appear in any Latin version, the opening words, which suggest setting out, and the final words of destination ('the heavenly Jerusalem' etc.), taken together suggest a journey. In addition, the idea of the journey of a soul was well established in medieval spirituality. Dying people received the *viaticum*, the bread and wine of Holy Communion, which was food for the journey. A writer called Pseudo-Dionysius (hereafter called Dionysius) from the eastern Church, whose work was known in the eighth-century western Church, suggested a structure of procession and return.

Inspired by the Father, each procession of the Light spreads itself generously towards us, and, in its power to unify it stirs us by lifting us up. It returns us back to the oneness and deifying simplicity of the Father who gathers us in.[2]

Dionysius supported his argument by using two biblical verses, James 4.8, which is the procession from the Father, and the doxological ending of Romans (Rom. 11.36), 'from him (and through him) and to him are all things',[3] which is both procession and return. The writer of this prayer can be said to view the moment of death as a moment when the soul is separated from the body, and then joins the second half of the procession to return to its creator in 'the heavenly Jerusalem'. 'The motif of procession and return ... clearly influenced Dionysius. Through him, among others, it profoundly shaped Christian theology and its systematic organisation, especially as *exitus* and *reditus* (going out and returning).'[4] In death the soul sets out on a journey where it is accompanied home by the returning heavenly host which has come out to greet it.

'Christian'

The two earliest manuscripts containing the *Proficiscere* are known as *Gellone* and *Rheinau* (we will learn more of them in the next chapter). It is a matter of note and some speculation that *Gellone* did not include the word 'Christian', and that *Rheinau* was the first text to include it (assuming that *Gellone* pre-dates *Rheinau*). Whichever was the first text, it is clear that one did not refer to the soul as being 'Christian'. In fact *Gellone* is only one of three medieval texts of the *Proficiscere* to commend a 'soul' rather than a 'Christian soul'. It is always possible that these were copying errors, although the omission of such a significant word as 'Christian' at the beginning of the prayer might be judged to be a surprising type of omission.

Other comments can only be more speculative. Did the author or copyists assume the soul was Christian, especially if the person concerned was a monk or a nun, so they did not need to be addressed with the adjective? All such speculation is only argument from a lack of information.

'Soul'

The instruction to depart is made to the soul, clearly suggesting a concept of the separation of the body and soul at death. It is not easy, and some would argue impossible, to enter into the cultural mindset of the monk who first wrote this prayer, as he contemplated the passage of the soul. As far as it is possible to achieve it, an understanding of the contemporary view of the relationship between the body and the soul is necessary for an appreciation of this part of the prayer. The Bible is often thought to speak of body and soul (Hebrew *nephesh*; Greek *psyche*; Latin *anima*) in both unitary and dualistic ways. In other words, they are sometimes thought of as being inseparable as if one, but at other times they are thought of as two distinct entities.

It is a matter of much dispute among biblical scholars as to the extent or accuracy of this picture. However, in medieval times, under the influence of Platonic thought, a clearer dualism developed. In Platonic thought the soul was both pre-existent and immortal. It inhabited the human body and was imprisoned in it until death, when it was set free to return to God. This model of embodiment suggested that the soul needed divine help and assistance, beyond its own capability, as it struggled to free itself from the body as the body approached death. The body could not live without the soul, but the soul would continue to live without the body after death.

However, before entering into heaven, the soul of a fundamentally just person had to spend a time of journeying, particularly in early medieval thought, passing through a cleansing purgatorial fire. This was necessary because the soul was still encumbered with the effects of temporal sins, although they had already been forgiven. This was seen as a cleansing process, because in early medieval thought no concept of purgatory as a place had begun to develop. Jacques Le Goff said that the idea of purgatory as a place did not develop until the twelfth century and added, 'The Carolingian Church [Frankish Church] showed little interest in purgatorial fires and introduced no innovations.'[5] The prayer clearly reflects a dualistic view, with the soul as a distinct entity. It was first written to assist the soul in its journey to heaven, as it wrenched itself from the prison of the body, in what is often referred to as the 'agony'.

'From this world'

These words emphasize what has already been said. Death involved a journey for the soul from earth to heaven. This was a different idea from that of the early Church, where the concept of resurrection held together body and soul as one, without any idea of a journey.

'In the name of God the Father Almighty who created you. In the name of Jesus Christ, Son of the living God, who suffered for you. In the name of the Holy Spirit, who was poured out upon you.'

The strong trinitarian statement repeats the common formula for the work of God as Father, Son and Holy Spirit. A number of the later texts, such as *Nursia*, contain the mark ε before or after each of the names of the three persons of the Trinity, indicating, presumably, that the sign of the cross was to be made at this point. Each of the three lines begins with the words 'In the name of ...' emphasizing an authorization, and an authorization which has divine power and influence.

This use of 'In the name of ...', repeated for each person of the Trinity, may have two reasons for it. First, it allows three different attributes to be given to the named person of the Trinity, that is, creation, suffering and pouring out (with the blessing of the attribute assigned to the dying person). Second, 'In the name ...' is a powerful linking phrase, which holds

The Proficiscere, 'Depart, Christian Soul'

together the work of the Trinity, the angels and the people of the Church.

It is interesting to note that only one manuscript adds to the reference to Jesus' death the words 'on the cross', to signify the cross as the place of death.[6] This is an example of a creative flourish by one copyist which was not adopted by others.

'In the name of angels and archangels. In the name of thrones and dominions. In the name of principalities and powers and of all the heavenly authorities. In the name of cherubim and seraphim.'

The third part of the opening section of the prayer authorized the departing in the names of nine types of angelic being; angels, archangels, thrones, dominions, principalities, powers, heavenly authorities, cherubim and seraphim. According to Dionysius, angels (a generic title which includes all of these) were messengers and agents of God who communicated with people and interceded for them. The following biblical references indicate that there is stronger biblical authority for some types of angelic being than others.[7] (Different translations of the Bible sometimes use different terms for some of these.)

Angel		Numerous references in the Old and New Testaments
Archangel	2	1 Thess. 4.16; Jude 9
Thrones	1	Col. 1.16
Dominions	2	Eph. 1.21; Col. 1.16
Principalities	5	Rom. 8.38; Eph. 3.10; 6.12; Col. 1.16; 2.15
Powers	8	Eph. 1.21; 3.10; 6.12; Col. 1.16; 2.15; Titus 3.1; Hebrews 6.5; 1 Peter 3.22
Authorities	2	Eph. 1.21; Col. 1.16
Cherubim	1	Heb. 9.5
Seraphim	0	(in NT) but in OT see Isa. 6.1–7; 14.29; 30.6; Ezek. 1.27 (and cf. Num. 21.6–9 and Deut. 8.15)

It is clear from this rather sparse and unco-ordinated listing that New Testament writers had not developed any systematic theological understanding of the work and role of angels, nor any sense of hierarchy. It was left to the theologians of the early Church to bring order, meaning and importance to these nine categories of angel.

In the early Church, as the theology of angels developed, there was no settled order of importance, different writers listed them in different ways. What is noticeable is that once the original author of the *Proficiscere* had settled on an order (different from all the others in the early Church) it remained one of the most settled parts of the text.

'In the name of all the human race which is sustained by God'

The whole human race is summoned in the last part of the triad to play its part and offer its authority. Thus the triune God, angels of all ranks and all humanity, together join in authorizing the soul to depart. The *Proficiscere* then follows the pattern of linking pairs of ranks, echoing the linked pairs of angelic beings earlier in the text.

'Patriarchs and prophets'

The patriarchs were considered to be the fathers of the human race and the great figures in the formation of the People of Israel. They were Abraham, Isaac and Jacob, together with the twelve sons of Jacob (Gen. 35.22–26). In Stephen's speech in Acts 7.9 he says, 'The patriarchs, jealous of Joseph, sold him into Egypt', and the writer of Hebrews refers to Abraham individually as a patriarch (Heb. 7.4).

The prophets were the inspired deliverers of God's message. In a narrow sense they were Isaiah, Jeremiah, Ezekiel and the twelve 'minor' prophets. However, the title could be applied more widely to include Moses (Deut. 18.15–18), and David (Acts 2.29–30).

The Proficiscere, *'Depart, Christian Soul'*

'Apostles and martyrs'

The apostles were, of course, the twelve primary followers of Jesus, although there is not complete agreement as to the names (cf. Matt. 10.2–4; Mark 3.16–19; Luke 6.13–16). The title was also bestowed on Matthias after the death of Judas Iscariot (Acts 1.26) and on Barnabas and Paul (Acts 14.14). Paul also frequently claimed it for himself as God's gracious act (e.g. 1 Cor. 1.1; 2 Cor. 1.1).

The martyrs (literally 'witnesses') were originally those who had witnessed Jesus' death and resurrection (Acts 1.8, 22), but when persecution developed, especially under the Roman emperor Diocletian, martyrdom involved suffering and death for faith in Jesus Christ. Those who remained faithful, even to death, were especially honoured by the Church. The significance of 'martyrs' in the context of the *Proficiscere* may be related to the fact that they were honoured as powerful intercessors. The word 'saint' does not appear in any of the early medieval versions of the text, but they were counted as saints and held rank before them.

It is also worthy of note that two later texts, after 'apostles' add the words 'and evangelists', reflecting an emphasis in the later medieval Church on a new minor order of ministry, judged to be of increasing importance. The word 'evangelist' is used in the Vulgate (a translation of the Hebrew Old Testament into Latin) for the announcer of good news (Isa. 41.27) and for a preacher of the gospel, from the end of the fourth century.[8]

'Confessors and bishops'

Confessors in the early Church were those who suffered in some way for holding their faith in Jesus Christ, but did not actually die as a martyr. It was later a title conferred by the Pope on men of notable holiness. The English king Edward the Confessor (1003–66) was declared as such by Pope Alexander III in 1161, when he was also declared a saint.

Bishops were the highest of the three orders of ministry in the Church, distinguished from priests mainly by their authority to confer holy orders and to confirm people.

'In the name of priests and deacons and of every rank of the catholic church'

Priests were the middle rank of the three orders of ministry. Deacons were the lowest of the three ranks, traditionally traced back to the appointment of the seven in Acts 6.1–6. They were appointed so that the twelve apostles could devote themselves to prayer and the ministry of the word. The fact that, as soon as he was appointed a deacon, Stephen promptly preached the longest sermon recorded in the New Testament, Acts 7.2–56 (and became the first Christian martyr) is generally overlooked in writings about the diaconate. The role of deacons grew and then diminished in the Church, until generally the rank had become one held for a year or so before ordination to the priesthood. Vatican II did reintroduce a permanent diaconate, but every church seems to be struggling creatively to understand what this is.

The phrase 'every rank of the catholic church' introduces the final categories in this section. It can be noted that, for Dionysius, the laity consisted of three groups, monks, communicants and those being purified (catechumens, penitents and the possessed).[9] However, he later abandons this strict hierarchy and at least implies other groups.[10] It would appear, although there is no direct evidence, that the writer of this prayer included this concept of 'rank'.

'Monks and anchorites'

Monks belonged to a number of different orders, such as the Benedictines and the Cistercians, and lived in monasteries. The 'rule' they lived by dictated the nature and style of life they lived.

Anchorites were people who withdrew from the world to

live a solitary life of prayer, silence and mortification of the flesh. The *Rheinau* and one other text are the only manuscripts to omit the mention of anchorites and not to substitute any other word in its place. Because of this omission, and the fact that there is no substitution, means that the flow of the lines with two groups in each is strangely lost. It is not clear why these two versions of the *Proficiscere* should have omitted them. Perhaps a too-simple solution is that anchorites were not present in the community where this version of the prayer was developed so they were not included, but if this is the case why is there such a strange break in the rhythm of the prayer? 'Hermits' was an addition in place of 'anchorites' in many of the later texts. The difference between the two is not an easy one to define as the interrelated relationship between hermits and religious communities varied over time.[11]

Part of the problem lies in the fact that definitions altered over the medieval period. In the Rule of St Benedict, written in c. 540, the two words are used as titles interchangeably. Writing about different types of monks, Benedict mentioned 'anchorites or hermits, who have come through the test of living in a monastery for a long time, and have passed beyond the first fervour of monastic life'.[12] Clearly there is no distinction in his mind. However, by the late Middle Ages,

> a distinction was drawn between 'hermits', solitaries who lived in cells which were often (though not always) in isolated places and many of whom begged for or grew their own food, and 'anchorites', solitaries who were permanently enclosed in cells which were attached to churches and who, as a result, usually lived in the middle of villages or towns.[13]

'Virgins and faithful widows'

Virgins were honoured from the second century onwards because abstinence from marriage was favoured as an act of religious devotion. For example, the second-century *Apostolic Constitutions* 8.24 states, 'Concerning virgins. Virgins are not ordained, for we do not have an instruction from the Lord. Indeed, this is a glorious voluntary struggle, not towards the reproach of marriage, but towards the vocation of piety.'[14]

Widows held an ambiguous role in the medieval Church. As sexually experienced 'single' women they were, in the eyes of the Church, capable of threatening a stable sexual world, but as a significant segment of the Church they could provide both pastoral and practical contributions. The role, and also the ordination, of widows was sometimes confused with that of deaconesses in the liturgies of the medieval Church. The term 'widow' was also used of a woman who lived in voluntary separation from her husband. In the eighth century, in the Frankish Church, widows who had taken a vow were allowed to continue living in their own houses. This right was abolished in the ninth century when they were required to live in monasteries as the only safe place free from temptation.

One manuscript includes 'innocents' in this line. This may be a reference to the 'Holy Innocents', the children of Bethlehem and its surrounding area killed on the orders of Herod (Matt. 2.16–18). The phrase also appeared in a number of the *Ars Moriendi* (*The Art of Dying*) mentioned in Chapter 4.

'Today his place is made in peace and his dwelling in heavenly Jerusalem'

There is wide variety in the manuscripts between 'his' and 'your' in this line. The difference is indicative of the direction of the prayer. 'His' indicates that the prayer is now clearly addressed to God; 'your' indicates that it is addressed to God through the dying person. To rest in peace in the heavenly Jerusalem is the perfect destiny of the soul.

'May the holy angel Michael, who won the leadership of the heavenly army, uphold you'

The archangel Michael is referred to in both the Old and New Testaments. In Daniel 12.1, Michael, the great prince, will appear at the end time. In Jude 9 his example is invoked, 'not even the archangel Michael, when he was disputing with the devil for possession of Moses' body, presumed to condemn him in insulting words, but said, "May the Lord rebuke you."' He was widely venerated in the developing medieval world. The growth of his importance is evidenced, for example, by the Order of Saint Michael. He is usually depicted with a sword, standing over a dragon.

'May the holy angels of God come to meet you, and may they lead you into the holy city Jerusalem'

The imagery here is not one of a soul fearfully wending its way towards the holy city, but one of a joyful 'advanced party' of angels coming out to greet and accompany it safely home. It is a phrase since used many times in other prayers.

'Peter', 'Paul' and 'John'

The reference to Peter is found in Matthew 16.19 where Jesus promises to give Peter the keys of the kingdom of heaven. The prayer speaks of Paul as being worthy to be a vessel of God's choice, although Paul himself spoke of his sense of unworthiness to be an apostle (1 Cor. 15.9). There is no direct biblical evidence that to John was revealed the secrets of the kingdom of heaven. The tradition no doubt stems from the closeness of John, the beloved disciple, to Jesus, and possibly the reference in John 21.23–24, which may be taken to hint at special knowledge.

'May the saints, chosen apostles of the Lord, to whom have been given the power of binding and loosing'

The power to bind and to loose was given to Peter (Matt. 16.19), and more generally in Matthew 18.18. In modern translations the meaning is given as a reference to what the apostle might forbid and allow, rather than literally binding and loosing.

['May all the saints who are with Christ, who suffered in this world, intercede for you']

This is a 'catch-all' found in some manuscripts, which draws in all possible saints, as this part of the prayer moves to its climax.

'Go in peace, in the name of the Father, and of the Son, and of the Holy Spirit, who is to lighten your way into eternal life. (Amen. Pray for us.)'

The summons to 'depart' here is not a repetition of the opening *Proficiscere*, as a different Latin word is used. The persons of the Trinity are invoked to light the way of the departing soul into life eternal.

A trinitarian blessing is added to by a request that God will light the way of the soul as it journeys towards heaven, perhaps so that it might not stumble on the way. The addition of 'Amen. Pray for us' seems a strange interpolation at this particular point. It may be that the writer intended, in this version, that the next two lines were to be the opening part of the *Libera*.

['And raise you on the last day in the first resurrection. Lord Jesus Christ, good pastor, receive the soul of your servant in peace, and forgive all his sins, Saviour of the World']

The invocation continues, in some manuscripts, that the soul may rise on the new day of the first resurrection. In Pauline theology three resurrections can be determined (although only the second two are referred to in this passage). The first is Christ's, second the first fruits, those who belong to him, and third the resurrection at the end time (1 Cor. 15.23–24). The book of Revelation offers no such precise order. 'First' in this context may be 'first fruits', although the reference may be to

The Proficiscere, 'Depart, Christian Soul'

Revelation 20.5. Christ the good pastor, 'shepherd' in some versions, is asked to receive his servant in peace and to forgive all his sins.

'Lord, Holy Father of Jesus Christ, receive the soul of your servant in peace and forgive all his sins'

In this very understated way God is asked to forgive the sins of the person who is dying.

'Saviour of the world, who with the Father and the Holy Spirit, receive, Lord, the soul of your servant into your blessed abode'

Jesus, as Saviour of the world, is asked to receive the soul into 'your blessed abode', another image of heaven/Jerusalem.

'Set free, Lord, the soul of this your servant from all the dangers of hell and from all evil tribulations'

The third part of the prayer begins with these lines, reflecting an awareness of dangers that can face the soul after death, but they are noticeably modest images compared to the more dramatic pictures painted in some of the contemporary writings.

Before commenting in detail on the next lines, it is worth noting that the sequence of events from the Old Testament recalled in the prayer follows no logical order. Peter and Paul are the only ones from the New Testament.

'Set free, Lord, the soul of this your servant, as you set free …'

These are the beginning lines, repeated in relation to each biblical figure in the *Libera* part of the prayer. Some texts have 'your servant', while others have 'this your servant'.

['Abel']

Abel was Adam and Eve's second son (Gen. 4.2), who was murdered by his elder brother Cain because the Lord looked more favourably on the sacrifice that Abel had offered. Only two manuscripts, which are identical at this point, include this figure. The reason for the lack of popularity may be that, although he can be seen to be the first biblical martyr, his 'setting free' only comes through his death. Apart from Enoch and Elijah (see below) all the other figures are set free in the context of the threat of death.

'Noah'

Noah and his family alone were miraculously saved in the Ark from the world-destroying flood (Gen. 7.1—8.19).

'Elijah and Enoch'

Elijah and Enoch are two Old Testament figures who, it is recorded, did not die. Elijah was taken up into heaven in a whirlwind (2 Kings 2.11). Enoch 'lived three hundred and sixty-five years. Enoch walked with God; and then was no more, because God took him' (Gen. 5.23–24).

'Abraham'

Abraham, uniquely, figures in different versions of this prayer in three different contexts. He is mentioned in the 'negative' context of being the near perpetrator of Isaac's death. Then in two different groups of documents he is included as being saved from Ur of the Chaldees, the home of his father (Gen. 11.28—12.1), and in the other group he is saved through his faith and trustfulness. In the first case his 'salvation' cannot easily be seen in the same context of other figures who faced life-threatening danger, and in the second case he is saved because of his faith. The fact that he is not a popular choice, in spite of his biblical stature, may indicate that some liturgical writers had difficulty in fitting him into the formula of this prayer.

'Lot'

Lot, along with his two daughters, escaped from the destruction that befell the people of Sodom (Gen. 19.1–26), after his wife was turned into a pillar of salt, so he is well chosen as an example of God's miraculous saving power. As so often happens in the way the Bible is used, the negative side of people's characters is ignored. The fact that he offered his two daughters to a gang of rapists did not stop Lot being held up as an example in prayer, as might well happen today.

['The People of Israel']

This reference is only found in one manuscript and is a reference to the Israelite nation that was the focus of God's saving activity. The fact that a group was saved, rather than a specific biblical figure, suggests that it was a local invention, which did not find popularity with other liturgical writers.

'Isaac'

The near sacrifice of Isaac (Gen. 22.1–18) at the hand of his father Abraham, and his salvation, figures frequently in the manuscripts as a sign of God's saving power.

'Jacob'

Jacob is far less popular in the manuscripts. Like Abraham, he is remembered for being majestically blessed, rather than for being saved (from the hand of his angry brother?). His blessing took place at Luz, which he renamed Bethel (Gen. 28.10–22).

'Moses'

Moses and the children of Israel were set free from Egypt at the climax of the battle between Moses and Pharaoh (Ex. 6.26—14.31). He was a popular figure in versions of the prayer, representing God's saving activity especially through the miracle of the Red Sea, and appears with great regularity.

'Jonah'

Jonah was released by the Lord after spending three days and nights in the belly of a great fish (Jonah 1.17—2.10). In view of the powerfulness of the salvation miracle contained in this story, it is not easy to understand why Jonah does not feature as frequently as many of the other Old Testament figures. Perhaps, even in those days, although it was a miracle they recognized it was a truth told in the form of a story, rather than being considered a historical fact.

['Job']

The poem about the suffering of Job is found in the book of his name, which debates, among other matters, the question of suffering in the light of Job's own suffering at the hands of the 'Adversary' or 'Satan' (Job 2.1). At the end of the story he is relieved of his sufferings by the Lord and his fortunes are miraculously restored (Job 42.10–17). It is, perhaps, surprising that *Nursia* is one of the few manuscripts not to include this figure.

'David'

During the period of Saul's reign, when David was hunted as an outlaw, he had a number of narrow escapes from Saul's anger, until Saul was himself killed in battle (1 Sam. 18.9—31.13). Before these events the young David had killed the giant Philistine warrior Goliath, by striking him with a stone from his sling (1 Sam. 17.51).

The Proficiscere, 'Depart, Christian Soul'

'Daniel'

The wording of the prayer concerning Daniel indicates a slight lack of accuracy in some versions. In the book of Daniel, the hero is placed in a lion-pit by King Darius for his refusal to obey an edict which stated that prayers should not be offered to any god or human being for a period of 30 days. The prayer in some versions refers only to one lion, while Daniel 6.22, 24 clearly indicates that there were several lions.

'Three young men'

This is a further reference from the book of Daniel (3.1-30). King Nebuchadnezzar threw the three boys or young men, Shadrach, Meshach and Abednego, into a blazing furnace because they refused to bow down to a gold image. They were unharmed by the fire, for 'The hair of their heads was not singed, their tunics were not harmed, and not even the smell of fire came from them' (Dan. 3.27b). This can be seen as a particularly miraculous act of salvation and is one of the most popular images.

'Susanna'

The story of Susanna is found in chapter 13 of the Greek version of Daniel in the Apocrypha, and is thus one of the least-known figures today. It is well worth reading for its skilful erotic tone. Susanna was 'a very beautiful woman and one who feared the Lord', and was married to a rich and honourable husband Joakim. Two elders in the community used to come to their house on business, but both developed a lustful desire to seduce her. Eventually they approached her when she was bathing alone in the garden, without her servants present. They threatened her that if she did not let them seduce her they would denounce her 'unfaithfulness' to her husband by saying that they had found her with a secret young lover.

Their attempt at blackmail did not persuade her to surrender herself, so next day in revenge, they arraigned her in a court and accused her of adultery. Because they were respected elders, their story about her concealing a young lover was believed, and she was condemned to death. As she was being led away, she cried out to God, who heard her and 'stirred up the holy spirit of a young lad named Daniel', who came to her aid. He managed to arrange a retrial at which he skilfully cross-examined the two men separately. Their two stories did not match and out of their own mouths they were proved to be false witnesses. It is hardly surprising that they then suffered the death sentence which Susanna so nearly suffered herself. The story of her salvation, after the false sexual allegations, was a popular one featuring in many of the manuscripts.

'The human race'

The human family is saved by the Passion of our Lord. Although it is a powerful and all-inclusive image, it only appears in one group of manuscripts.

'Peter and Paul'

It should be noted first that Peter and Paul are the only New Testament figures in the prayer. All other references are found in the Old Testament or the Apocrypha. The Bible offers a number of references to Peter and Paul in prison. The two most obvious escapes are by Peter (Acts 12.6–10), when he is rescued by an angel of the Lord, and by Paul, when an earthquake loosened his bonds and those of Silas while they were in prison in Philippi (Acts 16.25–26). In fact he was not set free by this event, but by the magistrates the next morning. There is a reference to 'tortures' in *Gellone*. Paul was on various occasions beaten, flogged and stoned as methods of punishment, but there is no evidence of torture (as a means of gaining a confession). Similarly there is no evidence in the Bible that Peter was tortured, apart from a possible interpretation of the prediction in John 21.18–19. Presumably other writers could not justify the inclusion of 'torture' on strictly biblical grounds so they did not repeat it.

'Thecla'

The inclusion of Thecla and her deliverance 'from the midst of the spectacle', or in other versions her 'three torments', is of particular interest as she is the only non-biblical figure included in the prayer. We will say something about her here, and then in the next chapter suggest a possible reason why she, alone of all the saints, was included, but only in the *Rheinau* text and not in *Gellone*.

In my more irreverent moments I picture a person very near death, probably prostrate on the chapel floor or perhaps in their home, dressed in sackcloth and lying on ashes. As they listen to the words of the *Libera* they nod or groan assent to each of the long list of examples of God's saving acts, through the Old Testament, and then on to Peter and Paul. But at the mention of the name of Thecla, the dying person suddenly sits up and asks 'Who was she?' It is a not uncommon response from people who come across the prayer today (and it was mine when I first read it). We can only speculate how many thousands of Christians have died, listening to the *Libera*, and not knowing just what it was that made Thecla so famous and significant that she alone was considered worthy to gain a place in the liturgy of dying as the climactic representative figure of God's grace, for well over one thousand years.

After her first mention in *Rheinau* she is one of the most popular names among the many medieval versions of the *Proficiscere*, gaining more mentions than Jonah, Abraham or Jacob.

The search for the source of the reference to Thecla involves a study of early church hagiography. Among the many books which did not make it to the canon of the New Testament was the apocryphal *Acts of Paul*, which contains a section entitled the *Acts of Paul and Thecla*. It may not have made the ranks of holy scripture, but its popularity in the early Church is indicated by the wide variety of languages into which it was translated, including Latin, Coptic, Syriac, Ethiopic, Arabic, Armenian and Slavonic, apart from a number of Greek versions.[15]

The *Acts* tell the story of Paul preaching on his missionary journeys in Iconium and deeply influencing a young woman, Thecla, who heard him. This led her to desert Thamyris, the man to whom she was betrothed, in order that she could follow Paul. She watched and listened to Paul from a window, to which, said her mother, she was attached like a spider. She tells her daughter's betrothed partner Thamyris:

> for assuredly for three days and three nights Thecla does not rise from the window, neither to eat nor to drink; but looks earnestly as if upon some pleasant sight. She is so devoted to a foreigner teaching deceitful and artful discourses, that I wonder how a virgin of such modesty is so painfully put about.

Thecla would not even turn round to speak to her family as this would mean taking her eyes off Paul for a moment. Paul was in due course scourged for the effect he had had on her, 'making virgins averse to marriage', but Thecla was condemned to a worse fate, to be burned to death. Her mother encouraged this action saying, 'Burn the wicked wretch; burn in the midst of the theatre her that will not marry, in order that all the women that have been taught by this man (Paul) may be afraid.'

There then began a series of increasingly violent events, when opponents attempted to kill her, all of which miraculously failed. First, wooden faggots were built up around her and set ablaze, but she was not burned or even singed by the flames. On this occasion she escaped further punishment and later Paul took her with him to Antioch where Alexander, an influential citizen, became infatuated with her. She spurned his advances, and, 'taking hold of Alexander, she tore his cloak, and pulled off his crown, and made him a laughing stock'. It is hardly surprising that, once again, she was condemned to death, this time to be killed by wild beasts. At the first attempt Thecla was bound to a lioness, but instead of attacking her, the lioness merely licked her feet. The next day she was thrown into an arena with wild lions and a bear. One of the lions and a bear prepared to attack her, but a lioness defended her, and the other wild animals refused to join in the attack.

Her executioners gave up on wild beasts and instead threw her into a pool full of seals (or some sort of dangerous fish), but after a flash of lightning the seals floated dead on the surface and she alone survived. It was then back to the wild beasts again, but this time they failed to kill Thecla because her women supporters let loose a mass of perfumes which hypnotized the wild animals, stopping their flesh-eating instincts. Finally, she was placed among wild bulls, which had the misfortune to have red-hot irons placed under their genitals, 'so that they, being rendered more furious, might kill her', but even they failed to be sufficiently enraged. Admitting defeat the Governor put a stop to the games, much to the dismay of the people of the city. Thecla was summoned by the Governor and was able to make her testimony of faith to him.

One manuscript adds a further story of Thecla, set when she was in her old age and living in a cave near Seleucia. She healed so many of the people who turned to her for help that the local doctors were put out of practice. They plotted their revenge, not with wild animals, but in a more subtle way. They persuaded a group of drunken men to attack her so as to corrupt and defile her as a virgin. When confronted by them, after she had said a prayer, an opening appeared in the rock wall of her cave. She entered the large crack and it closed after her. The men could not follow, but were only able to catch part of her dress.[16] She had escaped for the last time.

Different versions of the 'Thecla' story refer either to her being saved from the 'spectacle' that is in the theatre with the wild animals, or from her three torments. It is not clear if the 'three torments' necessarily included the last story, as it is possible to divide up the other torments, from the way in which they are told in the text, into three: fire, wild beasts and water. These were the three classic ways in which people were martyred.

You may not be surprised that the story of Thecla failed to make its way into the New Testament, but this did not stop the cult of Thecla enjoying considerable popularity. She is one of the most enduring people in this biography and will reappear in the next chapter, and in Chapter 6, when her role in the prayer was reappraised by the Roman Catholic Church.

'So deign to set free the soul of this man and allow him to dwell with you in the blessings of heaven'

With these words the long prayer comes to an end. Everything possible has been said which might enable the person's soul to be set free and to journey and rest in the blessings of heaven. Because the moment of death is uncertain a few manuscripts have in the margin at the end of the prayer words such as 'and so on as necessary'.

I want to raise a concluding general question here. Why are these particular, mainly Old Testament, figures held out as models of God's saving activity? It is clear that, apart from Enoch and Elijah, they all died, but the biblical events which are projected in the *Libera* all concern danger. Each faced a potentially life-threatening situation. When the *Proficiscere* was being said, the person dying was facing a life-threatening situation, but the request is not that they be relieved from it, as were the biblical figures. The invocation is that a saving God, who demonstrated great power for people who continued to live in this world, will demonstrate the same miraculous power for a person who will not continue in this world.

There is thus clearly a disjunction between the type of setting free indicated in the Old Testament model and the type of setting free at death envisaged in the *Proficiscere*. The prayer foresees danger beyond this life, although there is no mention of the actions of devils and demons, popular in other imagery, which might impede the successful journey to the heavenly Jerusalem. So the 'set free' is from danger, but there is also a sense of the setting free of the soul in that dangerous moment of tearing apart of soul and body.

It may be that a modern reader, bringing modern cultural assumptions, can be misled by the constant repetition of '*Libera*'. Is it possible to seek to understand the mind of those who spoke these words? An interesting, if provocative, solution has been suggested by the historian Albert Mirgeler, who has written on the rise of Christianity from a German perspective. He explored what it was about Western Christianity that appealed to the early medieval German tribes, and how in consequence Roman Christianity 'mutated'. He provided a framework of understanding in which the figures in the *Libera* can, perhaps, better be understood.

The framework he looked at was the religious world that the Germanic tribes inhabited. He argued that, before the coming of Christianity, there was a strong belief in fate, which was countered by devotion to different gods on a 'trading' basis. Different gods were worshipped in the expectation that a particular god would support the interests of the tribe. 'If the god did not act as such a "friend in need", his client was very ready to change his allegiance or to abandon it altogether.' [17] With the introduction of Christianity the tribes were made aware of a strong Christ who demanded total allegiance. The change he introduced was that there was no going back to one of the old gods.

> (T)he Christian God had to reveal himself less as the announcer of salvation to come than as the guarantor of every earthly success. He had to show that he was above the course of earthly destiny by an uninterrupted series of interventions from the world beyond, in brief, to present himself as the great miracle-worker. The atmosphere of primitive Germanic Christianity could therefore only be that of belief in the miraculous, the hourly expectation of supernatural events.[18]

Mirgeler then adduced evidence of the power of belief in miracles in the early medieval Church, and that religious life for the majority of people was dominated by the miraculous rather than by the formal theology of the Church. He argued that the role of the saints changed in the Middle Ages, from that of fellow travellers who had reached their goal, to one of those who helped in time of need.

It is, perhaps, in this context that the list of biblical figures can better be understood. They were venerated in this prayer, not because they escaped the perils of death in the event referred to, but that their liberation from peril was a miraculous example of the saving power of God.[19] If God worked miracles in their lives, so God could be called on to work a miracle in the life of the dying person, not to restore them to health, but to work the miracle of bringing them safely to the heavenly Jerusalem.

One caveat needs to be entered, which was expressed by David Knowles who wrote an introduction to Mirgeler's book. He said that it was difficult to characterize Christianity in another age, in particular the less formal aspects of the faith and the mindsets of earlier Christians. He warned against accepting the judgements in Mirgeler's book as 'the findings of history' but concluded, 'if [the reader] uses them to illuminate his own reading and to break down a narrow, formal or tendentious attitude to the past they will enrich his mind and help him towards a penetration in depth of the religious history of Europe'.[20]

The final point to be made in this detailed study of the prayer is that there is a wide variety in the manuscripts about the inclusion of the word 'Amen'. In some it appears only at the end, in others it appears irregularly. (I suspect the monk copying the text put it in if there was space at the end of the line.) In others it appears with great regularity. I like to picture it being said by the other monks, or the family who were assembled around the deathbed, as a communal response to each line. Each cries out for a response of 'Yes' or 'So be it'. You might like to try reading through part of the *Nursia* text, at the beginning of this chapter, and say 'Amen' after each line. It can certainly add to the power of the prayer.

Now the content of the prayer is familiar to you, we can begin to develop a better understanding of the changes which took place in the medieval world which led to the birth of the new prayer *Proficiscere*.

2

From Birth to Maturity

I have often wondered, if I had lived in the eighteenth century, how I would have reacted to the fact of slavery. Together with the majority of the population, I would have been aware that it was a fact of life, that my country's economy was greatly strengthened by it, and that it was accepted, and could be justified, by the Bible. I suspect that, as a man of those times, I would have accepted it as morally neutral and lived with an untroubled conscience. If I had lived 100 years later I like to think that I would have viewed slavery as morally, socially and theologically abhorrent and evil. I would have wanted to join with most other people in proclaiming that the attitude of former generations to slavery was wrong and that we should now all act very differently. The point I want to make is that, over a period of time along with the population at large, my attitude towards the same objective fact, the existence of slavery, would have changed dramatically. The change in attitude would have been brought about by changes in religious, social and economic perceptions.

This illustration came to mind as I was trying to think about the way in which people's attitude to death changed in the eighth century. Death was still death, but for reasons we will explore in this chapter, people's view of it changed from one of calm and sometimes joyful acceptance to one of fear. The best way to explore this change is to ask such questions as, why did the *Proficiscere* ever come to birth, what was it like to live in the Frankish Church which brought it to life, and what changed in people's attitude to death, which led them to want to use this new prayer?

The birth of the *Proficiscere*

In order to construct the early life of the *Proficiscere* we need to turn to two groups of scholars for help. The first are the textual critics who have examined many manuscripts and are able to tell us about their age and provenance. The other group are historians who can tell us about what was going on in the world at the time the texts were written. Obviously there is an overlap between the two groups, neither can work in a vacuum, but they represent the two poles of research for our biography. As outlined in the Introduction, these two poles are first the texts, which are the immediate life of the biographer's subject, and second the historical context in which that life was lived.

The accurate dating and detailed analysis of the content of medieval manuscripts is a comparatively modern science, although scholars have for many years published books containing extracts of older manuscripts. One of the most famous and valued is that of a scholar called Edmund Martène. At the beginning of the eighteenth century he published three massive volumes, *Ancient Rites of the Church* (*De antiquis ecclesiae ritibus*), which was the result of a massive trawl through the scholarly libraries of Europe. He set out some texts in full and summarized others, also giving his estimate of the age of the manuscripts. Although his judgement on the dating of many texts is now questioned, his works are a valuable source of information, particularly as he sets out the text of some manuscripts which have since unfortunately been lost by theft, warfare or by fire, so that in some cases his information is all that we have. He refers several times to liturgies which contain the *Proficiscere*.

We are fortunate that, more recently, manuscripts have been copied on to film, so that they can be reproduced and studied in any country. Valuable as this is, there are two problems for scholars. The first is that irreparable damage can occur to manuscripts during the process. Inside the front of a manuscript I studied in the Bibliothèque Mazarine, in Paris, which contained a version of the *Proficiscere*, is a handwritten note indicating that it was necessary to rebind the manuscript in 1933 as the result of it being opened so that the contents could be photographed. The rather brutal treatment old manuscripts have received, so that microfilms could be made, is the price paid for the increasing ease with which old manuscripts can be studied throughout the world. Methods used today are more careful than they used to be, but the risk of damage still exists.

The second problem is that, while a photograph may be very helpful, it can lead scholars astray, as they can miss things on a photograph or microfilm which they would notice on an original. Also, for experts, a detailed study of the binding of a manuscript can reveal all sorts of secrets. Photographs of the leaves of the manuscript cannot reveal these details. There is no substitute for looking at the original, unless the manuscript has already been the subject of a scholarly analysis.

The days of scholars listing the contents of entire libraries are now over. During the last hundred years or more, individual scholars have concentrated their work on just one or two manuscripts each and spent many years setting out the text and writing a scholarly commentary. Once their work is done there is less need to look at the original, as they set out in minute and expert detail everything there is to say about the manuscript. This enables another group of scholars to work from these published sources and write about both the text and the context. Of course only a fraction of all the medieval manuscripts available have received this treatment, but it is fortunate that the two manuscripts that contain the earliest examples of the *Proficiscere* have received this careful attention.

Bernard Moreton examined the historical and geographical backgrounds of the first two sacramentaries to contain the *Proficiscere*, namely *Gellone* and *Rheinau*, which were virtually contemporaneous.[1] These two manuscripts are called either the eighth-century Gelasians or the Frankish Gelasians, because they were written in the eighth century and were the products of the Frankish Church, based on earlier material known as Gelasian. Gelasius was a pope (492–496) who was supposed, incorrectly, to have been the author of the original Gelasians. There are about ten such Frankish Gelasians (or parts) but only two contain the *Proficiscere*.

The Frankish Church, into which the *Proficiscere* was born, covered roughly the area of modern northern France round into Germany and south into Switzerland. How did this Church put its manuscript material together when it produced these two sacramentaries? Traditionally, scholars had worked on the assumption, challenged by Moreton, that a copy of an earlier text like one called the Vatican Gelasian, which was produced in Rome, was taken north in the period 750–760 and was one of the sources of the eighth-century or Frankish Gelasians. According to this theory, under the direction of the Frankish King Pepin, an unknown cleric of the Frankish Church, working in a Benedictine monastery, blended it with material from a Gregorian sacramentary (a sacramentary associated with Pope Gregory (590–604)), and added distinctively Frankish material, which included the *Proficiscere*.

Against this traditional view, Moreton argued that all that travelled north from Rome were individual booklets, or prayer collections, containing different orders for Mass and groups of prayers (rather than 'finished' sacramentaries) and these were incorporated by the Frankish Church, in a creative way, into distinctive new sacramentaries. He summarized his judgement in this way. 'The eighth-century Gelasians are contemporary derivations with the Vatican Gelasian and the Gregorian, not dependent on them but stemming from the same sources, the earlier prayer collections.'[2]

However, there is no evidence that the text of the *Proficiscere* itself was part of any of the group of books of prayers which travelled north from Rome. Part of its fascination is that it seems, along with other material, to be an original creation within the Frankish Benedictine community. How do we know that this type of sacramentary originated in a Benedictine monastery? Moreton pointed first to the fact that these manuscripts contain a special Mass for the feast of Benedict on 11 July.[3] Second, 'his name appears ... together with Augustine, Gregory, and Jerome, all of whom have a great significance for monasticism, and those sacramentaries which give an extensive additional section after the Canon devote considerable attention to the monastic rites'.[4]

As far as dating is concerned, Moreton indicated that there has been disagreement among scholars, but only over the matter of a few years. Most scholars date the Frankish Gelasians to between 750 and 800.[5] One scholar, Cyrille Vogel, dating *Gellone* between 790 and 800, judged that it was probably copied at the Holy Cross Abbey at Meaux, possibly for Cambrai Cathedral (in north-eastern France) during the episcopate of Hildoard (790–816). It was donated to the Abbey of Gellone, in south-western France, in about 807.[6] The manuscript's journey from northern France to Gellone was of some 400 miles, and its presence in Gellone gave it its title.[7]

The other Frankish Gelasian manuscript containing a version of the *Proficiscere*, known as *Rheinau*, is virtually contemporaneous with *Gellone*, and Moreton dated it as late eighth or early ninth century. He detailed the disagreements among scholars over the place of writing of this manuscript,[8] but said that palaeographical evidence (that is, the style of handwriting) points to the likelihood that the manuscript was written in a Swiss scriptorium.[9] A scriptorium was the room in a monastery where manuscripts were copied by the monks.

Moreton goes on to comment helpfully on the social and cultural milieu in which *Gellone* and *Rheinau* were composed. While there is no unanimity among scholars, as far as geography is concerned, Moreton said:

> Here there is some foundation for a belief that the eighth-century Gelasian tradition had its home in the region of the Rhaetian Alps, and that the redaction [rewriting] of the Sacramentary took place in a Benedictine House somewhere in this region early in the third quarter of the eighth century.[10]

Rhaetia is the area south of Alemannia (in present-day Switzerland), including Chur in the south and St Gall in the north. At various points in time there were political and ecclesiastical links with the north-eastern provinces of Italy. The Brenner Pass in the Alps was a link over what was otherwise a barrier between the two geographical areas. During much of the year it would not have been possible to travel across the Pass, because of the snow, but it was capable of being a means of communication between north and south, and the Roman and Frankish Churches.

We know quite a lot about the Frankish Church so, inevitably, scholars have tried to say who they thought composed the new sacramentaries. One scholar, Eric Palazzo, thought that the Frankish Gelasians were part of a project undertaken by Frankish monks under the direction of King Pepin, who wanted to establish liturgical unification in his kingdom through the creation of a new sacramentary. This was on the basis that you can unite your kingdom if everyone is singing from the same sacramentary. He dated this movement to the period 760–770.

However, it was a short-lived liturgical experiment, because it was soon overtaken by the use of the Gregorian Sacramentary (which did not contain the *Proficiscere*). Palazzo commented that it was 'the serious work of a team of competent liturgists' and discounts the theory, held by some scholars, that it was the work of Bishop Chrodegang of Metz, who had been to Rome.[11] Other scholars point to Bishop Remedius, who was the brother of Pepin, and it is known that he also was sent to Rome in 760 to study the liturgy. However, Moreton concluded that there is nothing positive that can be produced to point to either man.[12] As the *Proficiscere* was an original composition it is unlikely that it had a Roman origin, as there are no Roman parallels and, as has been seen, it was not included in early Gregorian material, which came north from Rome.

Moreton is to an extent supported in this approach, at least methodologically, by Paul Bradshaw. Bradshaw was writing about the development of manuscripts in the earlier centuries of the Christian Church, but what he said is equally relevant in view of the similar ways in which written material was transmitted between manuscripts in later centuries. He issued a warning about drawing conclusions too easily from manuscripts, and took what he called a 'splitters' view rather than a 'lumpers' view. 'Lumpers' are those scholars who have a tendency to unite texts because of similarities, as opposed to 'splitters' who tend to differentiate because of differences.[13] Adopting a 'splitters' view is a methodological assumption, also adopted by Moreton, which was current at the end of the twentieth century (and still is today) standing over against the previous predilection of 'lumpers' who were looking for similarities at the beginning of the twentieth century. In the next chapter we will see how the assumptions of 'lumpers' led a number of scholars into the error of linking texts and archaeological evidence to the *Proficiscere* on the basis of superficial similarities.

So far we have shown that the first manuscripts that contain the *Proficiscere* can be dated to a specific period (750–800) in the life of the Church, and that they were an original contribution by monks or others in the Frankish Church.

What was it like to be a Christian?

What was it like to be a Christian in the Frankish Church? In order to answer this question I now want to draw on the researches of a group of scholars (in addition to Mirgeler at whose contribution we have already looked) who between them offer a broader glimpse of the cultural environment in which the *Proficiscere* was created. Inevitably, it is only possible to offer a tentative picture of religious awareness in the Frankish Church, and the attitude to death, as it is so difficult for us to understand what it was like to inhabit the religious world of that period.[14]

In his detailed history of the Frankish Church, John Wallace-Hadrill offered a number of valuable insights or clues into some of the influences that may have shaped the

From Birth to Maturity 37

composition of the *Proficiscere*,[15] although the *Gellone* text is only mentioned in passing.

Although travel was never easy, the Frankish Church was not isolated and was influenced by all its neighbours. Wallace-Hadrill points first to the impact of Irish and Anglo-Saxon missionaries, who had travelled south-east to the continent and played a dominant role in the missionary work in the German Church about one hundred years before the *Proficiscere* was written. Why did they leave the shores of Ireland and England to risk all in what we would call today a dangerous war zone? Wallace-Hadrill, the pre-eminent historian of the Frankish Church, identified a restless, driven spirituality among the Irish monks, which led them to leave their homeland and go as spiritual pilgrims, to *peregrinatio*, to a sacrificial exile from home. This sense of spiritual and physical journeying was picked up from the Irish monks by Anglo-Saxon monks and both saw it as a means towards ascetic fulfilment. Another reason was the influence of Rome, which was powerfully encouraging the Church towards universal conversion. Wallace-Hadrill says, 'Stronger than either was the teaching of the Bible, because of which *peregrinatio* [going on a spiritual pilgrimage from home] dissolved into *missio* [missionary activity]. And what more natural for an Anglo-Saxon so inclined than the lands of his Germanic kindred over the sea?'[16]

Another scholar, Anton Wessels, was more careful to distinguish missionaries (whom he says were mainly Anglo-Saxon) from the Irish *peregrinates*, although he acknowledged that they were interwoven. A missionary might go abroad to a foreign country with the intention of returning, while a *peregrinatus* might set out for life and establish himself in a primarily pagan area for the good of his soul. 'The prime motive of the Irish monks and scholars was thus asceticism and not evangelization.'[17]

Wallace-Hadrill outlined the history of succeeding waves of missionaries from Ireland and England who penetrated ever further down the Rhine basin. In particular he wrote of the ministry of St Pirmin (scholars, he says, have not been able to determine if he was Irish, Frankish or a Goth) who attracted endowments for monasteries which followed the Rule of St Benedict. Before his death in 753 he had established major foundations at Reichenau on Lake Constance in 724, and Murbach in Alsace in 728. Not far from Reichenau was St Gallen, a foundation of Irish–Rhaetian origins.[18] In the eighth century the Frankish Church grew and developed, both as a home-based church and as a missionary church, extending its reach into the German (Saxon) regions. As the Church and the Frankish empire expanded eastwards, this area came under Frankish influence after the middle of the eighth century, and (although Wallace-Hadrill did not make the point) it can be said to form a realistic setting for the composition of the *Proficiscere* and the liturgy that encompasses it.

It was also to this area that the Anglo-Saxon Boniface came. We will say more about him in the next chapter, but he set out the boundaries of dioceses. As Wallace-Hadrill commented, 'Boniface's most lasting work in Bavaria was, as elsewhere, the introduction of Benedictine monasteries and their integration with indigenous monastic traditions.'[19] Boniface died in 754, at about the earliest possible dating of the two earliest manuscripts containing the *Proficiscere*. While no claims are made that he was the author of the text,[20] it is reasonable to surmise that he played a part in laying the foundations for the church culture in which it was written. One scholar, Anton Baumstark, has suggested that texts were brought from England or Ireland which contained either the *Proficiscere* or an earlier version of the *Proficiscere*. This is speculation, but in the next chapter we will look at a contemporary Irish manuscript that does contain a version of the *Proficiscere*.

Wallace-Hadrill outlined the complex interrelationship between individuals from the Irish, Anglo-Saxon, and Frankish–German Churches in the Lower Rhine area where the *Proficiscere* may well first have been composed.[21] He also emphasized the importance of this intermingling of the different north European Churches. His words are worth quoting at

From Birth to Maturity   39

length, because they illustrate the complex world out of which the *Proficiscere* in its earliest known forms, in *Gellone* and *Rheinau*, emerged:

> Frankish penetration over the Rhine, the motives behind which were more complicated than mere aggression, coincided, in the late seventh and early eighth centuries with isolated missionary activity which the Franks did not initiate but did encourage. There was nothing planned or coordinated about this activity. From Frisia in the north to Rhaetia in the south it assumed different forms and met with different fortunes. But its impetus was *peregrinatio*. Irish in origin, this affected Anglo-Saxons, Franks and possibly Goths. From Northumbria to Septimania, monks would now risk their lives in missionary journeys into the same hinterland of Germanic tribesmen, some pagan but mostly Christian, there to establish themselves under the protection of local chieftains and ultimately under that of the Frankish rulers.[22]

So the picture we have is of Frankish, Irish, Anglo-Saxon and Germanic Christians all mixing and sharing not only different understandings of Christianity but, more importantly, different cultural assumptions about the nature of the world.

Wessels contributed to this picture by outlining ways in which Celtic Christian life and culture were able to assimilate themselves into the prevailing pagan culture. He concluded that the Christian churches adapted themselves as much as possible to local customs and institutions, what is called today 'inculturation'. The result of this cultural flexibility was that the transition from 'paganism' to Christianity was remarkably peaceful.[23] The other contribution that Wessels offered, which helps towards an understanding of the significance of the *Proficiscere*, is the role of 'power' in Germanic religion. The German gods, such as Odin and Thor/Donar, were found to be less powerful than the new Christian God. 'The reason why many people in the Germanic world accepted Christianity was that belief in Jesus Christ was seen as more powerful than other religions or gods.'[24] The *Proficiscere* is nothing if it is not a powerful prayer.

The distinctive contribution of Michael Driscoll to the cultural scene in which the *Proficiscere* was first composed is that he outlined the development of penitential rites in the medieval Church, which are the outward liturgical signs of a deeper inner awareness of sin, its consequences and the need to remove that sin. The time when the *Proficiscere* was created was a time of increasing penitential spirituality and a new awareness of sin. Driscoll examined a variety of early medieval penitential books, which illustrate an increasing trend towards an awareness of a need to be in a right relationship with God. Writing about the contribution of Alcuin of York (c. 735–804), he commented: 'One could falsely presume that this age was populated by greater sinners than the world had known before or since.'[25] While it is clear that the 'Commendation of the Soul', which contained the *Proficiscere*, was not a penitential rite, its spiritual seriousness and its awareness of the fragility of the soul in death do indicate a pastoral response to a changing understanding of death and its consequences. The developing understanding of the need for a penitential life, as typified in the writings of Alcuin, influenced the way in which death was being interpreted, and the need for new rites associated with death.

None of these writers attempted to enter into the spiritual interiority of the Germanic people. However, Pierre Riché wrote of both Celtic and Germanic spirituality, saying that the conversion of these peoples 'radically changed the conditions of Western religious life'.[26] The Germanic social and religious life was dominated by a sense of warfare, and its members 'believed that the world was in a perpetual state of tension, subject to antagonistic, destructive and creative forces'.[27] While they believed in an afterlife, particularly for warriors (Valhalla), Driscoll said, they did not believe in immortality. However, their major fear was that after their death other people could harm them. Riché does not make the point, but the *Proficiscere* can perhaps be understood in the context of a safe journey beyond the reach of those remaining who might wish to do them harm, earthly or heavenly. It combined parts of each of the traditions, fear and immortality.

Adding to this understanding Russell commented that within the elusive medieval world view was 'the process by which the Christian ideological matrix of sin–repentance–salvation gained ascendency over Celtic–Germanic notions of fate and destiny, a process which may be identified with Christianisation'.[28] Again here, it is possible to see something of the background against which the *Proficiscere* offered a pastoral response of Christain hope.

Riché made two further points which offer possible insights into the development of the *Proficiscere*. First, he said that in both the Irish and the Germanic pagan background there was much use of magical incantations to offer protection from evil. To counter these the Christian Church introduced 'Christian incantations' which would, among other things, drive away thunder and tempests. 'In order to prevent a sick person from going to find some healer who was in effect a sorcerer, clerics recited formulas blending Latin, Greek, vernacular, and cabalistic words, all accompanied by many signs of the cross.'[29] You will no doubt be familiar with the hymn attributed to St Patrick, 'I bind unto myself today the strong name of the Trinity. By invocation of the same, the three in one and one in three.' Here is a Christian incantation, and you may even hear echoes of the *Proficiscere* in it.

Second, Riché painted an image of the Frankish court which influenced the picture of heaven held by converts.

> After 751, when the Carolingian [Frankish] kings were anointed by bishops, this reinforced their religious character. The Frankish king represented God on earth: his palace was described after the manner of paradise – he sat surrounded by his warriors and vassals, like God in the midst of the angels and the saints

– an image at least compatible with the first part of the *Proficiscere*.[30]

Among the unique prayer material found for the first time in *Gellone* and *Rheinau,* these two Frankish manuscripts, is the *Proficiscere*. There is insufficient evidence to support arguments that the *Proficiscere* was either composed in northern France and carried into the area of the Germanic Church, or in the area of the Germanic Church and carried into the Frankish Church. Its composer or composers are also unknown but, as will be seen, the *Proficiscere* was to shape both the prayer life and the theological perceptions of Christians concerning sickness and death for centuries to come. It was to express, in a new way, Christian hope to those who were dying, so that they might find the liberty to die within the context of the Christian faith, free from the powers of sin. Otherwise they would have faced death with a greater sense of fear than had previous generations.

The value of these contributions to the study of the *Proficiscere* is that they ground it (as far as it is possible) in the geographical, historical, religious and cultural settings of its time. Together they offer a credible 'world view' of the religious and spiritual life at the end of the eighth century, which resonates with the life of the *Proficiscere*.

Death gets grimmer

One other scholar, Frederick Paxton, has deepened our knowledge and understanding of what was happening in the Frankish world view, by tracing the changes which took place in liturgical documents of this time. These reflect the Christian response to the cultural changes we have just examined. The Church started to reflect a changed view of death in its liturgies.

We do not have any direct evidence of the attitude to death of the very early Church, as expressed in its liturgies, because we do not have very early Christian liturgies for deaths or funerals. It is clear from the New Testament that the death and resurrection of Jesus, and the hope of heavenly resurrection, played a central part when a Christian died, but what was said at funerals is lost to us. One of the oldest surviving documents, which consists of instructions (*Ordines*) rather than liturgies, is known as *L'Ottobonianus* 312, and can be found in the Vatican Library in Rome.[31] It outlines what was to happen liturgically when a Christian was approaching death, and sets out practices which dated back to about the third century. The text, which was still in circulation in the eighth century, is as follows (the translation is by Paxton):

> As soon as they see him approaching death he is to be given communion even if he has eaten that day, because the communion will be his defender and advocate at the resurrection of the just. It will resuscitate him. After the reception of communion, the Gospel accounts of the passion of the Lord are to be read to the sick person by priests and deacons until his soul departs from his body.[32]

You will probably have noticed from this that, having received Holy Communion, the dying person lived his or her last minutes listening to the account of Christ's passion and death. Their death was interpreted within the context of Christ's death, and through this understanding their own death would not be final. It can be read as a cool, calm, comforting and hopeful interpretation of death, a death with Christ and without fear.

Paxton then comments: 'Its optimistic celebration of Christian salvation in the face of death did not reflect the more penitential, less self-assured faith of early medieval Christians.'[33] Death became grimmer.

A second pointer towards a change is found at the end of the sixth century. In the West, the liturgy of the Mass began to play an increasingly important part in commemoration of the dead and in posthumous rituals of expiation, seeking forgiveness. Paxton drew attention to the pivotal role of Pope Gregory I (590–604) who in his *Dialogues* spoke of the Mass as the one thing which could possibly benefit the soul after death. There was a growing sense among Christians that their immediate situation after death was between heaven and hell. This change in understanding can be detected in the liturgical material of the time. New penitential practices, developed in Ireland and England, encouraged a sense that every sin had to be atoned for in life or it would have to be expiated after death.[34] The approach to death was changing from being joyful and resurrection-centred to heavy and fearful.

Then, in the latter part of the eighth century, in the period 750–850 under the reforms of the Frankish Church, liturgical texts and ritual practices blossomed, so that by about the year 900 funerary practices had been developed into a pattern which would become standard throughout the Middle Ages and beyond. As has been shown, part of the result of this creative period of development was the *Proficiscere*. Paxton shows us that the funeral rites developed into a threefold structure, namely pre-death, the moment of death, and post-death rites.[35] The *Proficiscere* became a significant part of the pre-death rites as the atmosphere of death became more uncertain and fearful. Also, at the end of the eighth century, two important changes came about in the liturgies, which Paxton detailed.

First, there was a general rearrangement of the liturgical material in the sacramentaries so that the old north Italian prayers for the deathbed reconciliation of penitents were moved from material for Holy Thursday to a new location, immediately before the funerary rites. This innovation, Paxton said:

> signals a fundamental change in ritual structure and tone. In one way or another, these books all record the development of a ritual accompaniment to death itself which focused the power of communal prayer on the deathbed as an aid to the dying person in his or her final agony. The ritual process around the deathbed mirrored the increasingly dense network of reciprocal ties between the living and the dead which marked the Frankish society of the eighth century, and placed each individual and the whole community within

a sacred history stretching from the Old Testament covenant to the final judgment.[36]

We have already tried to bring some understanding as to why the early medieval Christians lost faith in the more optimistic interpretation of death held by the early Church. We have seen how the Irish Church, which seems certain to have influenced the Frankish Church, developed a more rigorous and ascetic lifestyle. The rugged landscape of Ireland, and its lack of city life, produced a lifestyle which 'tended toward the asceticism of the desert fathers rather than the more pragmatic style of St Benedict of Nursia'.[37] This style of spiritual life was conveyed to the Frankish Church by monks during their *peregrinationes* across the Irish Sea and on into continental Europe. There is evidence for this in the growth of new penitential practices and rites in the liturgies of the Frankish Church. But these new spiritual influences would not have gained such a hold if they had not spoken to an existing spiritual insecurity within the Frankish Church.

Paxton also suggested that the cultural tension between the Christian Frankish Empire and the newly conquered Saxon (Germanic) regions, in which the Christian faith could only be communicated among the Saxons in what was for them a foreign language, added to this sense of spiritual insecurity for the new converts. We like to hear the faith proclaimed in our own tongue. Paxton also quoted from a sixth-century rite, possibly the work of Bishop Caesarius of Arles, which includes the following words in a prayer: 'Permit her to cross over the gates of hell and the paths of darkness and remain in the mansions of the saints.'[38] Although this prayer is said over a dead body, it reflects a measure of uncertainty about the future life and the need for prayer to effect a beneficial outcome. This ambivalence, Paxton argued, developed rapidly with the establishment of more elaborate Masses for the dead and votive Masses.

Prayers for the dead began to be organized first on an informal and then a more formal basis among fraternities of religious. These confraternities of prayer for the dead, in which each member was pledged to pray for the others when they died, were formed from groups of clergy, and there is evidence that monastic communities circulated lists of their members, living and dead, for commemoration by other houses.[39] By what may have seemed at the time to have been an imperceptible process, death was no longer a safe and secure process, first because the destination was no longer so certain and second because the journey of the soul to heaven was fraught with dangers. What was needed was a strong new prayer which would help a dying person in this difficult time of transition. The answer to this need was the *Proficiscere*.

This is now the right time to set out the text of the *Proficiscere* as it first appeared in the Frankish Church. This is the *Gellone* version with the *Rheinau* additions in italics. I have not set out all the repetitions of 'Set free, Lord, the soul of this your servant ...', but you will notice immediately how much shorter it is than the *Nursia* text.

> Set out, (*Christian*) soul, from this world.
> In the name of God the Father Almighty who created you.
> In the name of Jesus Christ, Son of the living God, who suffered for you.
> In the name of the Holy Spirit, who was poured out upon you.
> In the name of angels and archangels.
> In the name of thrones and dominions.
> In the name of principalities and powers and of all the heavenly authorities.
> In the name of cherubim and seraphim.
> In the name of all the human race which is sustained by God.
> In the name of patriarchs and prophets.
> In the name of apostles and martyrs.
> In the name of confessors and bishops.
> In the name of priests and deacons and of every rank of the catholic church.

From Birth to Maturity

In the name of monks and anchorites.
In the name of virgins and faithful widows.
Today his place is made in peace and his dwelling in heavenly Jerusalem.

Receive, Lord, your servant in good habitation.
Set free, Lord, the soul of your servant from all the dangers of hell and from all evil tribulations.
Set free, Lord, the soul of your servant, as you set free Noah from the flood.
Elijah and Enoch from the common death of the world.
(*Isaac from the sacrifice and from the hand of his father Abraham.*)
Moses from the hand of Pharaoh, king of the Egyptians.
Job from his suffering.
Daniel from the lion's den.
The three young men from the furnace of blazing fire and from the hands of an evil king.
Jonah from the belly of the whale.
Susanna from false witness.
David from the hand of King Saul and from Goliath and from all his bonds.
Peter and Paul from prisons and chains.
(*Thecla from her three torments.*)
So deign to set free the soul of this man.

You will notice that the first part of the prayer is to all intents and purposes the same as *Nursia* (although there is considerable alteration in spellings and endings in the Latin). To this early version later writers added to the *Libera* all the names in the *Nursia* text, such as Abel, Lot, Abraham, Jacob and all the human race. Perhaps most noticeably, the middle section, from 'Michael' to 'blessed abode', was not in the early texts and was the major later addition.

So this is how the 'young' *Proficiscere* appeared. Not only was the *Proficiscere* added to the new liturgy to be said when a person was dying, but another significant innovation took place in *Rheinau*. Here the words of the *Proficiscere* replaced the reading of the Passion and receipt of the *viaticum*, which were included in the earlier Roman instructions as being the procedure when a person was dying. The use of the *Proficiscere* thus carried considerable liturgical and soteriological weight and responsibility in the process of a rite for the dying. It is an indication of the significance it played that it was a replacement for the reading of the account of Christ's Passion.

Paxton did not comment on the possible source of the title which was later given to this section in the sacramentaries, 'The Commendation of the Soul', apart from the obvious biblical references to Jesus commending his spirit. While there can be no certainty, the source might also have been the increasing practice from the fifth century onwards of 'Commendatory Letters' which were given to pilgrims as they set off on their journey.[40] The letters were evidence that the bearer was a communicant. Those who did not have such letters could avail themselves of the hospitality offered by churches and communities when on pilgrimage, but not the sacrament of Holy Communion. To hold a commendation in one's hand was a passport to receipt of the sacred elements and was evidence of one's good standing. It is at least possible that the idea was extended to the final journey, but spoken in the words of the *Proficiscere* and not written.

We have evidence that, over the next 700 years, there were at least 40 different versions of the *Proficiscere* in circulation. Different churches or dioceses copied and developed their own versions. We can summarize the developments which surrounded the introduction into life of the *Proficiscere* as being a three-phase process, although not all texts as revealed in the manuscripts went through all the three stages.

Stage 1

Although there are not many manuscripts containing the prayer as part of the 'Commendation of the Soul' dating from 800 to 1000, after that there are numerous examples. All texts of the prayer contain both the *Proficiscere* and the *Libera* parts. Starting from *Gellone* and *Rheinau* at the end of the eighth century, the text later spread into a number of other books containing the 'Commendation of the Soul', but, as I have indicated, not all of them. The prayer thus took on a life of its own. The texts tended to expand in length, particularly in the *Libera* as further biblical names were added, although overall it remained stable over the centuries.

Stage 2

The major development in the *Proficiscere* is the addition in some later versions, like the *Nursia* text, of the names of additional saints in a new middle section of the prayer, beginning with Saint Michael: 'May the holy angel Michael, who won the leadership of the heavenly army, uphold you.' This first appears in the Sacramentary of Arezzo, which is dated to the tenth century and was placed at the end of the first part of the *Proficiscere*, as it is in *Nursia*. In its earliest form it was shorter, mentioning only Michael and Peter. It was then developed into its longer and familiar form in a number of eleventh-century manuscripts, including *Nursia*. Then, in the Hamburg Missal, which is late eleventh or early twelfth century, for the first time the text is not included as a part of the *Proficiscere*, but as part of a separate prayer: 'Remember not, we beseech thee, O Lord, the sins and ignorance of his wilful youth', which is placed independently at a later point in the 'Commendation of the Soul'.

Stage 3

During this stage the 'Michael etc.' prayer generally became detached from the *Proficiscere* itself and was incorporated into another part of the 'Commendation of the Soul'. It was in this form that it appeared as the sixth prayer of the 'Commendation of the Soul' in the *Ritual* of 1614. Also during the later part of this stage the list of biblical figures in the

Libera became standardized and incorporated in the 1614 *Ritual*.

The *Proficiscere* itself therefore expanded as it became part of the inflation of funeral material as new sacramentaries appeared. When death was interpreted as being a good event and the journey to heaven assured, there was little need for a long preparatory process on earth before or after death. Starting towards the end of the eighth century, what can be thought of as a double-mirror process developed, as new expectations of life beyond death were mirrored by new pastoral responses on earth. The simplicity of the pre- and post-death liturgies mirrored an understanding that what happened to a person after death was a certain process. As uncertainties about the post-death process grew, and death was interpreted in a more negative, grim and fearful way, both pre- and post-death liturgies developed in complexity and gravity, mirroring what people believed was the state of events beyond death. But one fed on the other in an increasingly vicious circle. The pre- and post-death liturgies needed to be further strengthened in order to meet a more fearful interpretation of death, and in turn this more fearful interpretation of death fed the need for ever more powerful and complex pre- and post-death preparation. By strengthening the pre- and post-death liturgies a new, more frightening picture of life after death was also evolving, which required ever more complex liturgies to counteract it.

During the medieval period people were dying, as they always have and always will. What had changed was the way in which people were interpreting, or understanding, the process of death and its aftermath. Whether or not they were ultimately 'right' about what they thought about the post-death experience (and that could not then, and cannot now, be verified) death, and what lay beyond it, was being interpreted in new and darker ways. This meant that pre- and post-death rituals changed by becoming ever longer and more complex to accommodate this new understanding of the seriousness of death.

From Birth to Maturity

During this time the *Proficiscere* matured as a familiar and accepted part of the liturgy associated with death. Different parts of the Catholic Church each developed their own liturgies, but increasingly the *Proficiscere* remained a constant throughout. In due course there would be a radical pruning of the texts, by both the Roman Catholic Church and the new Church in England, as once again the understanding of death changed. The effect this had on the *Proficiscere* will be explored in Chapter 4. Before that, having established the birth and growth to maturity of the *Proficiscere*, we can begin the search for its ancestors.

3
Discovering the Ancestors

I suspect that, like other people with access to the Internet, I am just one of many who has had a go at tracing the family ancestors. If I type in the name 'Lampard' and 'genealogy' into a search engine, up come an amazing variety of names and details of former Lampards, Lamparts and many other derivatives. Some come from parts of the country in which I know other relations have lived, others carry the same Christian names as members of the family I have already traced. There are fellow clergy, and many people with craft skills, such as jewellers, weavers and small businessmen, which links with the fact that my forebears were Huguenots, illegal immigrants to this country who fled from France to escape persecution. I can find all sorts of similarities and apparent links to my own immediate family.

But do the links actually exist? Just because there are similarities, am I right or wrong to try to fit them somehow into the family tree of my direct ancestors? Many of the problems found, and assumptions made, by an amateur genealogist apply when we try to discover the forebears of the *Proficiscere*. In fact this part of the biography is a fascinating hunt that takes us into many unexpected places. The criteria for sifting and accepting the evidence in the genealogy of the *Proficiscere* have become more rigorous and sceptical as the years have passed, so we are sometimes less certain about how direct an ancestor really is. We begin the story by looking at the scholars who first sought out the *Proficiscere* manuscripts, and then we move further back to the forebears.

Finding the texts

Edmund Bishop (1846–1917) can be called the father of the *Proficiscere* biography, because he was the first scholar to initiate research into it, early in the twentieth century, and to make a study of its forebears and earliest uses. He was entirely self-taught as a liturgist and was actually converted to the Christian faith by reading the massive volumes of early liturgies compiled by Martène. He developed a remarkable skill in deciphering damaged manuscripts that no one else could read. Visits to the continent of Europe enabled him to examine numerous manuscripts that he deciphered, and on which he made exhaustive notes. 'It may safely be said that he knew the western liturgies in their entire sweep, as no one else in his day.'[1]

Bishop's interest in the *Proficiscere* was triggered when he received a letter in April 1906 from Father Unsworth, the parish priest of Barnstaple in Devon. He asked about the origins of the prayer, *Proficiscere, anima Christiana*, in the *Ritual*.[2] This led Bishop to consider all the texts of which he was aware. Were it not for this letter from Father Unsworth, and Bishop's subsequent interest, this biography of the *Proficiscere* would have been more difficult, indeed it might never have started. We do not know what Bishop wrote to Father Unsworth, but Bishop's full response came in an updated article he wrote over ten years later, which is the starting point for any research. Perhaps the name of Father Unsworth should be included in the Acknowledgements of this book.[3]

Bishop's article, in 1918, on eighth-century burial rites, included his research on the *Proficiscere*. He identified its first use in the two Frankish Gelasian sacramentaries, *Gellone* and *Rheinau* (the subjects of the last chapter), which he dated as eighth century, and in six later manuscripts he had read.[4] This was the first accurate dating of the prayer. He added further that use of the prayer did not spread to other contemporary sacramentaries such as the Gregorian type. From the evidence available to him at that time, Bishop believed that there was a gap of more than two centuries before the prayer (or references to it) appeared again in church rituals.[5]

Nearly twenty years later, in 1935, Dom Louis Gougaud produced the next, more detailed, study of a number of the manuscripts containing the 'Commendation of the Soul', which formed the context in which the *Proficiscere* was usually set.[6] He identified a further eight manuscripts which contained versions of the *Proficiscere*, so the total now known was sixteen. It is an indication of how recent is accurate research into early medieval liturgy that Gougaud pointed out that in 1931 the German scholar Ludwig Fischer had provisionally dated the *Proficiscere* as a twelfth-century composition.[7] The fact that Fischer was apparently unaware of the work of Bishop is an example of the problem of international scholarship, particularly in the aftermath of a world war.

Most significantly in our search for the forebears, Gougaud listed a number of texts[8] which, he said, 'present the same characteristic traits as the *Libera*'.[9] In other words, these were texts which carried *Proficiscere*-type material, but were not examples of the prayer as such. However, he did not comment on them or indicate with any clarity which ones might be considered to be earlier than *Gellone*, contemporary with it, or later. Gougaud's work was therefore an excellent platform for further research, as he did not follow up many of the manuscripts he listed. Thanks to Gougaud we will be able to follow up these fruitful leads.

Damian Sicard

Quite early on in my research, when I was facing a number of initial difficulties, I was recommended by Paul Sheppy, a friend who is a Baptist liturgist, to visit a priest in France who, he said, would be able to help me. Father P.-M. Gy responded warmly to my letter and on a cold November day I travelled to Paris, where I met him at the Centre for Advanced Liturgical Research. I did not realize, when I first approached him, that he was one of the world's greatest and most highly regarded authorities in the field of medieval funeral liturgy. Indeed, I do not think I would have dared approach him, very green as I was, if I had known just how eminent he was. After my visit I seemed to find his name wherever I looked in my researches. Father Gy is one of the last of his generation who were young scholars when the Second Vatican Council was summoned by Pope John XXIII. He was one those with special responsibility for the renewal of the funeral services.

It is fortunate that Father Gy spoke excellent English and he welcomed me into his very modest study bedroom, crammed from floor to ceiling with books, papers and articles. Even the bed was covered with papers. I shared with him the nature of my research, in which he showed great interest, repeating several times, 'What you are studying is most important!'

After Father Gy had listened to an outline of my research, he asked some brisk and penetrating questions, recommended several books to me, and even photocopied some articles for me in the library. One of the books he recommended was in French, over four hundred pages long, written by another priest, Canon Damien Sicard, who had been in the same group with him at Vatican II. I had already read some of Sicard's articles in which I had found what seemed to be some errors and omissions. I shared these with Father Gy who was fascinated, and chuckled that his former colleague had apparently overlooked some material. After we had finished our discussion he took me into the chapel to pray. Liturgy and worship became one. My visit to him was one of those awe-inspiring moments, as I felt myself timidly stepping over the doorstep of a world I had never before seen and would never see again. In the early years of the twenty-first century we are witnessing the ageing of the last of the younger scholars, like Fr Gy and Fr Sicard, who actually took part in the momentous events of Vatican II. Fr Gy died in 2004.

Canon Damien Sicard, a Canon of Montpellier Cathedral, wrote the ground-breaking book on early Latin funeral rites,

The Liturgy for the Dead in the Latin Church from its Origins to the Carolingian Reforms, about which Father Gy had spoken.[10] Sicard's overall contribution as the greatest scholar of the medieval texts of the *Proficiscere* is invaluable in this biography, and much that follows in this chapter is built on his study of the prayer. Sicard discovered many more manuscripts containing the *Proficiscere* than Bishop or Gougaud had done. This was the result of increased scholarly interest in the early manuscripts, the availability of microfilms and the number of scholarly texts produced by groups such as the Henry Bradshaw Society.

You will remember that Bishop had originally identified eight texts containing the *Proficiscere*, to which Gougaud added eight more, together with '*Proficiscere*-type' material. Sicard found about another twenty-five, but I had spotted that he failed to include in his full list three of the eight manuscripts identified by Bishop sixty years earlier. One of these was *Nursia*; thus my interest in it. In my own researches I have noticed one further manuscript not included in anyone's list, and no doubt there are others to be discovered. We now have nearly all the material we need for our study of the cousins and ancestors.

Searching for the ancestors

It is clear that the earliest textual examples, or attestations, of the *Proficiscere* are to be found in the two Frankish Gelasian manuscripts *Gellone* and *Rheinau*. If these are the source documents (acknowledged or unacknowledged) for all later examples of the prayer, where do we find the ancestors, or possible pre-sources lying behind the earliest example of the text? A major problem to be borne in mind, when exploring possible ancestors, is that similarities do not necessarily indicate sources. A similarity only indicates a possible source, not a source itself. Not everyone older than I am with the surname Lampard is necessarily my ancestor.

Discovering the Ancestors 57

I suggest that there are seven categories for classifying possible sources for finding the ancestors of a liturgical text, which we can use in our search. They are as follows.

1 Biblical material

There are no prizes for guessing that the Bible as a whole is clearly a source, and that medieval liturgists would be familiar with it. In the first chapter we saw how clearly the writer of the prayer had used biblical material, so there is no need to repeat what was said there. It is possible that the idea of 'The Commendation of the Soul' can be traced back to Luke 23.46, where Luke tells us that, on the cross, Jesus seems to have quoted Psalm 30.6, 'Father, into your hands I commend my spirit.' But we need to be cautious here as the biblical record refers to 'spirit' and not 'soul'.

2 Apocryphal writings

Some of the writings from the time of the early Church claimed authenticity, but did not receive endorsement by being included in the canon of the New Testament. Among these are three possible claimants for ancestry: one has a very strong claim, one fairly strong and one weak. The first is the book *Acts of Paul and Thecla*, which we have already indicated is the most likely source for the reference to Thecla at the end of the *Libera*. We will say more about Thecla when the theme of 'Local cults of the saints' is explored as possible source material.

The second possible ancestor is the apocryphal *The Apocalypse of Paul*, which dates from the end of the fourth century. It is of particular interest because it offers a view from heaven of good and bad souls being accompanied together on the journey after death. As a good man was dying, holy and evil angels stood around, but the evil angels found no home in him. The holy angels told the soul to take note of the body, as the soul would return to it on the day of resurrection. These angels received the soul out of the body and kissed it as one they had known every day. Coming into the presence of God the soul met Michael, angels, archangels, cherubim and the 24 elders. The soul then met Enoch, Elijah, virgins, and then later Isaiah, Jeremiah, Ezekiel, lesser prophets, Abraham, Isaac, Jacob, Lot and Job, and other unnamed saints. Finally the soul met David in the City of Jerusalem.

While there is no evidence, beyond the very obvious similarity, that this text was of direct influence in the composition of the *Proficiscere*, it does suggest a milieu out of which it might have developed and to which the prayer is, in part, a pastoral response. As J. K. Elliott has said, 'The Apocalypse of Paul more than any other of the apocryphal apocalypses was responsible for the spread of many of the popular ideas of Heaven and Hell throughout Christianity and especially in the Western church of the Middle Ages.'[11]

Finally, reference can be made to the identity of the 'Enoch' whose name appears in many versions of the *Proficiscere*.[12] The reference was either to Genesis 5.24, 'Enoch walked with God; then he was no more because God took him', or to the apocryphal Book of Enoch. Enoch, Books 1–2 (Book 3 is fifth to sixth century AD) is an expansion of Genesis 5.21–32, the life of Enoch up to the Flood. There does not appear to be a compelling case that the Book of Enoch, rather than Genesis, was a source or inspiration to the creator of the *Proficiscere*.

3 Patristic writings

The opening section of the *Proficiscere* may have been influenced by the writing of the sixth-century eastern writer Pseudo-Dionysius whose writings were referred to in the first chapter.[13]

There is more certainty that the trinitarian formula (In the name of the Father ... In the name of the Son ... etc.) was received from early writings of the Church, but no particular ancestor source can be identified. It is clear that the *Proficiscere* was the product of the western Church, as there are no examples of it in eastern liturgy, but there was a continual interplay of liturgical books and ideas throughout Christendom. Is there any firm evidence of eastern ancestry in the creation of the *Proficiscere*?

It is possible that both the innovative language and shape of the prayer, and its theological and liturgical intent, were influenced either directly by the writings, or indirectly by the milieu, created by the work of Dionysius. His writings provide both the material and the theological shape for the first part of the *Proficiscere*, illustrating his favoured hierarchical and triadic system. The threefold structure for the 'going forth' is set in trinitarian, angelic and earthly terms, much used by Dionysius.

But were his works known in the Frankish Church? We do know that the Byzantine emperor Michael sent a copy of the works of Dionysius, which were in Greek, to Louis the Pious, a Frankish king in 827.[14] Charles the Bald later had this text translated into Latin by the Irish scholar Eriugena.[15] However, this was after the likely date of the *Proficiscere* in the *Gellone* text, so no direct link can be proved. However, Judith Herrin has recently drawn attention to evidence of an earlier gift of a copy of the works of Dionysius. During the period around the Lateran Synod (769) Pope Paul I (757–767) had sent to the Frankish Church 'Greek texts as well as the more familiar extracts from pseudo-Dionysius.'[16] Perhaps more importantly, Herrin draws our attention to the broader influence of the theology of the eastern Church on the Frankish bishops who attended the Lateran Synod:

> Their presence in Rome had the result of incorporating them into the Orthodox Christian universe ... Through the declaration of iconophile doctrine, accompanied by the eastern creed, which was also read out in translation, they gained a broader vision of Christianity.[17]

There was much debate at this time over images of God, brought on in part by the influence of Islam, which allows no such image. Herrin also offered evidence of the pattern of wanderings of both scholars and manuscripts within the churches East and West, and it is not inconceivable that some of Dionysius' influence circulated within the churches of the West as well as the East.

Paul Rorem wrote of the major influence that the writings of Dionysius had on the medieval world, in particular in the fields of theology, liturgy and mysticism, and adds:

> Interpreting the Areopagite is a major challenge for any reader, and assessing the relative influence of the Dionysian texts in medieval Christianity would require several lifetimes. A major purpose of this book is to invite others to undertake the task of interpreting the Dionysian writings and evaluating their influence.[18]

Perhaps we can say that there is good evidence for some ancestral material here.

4 Archaeology

Archaeology may seem a strange place in which to look for the ancestors of the *Proficiscere* but it was the most popular hunting ground for all the early scholars who wrote about the prayer.

In the 1870s a French scholar, Edmund le Blant, exploring Christian burial remains near Arles in France, discovered something that excited him. On a sarcophagus (a stone coffin) he found engravings of Old Testament figures, which he identified as being some of the same Old Testament figures featured in the *Libera*. As the tombs were second or third century he thought he had discovered a very early source for the prayer, and that the prayer dated from that age. Edmund Bishop was not persuaded that an early ancestor had been found, and made two critical points. First, that le Blant used his discovery of these engravings as evidence for the 'first attestation (or, as I should say, origin) of the *Proficiscere*, and of the *Libera* invocations which originally formed an integral part of it'.[19] The engravings clearly were not an attestation, nor were they evidence of the origins of the prayer. Second, said Bishop, the *Proficiscere* was of a much later date than the evidence from the Arles sarcophagus, therefore it was not evidence of the prayer's origins.

This second point of Bishop's begs the question about the gap between the dating of archaeological findings and the possible dating of a liturgical text. An obvious parallel is that there can be a wide time-gap between the composition of a biblical book and use of part of its material in a prayer. Evidence that an illustration on a grave is much earlier than a liturgical text, which refers to the subject matter illustrated on the grave, is not conclusive evidence either way that the first did not influence the second. Bishop was therefore both right and wrong in his judgement.

More excitement occurred in 1873 at an excavation in Podgoritza, which is now the capital of Montenegro, in former Yugoslavia. Archaeologists unearthed a cup, now known as the Cup of Podgoritza. It was originally dated as being third century, but more recent research has put the date as being fifth century. This fascinating object measures 0.24 metres across and is made of coloured and transparent glass.[20] The cup shows nine biblical figures, five of which are also included in various versions of the *Proficiscere*, and four of which are not. Again it was claimed to be an ancestor. Even if we dismiss the early attempts to date the prayer from the date of the Cup, such evidence can hardly be sufficient to describe it as an ancestral source. The most that can be said is that it represents further evidence that groups of Old Testament figures were often brought together in the liturgy.

We can parallel all these attempts by liturgical scholars to find 'evidence', with attempts by biblical archaeologists at the end of the nineteenth century to link any archaeological find, such as smashed ruins at Jericho, with a biblical narrative as a way of 'proving' a link between the two.[21] It appears that liturgical scholars have suffered from the same desire to prove archaeological linkages. There does not seem to be any strong ancestral linkage of the *Proficiscere* in either France or Yugoslavia.

Some liturgists were also excited by a further archaeological source which I was able to examine for myself. During my visit to Rome to examine the *Nursia* text, I also went to the Catacombs of Priscilla underneath the old *Via Salaria*, a road leading north-west out of Rome. The only way to get there by public transport was on a 'round the houses' shuttle bus, which weaved in and out of estates and shopping areas. Eventually I arrived at the *Via Salaria* and after some difficulty found the catacombs, which are in the care of a religious order. The coolness of the catacombs after the temperature of the hot spring day made me glad I had remembered to bring a sweater with me.

The nun who showed me round took me along the many winding passages to a number of large cubicles carved out of the rocks. Several of the cubicles had wall paintings on them, still quite clear although they date from the third century. I quickly identified illustrations of Daniel and the lions, the three young boys, Susanna, Abraham and Isaac, and Jonah. It is easy to imagine how excited liturgical scholars and archaeologists would have been when they linked the prayer and the illustrations together. Writing about the ways in which the afterlife is illustrated in catacombs, such as the Catacombs of Priscilla, the *Atlas of the Early Christian World* said the theme of 'deliverance through prayer from mortal danger' was a common one. Among those often cited are Daniel, Jonah, Susanna, Noah, Isaac, the three young men and a few others.[22]

Overall the discipline of archaeology, one of the most popular sources a century ago, is not directly helpful as far as the ancestry of the *Proficiscere* is concerned. What it does show is that the use of biblical figures representing salvation in the *Proficiscere* has a long, indirect lineage.

5 Early prayers and liturgical material

We have a considerable volume of prayer and liturgical material from the early Church. As we have already mentioned, Gougaud listed several manuscripts he had discovered that had similar characteristics to the *Proficiscere*. Three manuscripts are very much earlier than the *Gellone* text, dating from the fourth century.[23] These are a prayer of St Severus and two prayers of Pseudo-Cyprianus, and a prayer of St Euplus not noticed by Gougaud. We will look at each of these for possible ancestors.

The prayer of St Severus

St Severus was priest of Adrianopolis, and was martyred in about the year 303. As he was about to die he is recorded as offering the following prayer:

> You who preserved Noah and provided riches for Abraham, who delivered Isaac and provided a sacrificial victim instead of him, who engaged in a joyous wrestling contest with Jacob and led Lot out of Sodom from an accursed land, who appeared to Moses and made Joshua son of Nun prudent, who deigned to journey with Joseph and led out his people from the land of Egypt, bringing them to the land of covenant, who aided the three young men in the furnace, whom the fire did not touch, as they were besprinkled by the holy dew of your majesty, who closed the mouths of lions, giving life and food to Daniel, who saved Jonah and did not allow him to be harmed either by the ocean depths or the bite of the cruel sea-monster or to perish, who armed Judith, who delivered Susanna from unjust judges, who gave glory to Esther, who commanded that Haman should perish, who led us forth from darkness to eternal light.[24]

It would be hard to deny that there must be some sort of link between this early prayer and the *Proficiscere*. So many of the familiar biblical figures are there: Noah, Abraham, Lot, Moses, the three young men, Daniel and Jonah etc. You will have noticed that Judith and Esther named here are not included in any version of the *Proficiscere*. Clearly there is a shared tradition between St Severus and this prayer, but to what extent can any ancestral link be traced? What we cannot say, as was said by some scholars earlier last century, is that the prayer of St Severus proves that the *Proficiscere* is fourth century. All we can say is that behind the eighth-century prayer lies a tradition, when contemplating death, of linking together a series of Old Testament figures.

The two prayers of Pseudo-Cyprianus

These are two long prayers, probably dating from the fourth century. Sicard, who argued for a link, set out only the parts of the two prayers that have similarities with the *Proficiscere*.[25] As you read them, once again you will feel that you are on familiar ground.

> *First prayer.* God of Abraham, God of Isaac, God of Jacob, God of the prophets, God of the apostles, God of virgins, God of those who live good lives ... for we bend our knees and bow our necks to you to whom the angels, archangels, countless martyrs and choirs of apostles and prophets give praise ... And as you showed mercy to the three young men in the furnace and to Daniel, do the same for us your servants ... Be with us as you were with your apostles in chains, with Thecla in the fire, Paul among his persecutors, Peter amid the waves ... free us from the destruction of everlasting death.

> *Second prayer.* I thank and praise you ... God of the prophets, God of the apostles, God of the martyrs ... free me from this world, and hear me as you heard Jonah in the belly of the whale ... Hear my prayer as you heard Daniel in the lion's den. Hear my prayer as you heard Susanna in the

toils of the elders. Free me from this world as you freed Thecla from the midst of the arena ...

The context of these prayers is not death, as it was with the prayer of St Severus, but prayers that are said when people, catechumens, are about to be baptized. There is a clear biblical link between baptism and death, as Paul says, 'We have been buried with him by baptism into death, so that ... we might walk in newness of life' (Rom. 6.4). Referring to the biblical figures listed in the *Libera*, Sicard said:

> the church invoked these in the hour of agony or death struggle just as it had invoked them on behalf of the catechumens in the ancient rites of initiation. The *Proficiscere* made it clear that in their deaths the dying were bringing their baptism to fulfilment.[26]

But this theological link does not strengthen his argument for the *Proficiscere* being in any way textually or directly linked to the prayers of Pseudo-Cyprianus.

Is the undoubted similarity between phrases and subjects in these prayers and the *Proficiscere* sufficient to say that they are in any meaningful way part of the ancestry of the *Proficiscere*? Were they known to the monk who first wrote the *Proficiscere*, either in written form or memorized? The likelihood of any possible direct link is greatly weakened when the full prayers and the extracts quoted by Sicard are compared, because of Sicard's selectivity. In the first prayer Sicard selected only 71 words out of 388 (18 per cent). The second, longer prayer contains 860 words, from which Sicard has selected only 55 words (6 per cent).[27] We should always be cautious about using statistical analysis when dealing with textual matters, but it is clear that, when the texts of the two prayers are read in full, the likelihood of the prayers of Pseudo-Cyprianus being in any meaningful way an ancestor is far less convincing than when apparent similarities are 'cherry-picked' and differences are ignored. Sicard himself was very much in two minds over the likely link between the *Proficiscere* and the prayers of Pseudo-Cyprianus. His conclusions are worth quoting in full:

> When we realise the popularity of these prayers and when we observe how close they are in construction, inspiration and at times even expression, to the *Proficiscere*, we must believe that the author of the latter could not have been unfamiliar with the earlier prayers.
>
> There is no point in my demonstrating that the whole of the Bible and of its major figures are present to the mind of the author of the *Proficiscere*; this is self-evident. I agree with Canon Martimort that we should think also of the same biblical images as used in the old Gelasian Sacramentary in the exorcisms of catechumens.
>
> While it does not seem arguable that the *Proficiscere* itself goes back to the second century or even to the fifth, it does seem that through its various sources it reflects an inspiration which belongs to the very early centuries of Christianity.[28]

You will notice that the more positive judgement in favour of a literary link contained in the first paragraph is countered by a far less positive, and distinctly vague, judgement in the last paragraph. The very tentativeness of Sicard's conclusions indicates the weakness of any obvious or explicit link between Pseudo-Cyprianus and the text of the *Proficiscere*. In looking for evidence of an ancestral link, variances are as significant as similarities, and the variances include the 'omissions', if they are such, of Mary, Tobit, the Sons of Israel in the land of Egypt, and Ezekiel from the *Proficiscere*, if Pseudo-Cyprianus was a true ancestral document.

The prayer of St Euplus

St Euplus was martyred at about the same time as St Severus. When I first read his prayer I felt a frisson of excitement because I thought that perhaps I had found evidence for a clear ancestral link. The reason for this is that I first discovered the prayer in English:

> Listen, dearest brethren; pray to God and fear with your whole heart, for he is mindful of those who fear him, before they *go forth from this world*: and when they go forth the angels will hasten to meet them and will bring them to the holy city of Jerusalem.[29] (my italics)

I checked out the Latin original in Ruinart's book, only to discover that 'go forth from this world' is in fact a disappointing *'antequam exeant de hoc saeculo'*,[30] rather than the familiar *'Proficiscere de hoc mundo'* etc. Alas, there is no similarity with the first line of the *Proficiscere*, although there is a modest parallel with the end of the prayer.

In conclusion, it can be said that, although the similarities with ancient prayers are stronger than in some other categories, it is not possible to conclude with any confidence that a direct ancestral link can be made to any one original source. The most that can be claimed is that these prayers indicate a continuity of themes from the earliest days of the Church.

6 Contemporary liturgical and non-liturgical material

Non-liturgical material can be dealt with briefly. Some insights can be gained from near-contemporary records of the moments before death contained in the accounts of visions, which today might be classified as 'near-death experiences'. Two examples, which offer visionary material, at least provide a cultural framework or 'mould' that may have shaped the form that the *Proficiscere* took. The Venerable Bede, writing in about 731, said that after his death the soul of Drycthelm was led on a journey by a guiding spirit, during which a number of sins were dealt with by the use of fire and ice as punishments. He also looked into the mouth of hell where he saw the souls of the dead rising and falling. Between heaven and hell was a place where souls awaited a favourable judgement.[31]

Another vision, Wetti's, comes from about 824, and was written in Reichenau in Rhaetia, interestingly enough a possible place of composition of the *Rheinau* text, although the date of the first written version of Wetti's vision is after the earliest likely date for the *Rheinau* version.

In this vision Wetti is met by a shining angel and acknowledges that patriarchs, prophets, apostles and all the other dignitaries are working for humanity in heaven and on earth. After the first part of the vision, Wetti fell to the floor in front of his brothers and lay in the shape of a cross while they sang the seven penitential psalms (these became part of the 'Commendation of the Soul'). In the second part of the vision, again led by the angel, he encounters the King of Kings and Lord of Lords, the multitude of saints, holy priests, innumerable numbers of blessed martyrs and holy virgins,[32] and finally he is warned that widows living in pleasure are as dead.[33] If nothing else, these visions provide a helpful 'feel' for the dangers of the world envisaged by contemporary writers, against which the *Proficiscere* offered assistance.

As far as liturgical sources are concerned, it is worth mentioning at this point a very different theory of the origins of the Frankish Gelasians, put forward by Anton Baumstark.[34] You will remember that the generally accepted theory is that they were of Frankish origin, drawing on a number of sources. Baumstark argued for an English composition. He proposed that Boniface carried the texts from Wessex to the Continent when he worked as a missionary in the Frankish Church. Baumstark's theory has its attractions, particularly if you are English, but he did not support it with sufficient evidence.

As far as liturgical material is concerned, it is clear that there are similarities between the text of the *Proficiscere* and three contemporary manuscripts, two Irish – the Stowe Missal and *Oengus* – and an English text, the Book of Cerne. All of these were first identified by Gougaud, but were not further examined in his article. As far as the Irish texts are concerned, the problem lies in accurate dating, which might then indicate which documents were first. The English text is dated as from the first half of the ninth century.[35] We will look at these three possible candidates for more contemporary family links.

The Stowe Missal

A possible link is found in the first prayer in the Ordinary of the Mass in the Stowe Missal, parts of which have been translated by Esther de Waal. The relevant text of the prayer reads:[36]

> We have sinned, O Lord, we have sinned, have mercy upon our sins and save us; Thou who didst guide Noah over the waves of the deluge, hearken unto us; Thou who didst call back Jonah from the abyss by a word, deliver us; Thou who didst hold out Thy hand to Peter drowning, be aiding unto us; Christ son of God, Who didst bring to pass the miracles of the Lord with our fathers, be propitious in our time, stretch forth thy hand from on high, deliver us O Christ. O Christ hear us, O Christ hear us, *Kyrie eleison*.[37]

The dating of the Stowe Missal is a matter of much debate,[38] but a likely date is very early in the ninth century, which makes it not far from being contemporaneous with *Gellone*. An Irish–Frankish link is not proved by this evidence, but it indicates the possibility that Baumstark might have been partly correct if he had surmised at least an Irish, if not an English, link.

The martyrology of Oengus

In the last chapter we looked at the strong evidence that there was an Irish connection with the Frankish Church. A prayer of the Irish St Oengus confirms this.[39] You will appreciate the excitement I felt when I read the following words for the first time. Surely I had found an ancestor? (I have omitted the repetitions.)

Mayest Thou save me, O Jesus, my body and my soul, from every evil that exists, that offends on the earth.

Mayest thou save me, O Jesus, O lord of fair assemblies, as Thou savedst Elijah, with Enoch, from the world.

Noah son of Lamech from the Flood.

Abram from the hands of the Chaldeans.

Lot from the sin of the cities.

Jonas from the belly of the great whale.

Isaac from his father's hands.

Thecla from the maw of the monster.

Jacob from the hands of his brethren.

John from the poison of the serpent.

David from the valour of Goliath's sword.

The noble Susanna after the lie concerning her.

Nineveh in the time of the plague.

The people of Israel from (Mount) Gilboa.

Daniel out of the den of lions.

Moses from the hand of the Pharaoh.

The Three Children from the burning furnace.

Tobit from the misery of blindness.

Paul and Peter before kings from the punishment of the prison.

Job from the devil's tribulations.

David from Saul, from his accusation.

Joseph from the hands of the brethren.

Holy Israel from the bondage of Egypt.

Peter from the waves of the sea.

John out of the fiery vat.

Samson, who escaped out of the city.

Martin from the priest of the idol.

Patrick from death by poison in Tara.

Cóemgein from the falling of the mountain.

Mayest Thou save me, O Jesus, everlasting are Thy miracles! O Lord whom I entreat, I expect Thy messengers.

When the great boon may come to me, whether at Easter or in Lent, may the kinfolk I have commemorated convey me into paradise!

Discovering the Ancestors

I have commemorated the King above the clouds, etc.
IT ENDETH. Amen.

Unlike any of the other possible ancestors, the flow and style of Oengus's prayer shows a very marked similarity to that of the *Libera*. You will have noticed that the prayer exhibits an important difference in that it is addressed to Jesus, but the repetitive 'as thou savest' linked with Noah, Abraham, Lot, Jonah, and Daniel *et al.* demonstrates some sort of link between the two manuscripts. Oengus is a fascinating document because, although very early, it shows a creativity far exceeding that of any of the other versions. You may have noticed the following, which are unique to this document.

Jacob from the hands of his brethren. This reference is not entirely clear. It may refer to Jacob being saved from his brother Esau (Gen. 33), or 'Jacob' may be a copying error for 'Joseph' (Gen. 37.26–28), which was corrected 13 lines later.

John from the poison of the serpent. Again this is not clear. John could be an Irish saint (several are mentioned at the end) who appears earlier in the list, or it could be a reference to the legend that the apostle John was given a cup of poison by a pagan priest, or perhaps a mistaken reference to Paul and the serpent (Acts 28.3–6). It is worth remembering that, in a community that contained few books, inaccurate memories could produce errors.

Nineveh in the time of the plague. This is clearly a reference to the story of Jonah, but there is no reference to a plague, only a potential destruction that was averted.

The people of Israel from (Mount) Gilboa. This is a puzzling reference as it was on Mount Gilboa that Saul and the Israelites fought and were defeated by the Philistines. Many of the Isrealites were killed, Saul was injured and fell upon his own sword (1 Sam. 31.1–13). It seems too sophisticated to adduce from this reference the fact that Saul's reign was followed by the house of David, and thus the people of Israel were saved.

Tobit from the misery of blindness. Tobit was blinded by fresh sparrows' droppings (Tobit 2.10), but later his sight was restored by his son, through the medicinal application of the gall of a fish (Tobit 11.7–13).

Joseph from the hands of the brethren. Joseph's brothers planned to kill him, but sold him in to slavery in Egypt (Gen. 37.26–28).

Holy Israel from the bondage of Egypt. This refers to the escape from slavery in Egypt (Ex. 14).

Peter from the waves of the sea. Jesus saves Peter, who has started to walk on the water, as he is about to sink into the Sea of Galilee (Matt. 14.28–31).

John out of the fiery vat. There is a tradition that the apostle John was plunged into a cauldron of boiling oil by the Emperor Domitian, but escaped unharmed.

Samson, who escaped out of the city. Samson escaped from the Philistine city of Gaza, where he had visited a prostitute, by removing the gates of the city at midnight and carrying them away (Judg. 16.1–3).

Martin from the priest of the idol. This may be a reference to Martin of Tours, who is famous for cutting his coat in two to help a beggar. There were several attempts on his life by opponents and this may refer to one of them.

Patrick from death by poison in Tara. Patrick of Ireland visited Tara, where the King of Ireland lived, and where he faced opposition and attempts on his life, but I have found no reference to poison.

Cóemgein from the falling of the mountain. This is the Irish name for Kevin, a Bishop of Leinster, but again I have found no reference to what sounds like an escape from a landslide.

Oengus' martyrology is a wonderfully rich and varied version of the *Libera*. Not only does he draw on a wider variety of biblical figures and saints, but each one is introduced by an individual attribution to Jesus, such as 'O king of pure brightness' and 'whom thy Mother's folk rejected'.

In his martyrology, Oengus commends himself to God but, apart from the fact that it comes at the end of his manuscript, there is little sense that it is said *in extremis*. While Oengus is aware of his mortality, and hopes that he will be taken up into heaven when his time comes, there is little immediacy that would suggest a direct link with imminent death. De Waal actually commented that Oengus versifies the 'Commendation of the Soul' prayer,[40] assuming a causal link to the Celtic and from Frankish documents. It appears that her knowledge of the *Proficiscere* had led her to assume this is so.

But what is the strength and weakness of the case for arguing for an Irish ancestor for the *Libera*? Clearly the earliest dates for the two documents are similar. O'Loughlin does not discuss the date of Oengus, only commenting in passing that it is later than 688.[41] But this is not in itself sufficient evidence. The two earliest examples of the text of the *Proficiscere* are found in only two of the ten or so Frankish Gelasian texts known to exist, and dates for *Gellone* or *Rheinau* are sufficiently close, particularly if it is accepted that material in these liturgies may have existed before known dates in *libelli*. Second, as we have seen, there is strong evidence for Irish–Frankish links.

Third, in both text and context, there do seem to be marked similarities between the two liturgies. While it must always be borne in mind that the differences are as important as the similarities, textual links between the two documents are apparent, even on a casual reading. Of the 22 characters (or situations) in Oengus (excluding Irish names), 10 are reproduced in *Gellone* (and there are none in *Gellone* not also in Oengus), and 11 in *Rheinau* (again with no originals of its own). Together these two documents only include 14 of the 22 names in Oengus.

As mentioned above, Oengus is pleading for himself to be saved from the dangers of this world (rather than for someone else) so it does not carry any definite suggestion that it is associated with a sense on the part of Oengus of impending death. The rhythm and style of the catena of mainly Old Testament figures do suggest a much more realistic family link than any in the earlier categories.

However, there are arguments against an Irish 'source'. First, Oengus has a more 'developed' list than any of the early texts containing the *Proficiscere*, in fact it is the most developed list ever created. If Oengus was copied by the Frankish Church, why were about 50 per cent of the characters not included? A case can also be made for reverse influence, that an early example of the *Proficiscere* travelled from the Frankish Church to Ireland, and that Oengus used and developed the 'simple' format of *Gellone* or *Rheinau* when composing his more developed work. Which way did a *libellus*, or other liturgical document, travel? O'Loughlin, an expert on Celtic literature, told me in correspondence that he doubted that Oengus was a possible source for the *Proficiscere*. He writes:

> the answer is almost certainly that the influence is *from* [his emphasis] the continent, Oengus's martyrology (written in Old Irish in the main) was not used on the continent. You can therefore view it as a witness to the larger picture, rather than as an agent in the tradition of that text.[42]

Oengus is probably as close as we can get to 'family', if not to an ancestor.

The Book of Cerne

Finally we turn to the Book of Cerne, the last manuscript on Gougaud's list of possible English or Irish relations. This is a Morning Prayer contained in it.

> May we walk in prosperity in this day of light.
> May the power of the most high God, greatest of the gods,
> In a manner pleasing to Christ,
> In the light of the Holy Spirit,
> In the faith of the patriarchs,
> In the merits of the prophets,
> In the peace of the apostles,

In the joy of the angels,
In the splendour of the saints,
In the works of monks,
In the power of the just,
In the martyrdom of the martyrs,
In the chastity of the virgins,
In the wisdom of God,
In much patience,
In abstinence of flesh,
In continence of tongue,
In abundance of peace,
In praise of the Trinity,
With our senses alert,
With constant good works,
With the spiritual realities,
With divine conversation,
With blessings,
In these things is the journey of all labouring for Christ who leads his saints after death into eternal joy
That I may hear the voice of the angels praising God and saying Holy, Holy, Holy.

This is a private prayer rather than a liturgical text. The material resonates both in content and rhythm with the *Proficiscere*. However, its likely date, after the end of the eighth century, and its content mean that it cannot be considered to be an ancestral document. However, it is an example of the prayer-genre that was prevalent at the time and at least its style might have influenced the writer of the first *Proficiscere*. One scholar notes:

> There seems then reason for thinking that we have in the *Book of Cerne* a product of the beginnings of English Christianity, at a time when the spiritual forces which created it had not yet been welded together into their final resultant ... We appear to have specimens of the devotional, as distinguished from the liturgical, prayers current in

England in the VII and VIII centuries. Such prayers the English missioners themselves probably used and carried to the Continent.[43]

The category of contemporary liturgical and non-liturgical material proves to be the most fruitful in terms of a search for ancestors. But although the evidence for ancestry is stronger in this category than in others, we still have not found a direct ancestor, only evidence of strong family relationships.

7 The cult of the saints

The fact that many churches are named after or associated with saints may well indicate the popularity of particular saints' names. In a similar way the inclusion or exclusion of the many Old Testament figures in different versions of the *Libera* may also be the result of local communities identifying with particular biblical figures. In addition to the biblical figures, the cult of Thecla enjoyed considerable popularity in the early Church and medieval periods. According to *The Book of Saints* she was one of the most celebrated of the saints of the early Church with a feast day on 23 September.[44] However, it is possible that this may not be all that can be said about the story of Thecla and the *Proficiscere*. About fifty years before the *Rheinau* text was written, the Anglo-Saxon priest Boniface had been sent from England to engage in missionary work in Germany. He needed assistance as his work was progressing, so he turned to St Tetta, Abbess of Wimborne, who sent him a nun called Thecla, who was clearly a woman of considerable power and influence. She arrived from England in 748 or 749, serving first in Bischofheim and then in Ochsenfurt, where she became abbess. Boniface then made her Abbess also of Kitzingen on the River Main, before she died in about 790. 'She was noted for her humility, gentleness and charity not only among her Sisters but also among the local people ... There is some late evidence of a cult in the area around the abbey.'[45]

Discovering the Ancestors

This at least raises the question about the possible influence of Thecla. If she was popular and well respected her name would be on the minds of those who worked with her. As we saw in the last chapter, the *Rheinau* text is believed to have been composed in either northern France or Switzerland in about 800, and neither area is very far from where Thecla of Kitzingen was influential. The fact that there was a highly popular Thecla working in the area where the *Rheinau* manuscript was first written at least offers the possibility that her name encouraged the writer to include or keep her namesake Thecla in the prayer. So the reason why Thecla's name appears in the *Rheinau* text remains a tantalizing question, perhaps answered here.

This chapter has provided a history of the discovery of the manuscripts containing the texts of the *Proficiscere*, and a trawl through a variety of early Church and medieval evidence, looking for possible ancestors. As we said at the beginning, to some extent success in finding ancestors depends on how strictly you apply critical methods when assessing similarities. My own judgement is that the apparent similarities are not generally sufficient to draw any very safe conclusions about the direct line of ancestors, other than the obvious biblical material. This applies to the *Libera*, in particular.

The best I can offer to those who long to establish ancestry is an awareness that the liturgy, writings and iconography of the early Church resemble a vast and varied 'alphabet soup' of images, saints, biblical and apocryphal material. Perhaps a more felicitous phrase than 'alphabet soup' is the one offered by Dionysius, who used the phrase 'mysterious mixing bowl' to describe the place where divine Wisdom prepares nourishment, both liquid and solid, and encourages all to partake.[46]

This means that the material displayed in any one document cannot easily be tied down to a knowledge, by the writer, of an earlier document or archaeological find, just because there are some similarities. To argue otherwise is a denial of the obvious creativity displayed, in spite of attempts made in the Frankish kingdom, and later centuries, to develop patterns of uniformity. The *Proficiscere*, although startlingly original in form and purpose, does have ancestry, that is clear, but probably we have gone as far as we can to establish it. We can now look forward to the next stage in the prayer's life. Having flowered to a settled maturity in the sixteenth century, it was to be hit by totally unexpected events that almost brought its life to an end.

4
Extinction and New Species

Until about 65 million years ago, giant dinosaurs happily roamed the forests and swamps of the earth. The favourable climate and conditions enabled them to feed, breed and grow ever larger, as there was no threat to stop their flourishing and continuation. Suddenly, and no one is quite sure why, the dinosaurs came to an abrupt end, and they inhabited the earth no more. One theory is that the earth was hit by a large comet, which threw millions of tons of dust into the atmosphere. The global environment changed dramatically as the sun became blotted out and a 'winter' covered the earth. The dinosaurs, which had thrived in one sort of environment, could not cope with a very different one. They became extinct, and were replaced by much smaller, dinosaur-like creatures such as lizards, which could survive in the very different climate.

This image of sudden and dramatic alteration, brought on by environmental change, is not an inappropriate one to illustrate what happened to the *Proficiscere* at the end of the medieval period. The environment in which it had lived happily for many centuries was one in which the liturgies of the Church were getting longer and increasingly ornate and complex. As has been shown, the *Proficiscere* almost doubled its size in the prevailing favourable climate, as it was a part of funerary liturgies that had expanded in a similar way. The 'large comet', which struck the world of the medieval liturgy, and for our purpose the *Proficiscere* in particular, with such dramatic effect, changing the whole religious environment, was the Reformation started in Europe by Martin Luther.

This chapter in the life of the *Proficiscere* shows how it

became extinct in its traditional 'large' or long form, but how it managed to survive in new environments in altered forms. This part of the biography covers the years between 1549 (when it was not included in Cranmer's Prayer Book) and 1928 (when it was reintroduced into the proposed new Prayer Book). These were the 'hidden years' during which the *Proficiscere* disappeared from official English liturgies, apart from a Latin version in the Roman *Ritual* used by the Roman Catholic minority in England. However, during this long period it survived by developing new forms, much 'smaller' than the old one, but which could survive the new religious climate. Survival continued mainly because the prayer found a new environment outside the liturgies of the Church in unofficial books of prayer and devotion such as the *Ars Moriendi* (*The Art of Dying*), and in unofficial Roman Catholic and Protestant prayer books published after the Reformation.

The impact of the Reformation

It is beyond the scope of this biography to reflect at any length on the reasons for the Reformation. We must, however, step outside the life of the *Proficiscere* in order to understand why the environment in which it had flourished suddenly became so inimical to its existence. We will suggest that at the Reformation the *Proficiscere* was the proverbial baby that got washed away with the bath water. The 'bath water' was the traditional 'Commendation of the Soul' (the *Commendatio animae*), of which the prayer was a part, because the reformed English Church did not believe it necessary, or theologically sound, to make liturgical provision for prayers for the dead. The reason for this lies in the change that took place during the Reformation in the way in which death was understood and interpreted. There was a suspicion of what traditional prayers associated with death might be thought to be saying and doing.

The Reformation brought about a new way of thinking

theologically about God and salvation (and thus also death), which can helpfully be understood in terms of a shift in emphasis between immanence and transcendence. In both periods God was understood in both ways, but in the medieval world people were more aware of the intimate, immanent presence of God in the world, through miracles and in holy objects, as the sacred and the profane or the everyday were intermingled. In the Reformed world view God was 'wholly other', transcendent, in a sense removed from the world he had made, but accessible through the individual's life of devotion. Grace and faith replaced the miraculous.

At the Reformation so many of the religious symbols and actions, which made God's presence seem near and mingled in with the profane, were abolished. Out went pictures and statues, images and ornaments, robes and candles, processions and saints' days. While God might still seem very real, God was now transcendent, worshipped with the mind rather than the eye, with simplicity rather than with complexity, individually rather than communally. Equally importantly, God was now worshipped more directly, through the heart of the believer. The mediation of priest and church, which had traditionally been expressions of God's immanence, were no longer considered so vitally important as God, although now understood as being invisible, remote and wholly other, could be found by the believer through faith and grace.

When the founders of the Reformation in England, and Cranmer in particular, started to prepare new liturgies, which would reflect their new insights, they inevitably reflected major changes in the attitude to death. In the traditional Catholic funeral liturgy, prayers moved seamlessly from prayers for the dying (including the *Proficiscere*) to prayers for the dead and prayers said while washing the body. There were then prayers for processions with the body from home to church, then a burial service, followed by prayers for the soul of the deceased and complex Masses for the dead. These latter prayers were intended to reduce the time the soul spent in purgatory. (It is worth noting that it was the faithful who went to purgatory, not those who would never be saved.) Much church life was concerned with the souls of those who had died. Endowments were made, legacies were left in wills and chantry chapels were built so that the overpowering effects of death might be ameliorated and finally overcome. This would be effected by the prayers of the faithful living, so that the faithful soul might eventually reach the joys of heaven.

The new, Protestant understanding of death meant that the decision about the final destiny of the dead person was decided at the moment of death, and salvation could come a moment before death. William Camden's 'Epitaph for "A gentleman falling off his horse [who] brake his neck"' is a wonderful example of this understanding of death and instant salvation: 'Betwixt the stirrup and the ground / Mercy I asked, mercy I found.' At the moment of death a person was either saved or not saved. Camden's 'gentleman' sought and found God's mercy in the split second between falling off his horse and hitting his head on the ground. Salvation by faith meant that you were not saved by any amount of good works, or other people's prayers. If you were not saved by grace by the time you died, nothing done on earth afterwards could have any effect. Instead of a period in purgatory, in preparation for the joys of heaven, the new understanding of death leaned towards Jesus' words from the cross, 'This day you shall be with me in Paradise.' You were in or out, with no prospect of an intermediate period of preparation for heaven.

The Reformers began a radical overhaul of the Church's worship, setting out their theological arguments against the traditional position. But there is a strange omission in what they wrote. It is common to find condemnations in their writings of the doctrine of purgatory: 'I do clearly reject and esteem as fables all the limbos of the fathers, and of young children, purgatory, and such other like, to be follies, mockeries, and abuses, which were invented and found out by man, without the word of the Lord.'[1] Prayers for the dead are equally condemned: 'In holy scripture ... we find neither precept nor ensample of praying for any, when they be departed this life.'² Strangely though, I have not been able to find any references to a similar condemnation of prayers for the dying.³ This is why I say it was the baby thrown out with the bath water.

If you try to put yourself in the minds of the Reformers, you can see that they did not like the *Proficiscere* because they could read late medieval dogma into it, and thus found it suspect. Perhaps they thought it was insufficiently Christ-centred, and it made no reference to faith or the justified state of the dying person. But the very lack of evidence suggests that the Reformers did not perceive a need to include such argument against prayer for the dying. This may be on one or more of the following grounds.

First, the Reformers do not appear to have made an intellectual differentiation between prayer for the dying and prayer for the dead. The arguments against prayer for the dead, in their thinking, applied equally to prayers for the dying. Such prayers were believed to be an unjustifiable attempt by the Church to exert influence from this world on the course of events in heaven. They thought that the Church could lay no claim to affecting what might happen in heaven.

Such an attitude suggested that the Church had been making far too great claims for itself. The new Reformed understanding of death was informed by the doctrine of justification by faith, so that once death had taken place the person who had died was either saved or damned. As Horton Davies puts it, 'With such a conviction he [the dead person] was delivered from the bondage of guilt and anxiety, condemnation and fear, and translated from the kingdom of darkness into the light, love, and liberty of the sons of God.'⁴ There was no chance, or need, for a period in purgation. Put simply, if people were in heaven as saved souls there was no need for prayer, and if they were in hell no amount of prayer could save them. Christopher Haigh stated the new Protestant view of death succinctly when he said, 'Salvation came not by prayers for languishing souls, but by divine grace through faith in Christ.'⁵ This was the triumph of a transcendent theology over an immanent one.

Second, and in more practical terms, the Reformers may

also have perceived that prayers for the dying could often merge into prayers for the dead because of uncertainty over the moment when death actually happened. The moment of death forced a change in the way in which the prayers were interpreted, or rather changed the intention and meaning of the prayer. The state of the soul at the moment of death was the decisive issue, and if you were not quite sure about the moment of death you dare not risk turning prayer for the dying into prayer for the dead.

Third, the banning of prayers addressed to the saints, a significant part of Catholic worship, may well have overflowed into attitudes to the *Libera* with its long list of biblical figures. Although the biblical figures were listed, there was no direct appeal to them in the prayer, but in the reformed liturgy they too had to go. In spite of the lack of direct evidence, it is apparent that the Reformed English Church viewed prayers for the dying with the same suspicion as they viewed prayers for the dead, or they would not have excluded them. This was the death knell for the *Proficiscere* and it disappeared from the Church of England liturgy from the first Prayer Book in 1549 and for many years thereafter. Its assistance with the liberty to die was no longer considered necessary, pastorally or theologically.

These lines of argument are endorsed by what the reformers did in terms of commendation at the funeral service. Although it contained no commendation of the dying, the first Prayer Book written by Cranmer did include a commendation of the dead at the moment of committal as the priest said, 'I commend thy soul to God the Father almighty, and thy body to the ground, earth to earth ...' This Prayer Book was still judged to be too catholic and in 1552 the commendation was omitted, with the words, 'Forasmuch as it has pleased almighty God of his great mercy to take unto himself the soul of our dear brother here departed, we therefore commit his body to the ground ...' These latter words were unchanged in the next, Elizabethan, Prayer Book of 1559. Any idea of commendation to God and prayer for the deceased was out.

Extinction and New Species

In this stage of the biography we will see how, in these very inclement conditions, the *Proficiscere* just managed to hang on by adapting itself to survive. In the *Ritual*, produced by the Catholic Church in 1614 as a response to some of the criticisms of the Church by the Reformers, the *Proficiscere* continued, although in a shorter form. In the non-Catholic world the prayer disappeared from the liturgy completely, together with the 'Commendation of the Soul'. Although the English Church produced four Prayer Books, in 1549, 1552, 1559 and 1662, only the last of these contained any prayer material at all for a dying person. None of them contained any version of the *Proficiscere*, and it became extinct in the prayer books of the Church of England.

For many hundreds of years two rival interpretations of dying ran together in parallel in the two churches, as they both sought to impose their own 'correct' interpretation of death on their followers. The *Proficiscere* only survived in one of them, the Roman Catholic Church.

The Roman Catholic Church and the 1614 Roman *Ritual*

The long road of medieval amendments to the text of the *Proficiscere* came to an end in the text of the 'Commendation of the Soul' in the *Ritual* of 1614. The text was settled, along with other liturgical material, after the Council of Trent (1545–63), which was called by Pope Paul III partly in response to the challenge of Martin Luther and the Protestant Reformation to the Catholic authorities, but also as part of the continuing eager desire for reform within the Church. One of the purposes of the Council was to produce a standardization of worship within the Roman Catholic Church, in order to exercise more centralized control. Worship material itself was not actually produced during the Council, so responsibility for this fell to Pope Pius IV. However, it was not until the time of his successor Paul V that a committee of cardinals was appointed to draw up a new *Ritual*, based on earlier *Rituals*.

The *Ritual* was officially approved in 1614, and it eventually prevailed as a standard work over local usages. Apart from three changes, the 1614 text basically became the settled text for the *Proficiscere* within the Roman Catholic Church until the reforms of Vatican II. Its text was as follows:

> Set out, Christian soul, from this world.
> In the name of God, the Father Almighty, who created you.
> In the name of Jesus Christ, Son of the living God, who suffered for you.
> In the name of the Holy Spirit who was poured out upon you.
> In the name of angels and archangels.
> In the name of thrones and dominions.
> In the name of principalities and powers.
> In the name of cherubim and seraphim.
> In the name of patriarchs and prophets.
> In the name of saints, apostles and evangelists.
> In the name of martyrs and confessors.
> In the name of monks and hermits.
> In the name of virgins and saints of God.
> Today his place is made in peace and his dwelling in heavenly Jerusalem.
> Through Jesus Christ our Lord. Amen.
>
> Welcome your servant, Lord, into the place of salvation, for which he rightly hoped.
> Set free, Lord, the soul of your servant from all the dangers of hell and from all evil tribulations.
> Set free, Lord, the soul of your servant as you set free Elijah and Enoch from the common death of the world. [*The repetitions are not repeated here.*]
> Noah from the flood.
> Abraham from Ur of the Chaldees.
> Job from his suffering.
> Isaac from the sacrifice and from the hand of his father Abraham.

Extinction and New Species 87

Lot from Sodom and from the flames of fire.
Moses from the hand of Pharaoh, king of the Egyptians.
Daniel from the lion's den.
The three young men from the furnace of blazing fire and from the hands of an evil king.
Susanna from false witness.
David from the hand of King Saul and from Goliath and from all his bonds.
Peter and Paul from prisons.
Thecla from the midst of the spectacle.
So deign to set free the soul of this man and allow him to dwell with you in the blessings of heaven. Amen.

You will notice that the editors of the prayer in the Roman *Ritual* have rearranged the order of some of the lines. They have dropped the reference 'In the name of all the human race which is sustained by God'. In addition, 'hermits' replaces 'anchorites'; 'saints of God' replaces 'faithful widows'; Abraham's qualities of faith and trust are omitted, and somewhat strangely replaced by the geographical reference to 'Ur of the Chaldees'. The 'heavenly virtues' have been dropped so that the groups of angels can be in three pairs. Also omitted are the examples of Jacob, Jonah and the whale, and, again, 'the human race'. However, Job and his suffering is added. Finally, the whole of the middle section (Michael, Peter, John and Paul) is excised from this prayer and placed later as another prayer in the 'Commendation of the Soul'. It is only possible to speculate on why these changes were made, but we do know that they follow amendments made in other earlier late-medieval manuscripts so, in a sense, they were following tradition.

This text became the settled one in the Roman Catholic Church until Vatican II, apart from some early twentieth-century changes. As this chapter details the life of the *Proficiscere* up to the year 1928, this is the most appropriate place to examine these additions. They are important in the biography because they reflect the way the prayer was able to adapt itself to significant changes in Roman Catholic thinking. In particular, for the first time, the names of Mary and Joseph were added in 1919 and 1922 respectively, and printed in the 1925 version of Pius XI.

In 1919 the words, 'In the name of the glorious and holy begetter of God, the Virgin Mary' (*In nomine gloriosae et sanctae Dei genitricis virginis Mariae*) were added and in 1922, 'In the name of the blessed Joseph renowned with his espoused virgin' (*In nomine beati Joseph inclyti eiusdem virginis sponsi*). The reasons for these additions, which were added after the opening trinitarian reference, may be a liturgical reflection of the movements in Roman Catholic social teaching in the early decades of the twentieth century. The liturgical and doctrinal significance given to the role of Mary, which developed particularly in the nineteenth century, is also marked by the additions.

Behind these innovations lies a developing cultural trend of devotion to both Mary and Joseph. For example, Pope Leo XIII instituted a Feast of the Holy Family in 1893. It is also worth noting that a number of orders of the Holy Family were established in the second half of the nineteenth century, such as the Congregation of Sisters of the Holy Family (1842), the Sons of the Holy Family (1864), the Sisters of the Holy Family (1872) and the Holy Family Missionaries (1895). The positions of Mary and Joseph in the *Sanctorale* (a list of the saints with their days) had both been elevated in the nineteenth century, making their inclusion at this significant point in the *Proficiscere* (between the Holy Trinity and the Angelic Hosts) a liturgical confirmation of their increased status. The rest of the nineteenth century also saw a number of missionary orders established in honour of Mary, and the development of shrines such as Lourdes, La Salette and Knock, which were highly popular with pilgrims. In 1921 (a date between the two additions to the *Proficiscere*) the Legion of Mary was established. In his Encyclical *Quamquam Pluries* Pope Leo XIII elevated Joseph to a new status for devotion when he wrote:

Joseph was the spouse of Mary and he was reputed the father of Jesus Christ. From these sources have sprung his dignity, his holiness, his glory ... but as Joseph has been united to the Blessed Virgin by the ties of marriage, it may not be doubted that he approached nearer than any to the eminent dignity by which the Mother of God surpasses so nobly all created natures.[6]

The other significant alteration in the Latin text of 1925 was the introduction of alternative female terms and endings (*ancillae tuae* etc.). This shows that the Roman Catholic Church, at least in this liturgy, was many years ahead of other churches, which did not include inclusive language until nearly the end of the century. These additions to the *Proficiscere* are good demonstrations of how a long-established text can alter and adapt itself in response to the combined forces of culture, theology and history.

Unofficial texts: the *Ars Moriendi*, Protestant and Catholic books of prayers

Although the *Proficiscere* almost became extinct in England, as mentioned earlier, it was able to survive to a small degree because it adapted itself to its new, more hostile environment. Just as smaller creatures survived when the dinosaurs became extinct, so shorter, or smaller, versions of the *Proficiscere* developed in unofficial, non-liturgical books, both Roman Catholic and Protestant. These unofficial books are of interest as they contain the earliest English versions of the *Proficiscere*, far earlier than Newman's famous translation in the nineteenth century, the subject of the next chapter. Further, they illustrate the changing pastoral role of the *Proficiscere* as it moved from public liturgy to private devotions.

First, the *Proficiscere* continued, amended and re-amended, outside the official liturgies of the Church in a series of books called *Ars Moriendi* (*The Art of Dying*), some of which carry illustrations. One early block-book version, probably published in Cologne in about 1450, shows a dying man facing five temptations offered by evil-looking devils, while being protected by his guardian angel. It is evocative of the way in which the dying moments of a person were viewed and understood in the fifteenth century. One of the temptations is 'impatience', and is illustrated by the emaciated dying man firmly kicking the physician who is attending him. Is this illustrating the wrongness of wanting to die too soon, and not in God's time, or is it an unconscious expression of belief that the dying man actually wants death, but that the physician is stopping this happening? Perhaps this second suggestion is a too modern reading of a medieval text.

The text of the *Proficiscere* can be found in both Latin and English versions of the *Ars Moriendi*. One English translation, *The Art and Craft to Know Well to Die*,[7] is of particular interest as it is a translation made in 1490 by William Caxton, about a year before his death. Caxton was the first English printer, who not only printed about one hundred books on a new moveable-type printing machine, but also translated books from French, Dutch and Latin before printing them. Caxton's fairly free translation reads:

> Christian Soul, depart thee from this world when it shall please God,
> in the Name of the Father, which thee created;
> in the Name of Jesu Christ, His son, which for thee suffered death;
> and in the Name of the Holy Ghost, which hath shed in thee His grace.
> Come to thy meeting and succour thee the holy Angels of God, the Archangels, the Virtues, the Potestates, the Dominations, the Thrones, the Cherubins, the Seraphins.
> Come to thine help and aid the patriarchs and prophets,
> the apostles and evangelists, the martyrs and confessors,
> the monks and hermits, the virgins and widows, the children and innocents.

Also help thee the prayers and visions of all priests and deacons, and of them of all degrees of the Church Catholic; to the end that thy place be in peace, and that thine habitation be in celestial Jerusalem.
Through Jesus Christ our Lord. Amen.

There are a number of other English texts of a similar nature, some of which also contained parts of the *Proficiscere*. The first of these, by the Reformer Thomas Becon (*c.* 1511–67), is *The Sicke Mannes Salve* (1561), which is of particular interest as it is dated only 12 years after Cranmer's first Prayer Book, which had dropped the *Proficiscere* from the funerary material. It is the first Protestant text of the *Proficiscere*, and it was an extremely popular book in Elizabethan England, running to at least 18 editions. Becon wrote from a Calvinist position, but reflected an attempt to balance the best of the old with the best of the new. 'The dominant concern of the *Sicke Mannes Salve* may be to convince Protestants of the duty of a (purified) traditional response to death; but its author must keep one eye on the Romish enemy at every instant.'[8] You will note the '(purified) traditional response'. The book is in the form of a deathbed conversation among friends, one of whom is dying, interspersed with prayers. Every so often the friends think the dying man has gone, but suddenly he joins them again in their conversations about death. It was probably not meant to be as amusing as it reads today. It is another example of the *Proficiscere*'s ability to re-establish itself in new literary contexts, so that its life can continue. Outside the official prayer books it could afford to be less theologically 'correct'. Among the prayers offered as the man is dying are some new Puritan prayers, but also abbreviated versions of both parts of the *Proficiscere*.[9] It is worth quoting the majority of the *Libera* part of the prayer as it is a free adaption and raises some interesting points:

> O Lord Jesu Christ, thou only Son of the heavenly Father, our alone Redeemer and omnisufficient Saviour, we most

humbly beseech thee, deliver this sick and weak person, now being in great pains and at the point to depart out of this world, from all ugsome [ugsome: frightful] and terrible assaults and temptations of the devil, sin, and hell. Deliver him, O Lord, as thou deliverest Noe from the raging waves of the sea, Lot from the destruction of Sodom, Abraham from the fear of the Chaldees, the children of Israel from the tyranny of Pharao, David from the hand of Goliah, the three men from the violence of the fiery furnace in Babylon, Daniel from the mouth of the lions, Jonas from the belly of the whale fish, and Peter from the prison of Herod: even so, O gracious Lord God, deliver the soul of this person, both now and whensoever he shall depart hence, from all peril and danger. Open unto him, at the hour of death, the door of paradise, the gates of heaven, and the entry of everlasting life.[10]

The freedom of the translation is immediately apparent, as is the Protestant emphasis on the saving role of Jesus, noticeably missing from the medieval versions. What is also of particular interest is that for the first and only time the figures appear in the order of their biblical books (although both Lot and Abraham appear in Genesis, the order might have been reversed to make it perfect), indicating perhaps the new biblical awareness of the Reformation.

The version of the first part of the prayer included in *The Sicke Mannes Salve*, which appears nine pages later,[11] is a very abbreviated version:[12]

God the Father, which made you, bless you. God the Son, which redeemed you, preserve you. God the Holy Ghost, which sanctifieth you, confirm and strengthen you. The blessing, defence, and saving health of the Almighty God, the Father, and the Son, and the Holy Ghost, preserve you from all evil, and bring you unto everlasting life.[13]

You will note that there is no 'go forth' language, and no mention of the soul. Nancy Beaty commented on the devotional slant of the book: 'We are not surprised to learn that private devotion was nourished, throughout this controversial era, primarily by Catholic aids carried over from the medieval tradition with only minimal revision to ensure their doctrinal acceptability.'[14] This comment is of particular significance as Becon was at one time a chaplain to Archbishop Cranmer, the author of the 1549 Book of Common Prayer.

A Roman Catholic Counter-Reformation text, containing a version of the *Proficiscere* by the Jesuit Robert Parsons (1546–1610), also known as 'Persons', was the *First booke of the Christian Exercise, appertayning to resolution* (1582). In Parsons' book the medieval deathbed scene is restored with all its intense drama filled with agony, horror and physical pain. However, as Beaty pointed out:

> the Jesuits followed personally quite another tradition of dying well – one that excluded even that minimal fearfulness postulated in their devotional exercises and published works. According to Meadows, Parsons himself died, following St. Ignatius, 'in typical Jesuit fashion … quietly, undramatically, and in the midst of work.[15]

Beaty then makes the following comment:

> A twentieth-century layman may perhaps be forgiven for finding *some* drama in Parson's calling for the rope with which Campion[16] had been hanged, and wearing it around his own neck during the recitation of the Prayer of Commendation, '*Proficiscere, anima Christiana*'.[17]

John Cosin, who became Bishop of Durham, composed *A Collection of Private Devotions* in 1627 at the request of King Charles I for the use of Queen Henrietta Maria's English maids of honour. Cosin was strongly anti-Roman Catholic, disinheriting his son when he converted. However, in his prayer book he was willing to compose a prayer, for 'commending the soul into the hands of God, at the very point of time when it is departing from the body'. He included a version of the familiar opening lines, and later offered a more christological phrasing: 'Christ that ascended into Heaven, and now sitteth at the right hand of God, bring thee unto the place of eternal happiness and joy.' Then, to make sure the dying person gets the message, he concludes with a number of biblical texts, prefaced by the rubric, *'Then let there be said plainly, distinctly, and with some pauses, these ejaculatory Meditations and Prayers.'*[18]

Lastly, mention can be made of the Anglican Bishop Jeremy Taylor (1613–67) who, in *The Rule and Exercises of Holy Dying* (1651), did not include an English version of the *Proficiscere* as such, but echoes of it are evident, as are other parts of the Commendation of the Soul. One of his prayers reads:

> Let his portion be with Abraham, Isaac, and Jacob, with Job and David, with the Prophets and Apostles, with Martyrs and all thy holy Saints, in the arms of Christ, in the bosom of felicity, in the kingdom of God to eternal ages. Amen.[19]

Recusant Catholics in England (Roman Catholics who refused to attend Church of England services in the parish church) were provided with a variety of religious material to sustain them in a situation of oppression, persecution and lack of pastoral church support. *A Manual of Prayer*, typical of others of its type, was discovered late last century in the Library of Oscott College, dating from 1614 (coincidentally the same date as the *Ritual*).[20] Its purpose is stated in the editor's preface, 'To the Devout Catholike Reader', that it is written 'for the benefit, of lay catholics: but especially for those that understand not the Latin tongue'.[21] The Manual is basically a book of private prayer, designed to meet the needs of Catholics who had to live much of their religious lives without the benefit of priests or of public worship. In the third part there is a section, 'Prayers for the Sick'.

There is no separate section entitled 'Prayers for the dying' as the prayers are subsumed under the main title. The patient is exhorted to receive the sacraments of the Church, to reflect on Christ's passion, to commend himself to the prayers of Mary, confess his sinfulness and desire for reconciliation, and make both formal and informal acts of faith. After several more prayers of confession, and of love of God, there is a series of prayers for the dying. These include, in English, a substantial part of the *Proficiscere*. For a reason that is not apparent from the Manual, the text of the first part of the *Proficiscere*, unlike all the other prayers in English in the book, is printed in italics.

I was fortunate to be allowed to see this volume at Oscott and make a copy of the following prayer (I have modernized the spelling):

Thou Christian soul, depart thou out of this world, in the name of God the Father almighty, who hath created thee, in the name of Jesus-Christ, the Son of the living God, who hath suffered for thee on the holy Cross, in the name of the holy Ghost, who was poured into thee, in the name of the holy Angels and Archangels, in the name of the Thrones and Dominations, in the name of the Powers and Potestates, in the name of Cherubins and Seraphins, in the name of Patriarchs, and Prophets, in the name of the holy Apostles, and Evangelists, in the name of the holy Martyrs and Confessors, in the name of the holy Monks and Eremites, in the name of the holy Virgins, and of all the Saints of God. Let thy place be this day in peace, and thy habitation in holy Zion, through Christ our Lord. Amen.[22]

There are a couple of interesting variations in this text, although it is impossible to tell with certainty from which Latin version the writer was working. The reference to '*on the holy Cross*' was either an original contribution by the writer or taken from only one other manuscript to use any phrase about the cross. The former seems more likely; an example of similarities not necessarily indicating sources. There are only eight of the usual nine angelic beings. 'Virtues', or 'heavenly authorities' are omitted. The word '*virtutam*' was also omitted from the *Ritual* until 1925.

In addition, the compiler of the Manual includes a translation of the *Libera*, which accurately follows the text found in the *Ritual* and its predecessors. The final prayer in this section includes a translation of the whole of the 'Michael' section of the *Proficiscere*. Crichton concluded his comments, 'It is difficult to resist the reflection that a manual like this provided much more adequately for the needs of the sick and dying than the prayer-books of the nineteenth or even twentieth centuries.'[23]

So recusant Catholics could continue to die with the words of the *Proficiscere* in their ears, now in their native tongue. Its promises of Christian hope in the face of death comforted them, while fellow Catholics were being persecuted and put to death. Finally, it might be commented that the shortage of priests enabled lay Catholics to play a more active part in ministering to the dying, using such a manual. It would be over 350 years before there would be anything similar, when in 1999 the Bishops' Liturgical Committee of the Roman Catholic Church in England and Wales published *In Sure and Certain Hope*, a book of prayers, including prayers for the dying, for the use of lay Catholics.

The Church of England Prayer Books

The words of the *Proficiscere* in the *Ritual* became settled within the Roman Catholic Church (apart from the minor additions) for some 359 years (1614 to 1973), until it was amended and officially translated into English. For a period longer by 20 years (1549 to 1928) the words disappeared from the official public worshipping life of the Church of England.

As has been mentioned, none of the Prayer Books after 1549 contain any form of prayer comparable in language or even in purpose to the 'Commendation of the Soul'. The *Proficiscere* disappeared along with any prayer which the reforming zeal of theologians might suspect of being an attempt to affect the future of the dead. Any prayers of pastoral concern for dying persons or their families were excluded. It was not until 1662, in the 'Visitation of the Sick', that there was a prayer that performed something of the function of the *Proficiscere*. The text is as follows:

> *A commendatory Prayer for a sick person at the point of departure.*
> O Almighty God with whom do live the spirits of just men made perfect after they are delivered from their earthly prisons: We humbly commend the soul of this thy servant, our dear *brother*, into thy hands, as into the hands of a faithful Creator, and most merciful Saviour; most humbly beseeching thee that it may be precious in thy sight. Wash it we pray thee, in the blood of that immaculate Lamb, that was slain to take away the sins of the world: that whatsoever defilements it may have contracted in the midst of this miserable and naughty world, through the lusts of the flesh, or the wiles of Satan, being purged, and don away, it may be presented pure and without spot before thee. And teach us who survive, in this, and other like daily spectacles of mortality, to see how frail, and uncertain our own Condition is; and so to number our days that we may seriously apply our hearts to that holy and heavenly wisdom, whilst we live here, which may in the end bring us to life everlasting through the merits of Jesus Christ, thine only son our Lord. Amen.[24]

As the long ecumenical winter in the relationship between Rome and Canterbury began, followers of the two churches were pastorally prepared to meet God, as they came to death, in very different ways. Catholic liturgies still commended the soul, with a pastoral confidence and hope, that it would journey to God in the name of the Trinity, ranks of angels, and the saints. The *Proficiscere* continued to play a part in their death.

Meanwhile, the 1662 Book of Common Prayer reflected a general suspicion towards any prayers associated with the dead. It offered a more modest and humble request for the safety of the soul, coupled with a reminder to those who remained that they might ensure their own fitness when death came to them.

The parted ways between the two churches would not begin to come together, liturgically speaking, until the twentieth century, when the *Proficiscere* re-emerged with new life in the midst of a more favourable ecumenical environment. This would result in a renaissance in the traditional use, and also in new uses of the *Proficiscere*.

Before we can examine this, however, we need to look at the way in which the nineteenth century brought the words of the *Proficiscere* to the attention of an English-speaking population, mainly through the works of Cardinal Newman and Edward Elgar. They paved the way for the triumphant return of the *Proficiscere* in the twentieth century.

5
Victorian Revival

For 300 years the *Proficiscere*'s life hung by a thread. Gradually the post-Reformation *Ars Moriendi* (*The Art of Dying*) and other prayer books appear to have been forgotten. The books became a lost form of spiritual preparation for death, as their publication ceased in the eighteenth century. So the prayer was rarely heard in Britain except by Roman Catholics, many of whom would not have understood it, as it was in Latin from the time of the Reformation until 1845. In that year an unofficial prayer book by an anonymous author was published,[1] which contains an English translation of the 'Commendation of the Soul' from the *Ritual*, under the title, 'The Order for the Commendation of a Departing Soul'. The opening word of the prayer is translated 'Depart'.[2] This book would probably have circulated among members of the Catholic wing of the Church of England, stimulated by the development of the Oxford Movement, but it would not be well known to the general public.

John Henry Newman

The change to a more 'Catholic' perspective is seen in unofficial writings or books of devotion,[3] the most significant of which was Cardinal Newman's *The Dream of Gerontius*, first published in 1865. This work played a significant role in the biography of the prayer as it enabled the *Proficiscere*'s excess of meaning to spill out into new areas, and new interpretations, although its apparent intention by Newman was not pastoral. He used the *Proficiscere* in *The Dream of Gerontius* in a new way as part of a religious poem. Its popularity had the effect of releasing the text, in English, to a society unaware of its words but open to new religious understandings.

The use of much of the text of the *Proficiscere* by Newman in *The Dream of Gerontius* marked the third, and most creative, phase in the evolving life of the prayer. It signalled a significant change in its use, and in the way in which it was perceived by the general public. Because *The Dream of Gerontius* plays such a significant part in the revived life of the *Proficiscere*, it is interesting to look briefly at the circumstances in which it was written, the text of the *Proficiscere* within it and then at responses to the poem. These give some indication of its influence on people's perceptions. The release of the text from the confines of the Latin liturgy opened knowledge of it to a wider public, reopening its pastoral possibilities.

As we have detailed, the text of the *Proficiscere* remained in its Latin format in the *Ritual* from 1614 onwards. Apart from its inclusion in the *Ars Moriendi* and other such books, appreciation and increasing knowledge of it among the lay public was due to the fact that it was included (in an amended form) for the first time in a popular modern English form, in Newman's poem *The Dream of Gerontius*. The words of the *Proficiscere*, previously heard only in Latin in a monastery, church or in the home of a dying person, now became widely read in English everywhere. The words of the Latin Mass had frequently been heard sung (in Latin) in such secular settings, thanks to the fact that it has for many years been a staple text for a wide variety of composers. Now a new sacred text was liberated from its ecclesial liturgical setting. Its excess of meaning meant that it now sat on the boundary of sacred and secular use and knowledge.

The way in which the story of the creation of *The Dream of Gerontius* has traditionally been told follows a fairly clear line, related with varying degrees of detail by Newman's many biographers. In the middle of his controversy with Charles Kingsley, and shortly after the strain of completing his

Apologia,⁴ Newman was seized with a sense of his own impending death. It appears that he had received a medical opinion, which led him to write a 'Profession of Faith' in March 1864, in which he said, 'I write in the direct view of death as in prospect. No one in the house, I suppose, suspects anything of the kind. Nor anyone anywhere, unless it be the medical men.'⁵ Some nine months later, on 30 December 1864, Newman wrote to his friend Father Coleridge, expressing his fear of paralysis, after hearing that John Keble had had a stroke. After saying that he had been told that good health can often be the precursor of an attack of paralysis, he wrote, 'This makes one suspicious of one's own freedom from ailments', and he then lists other literary figures who had apparently suffered paralysis.⁶ It thus seems from this evidence, that Newman wrote *The Dream of Gerontius* while under both internal and external pressures.

No one, until recently, has offered any comment on why the poem he wrote in this mood was named after a figure called 'Gerontius'. While there can be no certainty, it is possible that he took the name from the Greek word *Geron,* an old man, which in the genitive (of an old man), is *Gerontos.* However, Elizabeth Jay offered a more subtle suggestion. She says:

> The death-bed setting of the poem's opening seems to have encouraged allusions to the Greek word for old age, but a classical scholar such as Newman would never have produced so hybrid a form. The source seems rather to have been the fourth-century Bishop Gerontius of Nicomedeia whom the Church authorities attempted to depose on account of the scandal caused by his recounting the tales of his strange dreams.

If Newman was as subtle as Jay suggests, could not both possible roots for the title have been in Newman's mind? ⁷

One of his biographers, Wilfrid Ward, suggests that the abandonment of the Oxford scheme⁸ gave him the leisure time to set down in dramatic form the vision of a Christian's death on which his imagination had been dwelling.[9] But it also seems possible that it was the result of a sudden burst of inspiration, which would have broken out from deep within him whether he was busy or not. Indeed, Ward suggests it was the result of a massive and emotional outpouring of creative energy, spurred on within him by what he felt to be the sense of his own impending death. He began the work on 17 January 1865 and finished it three weeks later in February, but there is no indication of how long parts of it may have been coming together in his mind before this time. Jay, who takes a very sceptical view of traditional interpretations, argued that, as the *Apologia* with its complex arguments took less than three months, three weeks for *The Dream of Gerontius* 'is not in itself evidence of abnormal inspiration'.[10]

The poem appeared in the Jesuit periodical *The Month*, then edited by his friend Father Coleridge, in the numbers for April and May (1865). Before examining the text, it is interesting to turn to Jay's modern reading of the text, in which she challenges Newman's statement of authorial intention, by setting it alongside a traditional reading. Geoffrey Rowell offers a summary of the traditional view:

> Newman's picture is of an ideal Christian death, with the dying man being supported in his last agony by his friends;[11] but it is also a picture of a man, whose life could be described as good but not exceptional, reaching the point of death. Gerontius is indeed Everyman, but he is Everyman as believer.[12]

As we have indicated, Jay offered a more critical appraisal of the poem, placing it in its contemporary culture. She argued that neither its genre, in its use of a dream to carry its message, nor its use of a medieval Catholic world, would be unfamiliar vehicles in the mid-Victorian age as means of offering critiques of nineteenth-century deficiencies. As we have said, *The Dream of Gerontius* was written just after Newman had completed his *Apologia*, in which he had spoken about his departure from the Church of England. She quoted from the beginning of the penultimate chapter of the *Apologia*:

> From the end of 1841, I was on my death-bed, as regards my membership with the Anglican Church, though at the time I became aware of it only by degrees ... A death-bed has scarcely a history; it is a tedious decline, with seasons of rallying and seasons of falling back; and since the end is foreseen, or what is called a matter of time, it has little interest for the reader, especially if he has a kind heart. Moreover, it is a season when the doors are closed and curtains drawn, and when the sick man neither cares nor is able to record the stages of his malady. I was in these circumstances, except so far as I was not allowed to die in peace, except so far as friends, who had still a full right to come in upon me, and the public world which had not, have given a sort of history to those last four years.[13]

From this Jay argued that, in Newman's thinking, the poem begins where the *Apologia* left off. If the *Apologia* is, in a sense, his last will and testimony to his old way of life as a priest in the Church of England, *The Dream of Gerontius* is his entry into his new way within the Roman Catholic Church.

Further, Jay said that Newman used part of the language associated with death, the *Proficiscere*, in the context of 'Prayers for the Dying', but then added to it a new dimension of life beyond death, as the soul of Gerontius journeys on towards heaven. This was for Newman an image, or metaphor, for his own journey from the Church of England into the Roman Catholic Church. If Jay is right, the *Proficiscere* is used as a symbol of the moment when Newman found the liberty to die to the Church of England and find new life in the Roman Catholic Church.

This method of analysis is one of the creative ways in which literature can be studied and analysed. Thus Jay sought to move outside what the text, or its author, or its contemporaries had to say about it. Her reading of the text of *The Dream* of Gerontius is both a challenge and a stimulus to its study. Whatever judgements are made on its strengths (and Rowell's negative response has been noted), it does suggest that the *Proficiscere* was used in a new way, as part of a 'device' to achieve a new perception of death as a change from the old to the new (from Canterbury to Rome).

We are now ready to look at the way Newman cleverly reworked the familiar words of the *Proficiscere* in *The Dream of Gerontius*. While the old man Gerontius is dying, the Priest and his assistants are praying with him. This is the text as originally published in *The Month*.

ASSISTANTS.
1 Rescue him, O Lord, in this his evil hour,
2 As of old so many by Thy gracious power: – Amen.
3 Enoch and Elias from the common doom; Amen.
4 Noe from the waters in a saving home; Amen.
5 Abraham from th' abounding guilt of Heathenesse; Amen.
6 Job from all his multiform and fell distress; Amen.
7 Isaac, when his father's knife was raised to slay; Amen.
8 Lot from burning Sodom on its judgment-day; Amen.
9 Moses from the land of bondage and despair; Amen.
10 Daniel from the hungry lions in their lair; Amen.
11 And the children Three amid the furnace-flame; Amen.
12 Chaste Susanna from the slander and the shame; Amen.
13 David from Golia and the wrath of Saul; Amen.
14 And the two Apostles from their prison-thrall; Amen.
15 Thecla from her torments; Amen:
16   – so, to show Thy power,
17 Rescue this Thy servant in his evil hour.

In Newman's poem Gerontius then responds briefly:

GERONTIUS.
18 Novissima hora est; and I fain would sleep.
19 The pain has wearied me ... Into Thy hands,
20 O Lord, into Thy hands ...

These are his final words, and the Priest says a further part of the prayer:

THE PRIEST.
21 Proficiscere, anima Christiana, de hoc mundo!
22 Go forth upon thy journey, Christian soul!
23 Go from this world! Go, in the Name of God,
24 The omnipotent Father, who created thee!
25 Go, in the Name of Jesus Christ, our Lord,
26 Son of the Living God, who bled for thee!
27 Go, in the Name of the Holy Spirit, who
28 Hath been poured out on thee! Go, in the name
29 Of Angels and Archangels; in the name
30 Of Thrones and Dominations; in the name
31 Of Princedoms and of Powers; and in the name
32 Of Cherubim and Seraphim, go forth!
33 Go, in the name of Patriarchs and Prophets;
34 And of Apostles and Evangelists,
35 Of Martyrs and Confessors; in the name
36 Of holy Monks and Hermits; in the name
37 Of holy Virgins; and all Saints of God,
38 Both men and women, go! Go on thy course;
39 And may thy place to-day be found in peace,
40 And may thy dwelling be the Holy Mount
41 Of Sion:– through the Same, through Christ, our Lord.

You will have noticed, as you read this through, that the text of the prayer is not so much a translation as a reconfiguration by Newman of the traditional words into a poetic form set in part in rhyming couplets. You will also have noticed that the order of the two parts of the prayer has been reversed. As the poem begins, Gerontius is approaching his death. Newman changed the movement and intent of the *Libera*, by translating it 'rescue him in this his evil hour'. The order he uses gives the poem a greater dramatic impact and power, as the Assistants plead to God for him, before the Priest dismisses the soul of Gerontius with the *Proficiscere* prayer of sending forth. There is not the same suggestion of 'evil' in the Latin text, and Newman's interpretation is a little darker than that of any of the other texts examined, at least as far as the *Libera* is concerned. While the text is not an accurate translation of the Latin, but rather a paraphrase in verse form, you may have noticed that there is a theological shift. It indicates perhaps a more developed awareness of purgatory than is evident in the medieval text already examined.

The following numbers refer to the lines of text above.

1   The opening words of the Assistants may echo the prayers to a long list of saints, which occurred before the beginning of the 'Commendation of the Soul' in many of the medieval liturgical texts. As has been mentioned, Newman has achieved this by reversing the two sections of the prayer, putting the *Libera* before the *Proficiscere*.[14] There is therefore added drama as, before the soul is sent forth, the Old Testament figures, instead of the saints, are invoked by the Assistants. Newman uses 'Rescue' rather than either 'Deliver' or 'Set Free', for '*Libera*'. 'His evil hour' would seem to be a weak summary of 'From all dangers of hell, from the snares of punishment, and from all tribulations' in the traditional text.

2   This is an addition which introduces the Old Testament figures.

3–15   These lines contain all the figures in the *Ritual*, in the order in which they appear, but he does not show any consistency in how he treats the names. He introduces 'Elias' instead of the *Ritual*'s 'Eliam', he modernizes 'Moses' instead of 'Moysen', and 'Daniel' instead of 'Danielem', but not 'Goliath', choosing 'Golia'. The names 'Peter' and 'Paul' do not scan easily, so they are 'the two Apostles'.

17   This line is added by Newman, but it reflects back the opening line, thus completing the prayer of the Assistants.

Victorian Revival

18–20 These lines are Newman's own invention and are not part of the *Proficiscere*.

21 The prayer of the Priest begins with the opening line in Latin and then changes to English.

22 Newman translated '*Proficiscere*' in an original way with the inspired phrase, 'Go forth', which has become a popular choice among twentieth-century liturgists. In this line Newman also adds 'upon thy journey', introducing into the English text a phrase which is not supported by the Latin. 'Journey' is a very helpful concept in the context of the 'Commendation of the Soul' because it is linked with the *Viaticum*, food for the journey (the bread and wine of Holy Communion), which a Christian would receive before death, and which is included in most texts. It has been a powerful influence on liturgists who have included 'journey' in versions of the *Proficiscere*. Some liturgists may not have known, or cared, that it was not supported by the Latin original.

23 The sense of urgency and of dismissal is emphasized by the three 'Go's' in the first two lines, and its repetition in lines 25, 27, 32, 33 and 38.

24 This is a faithful rendering of the Latin.

25–26 Newman adds 'our Lord'. The sense of suffering, Christ's passion is transformed into 'bled for thee', an original contribution.

27–28 'Poured out' is a literal translation of the Latin.

29–38 These lines represent an accurate following of the text in the *Ritual*. 'Go on thy course' is an addition.

39–41 These words are an accurate translation of the closing lines of the *Proficiscere*, although *dominationem* is rendered as 'Dominations' rather than the more usual 'Dominions'.

In summary, Newman offered members of the public who did not know Latin a creative translation of the key part of the 'Commendation of the Soul'. For the first time (apart from the

Ars Moriendi etc.) they would be able to read, and have available as a spiritual resource in a popular form, the text of a prayer that had supported and sustained the living and the dying who had known the Latin text for over one thousand years.

The Dream of Gerontius was not the only use Newman made of the *Proficiscere*. His *Meditations and Devotions* is a collection of prayer material which would probably have formed part of a 'Year Book of Devotion' for reading and meditation. According to the editor:

> The intention of composing such a book had been in the Cardinal's mind as far back as the early years of his Catholic life, but, though it was never abandoned, various circumstances hindered him from pursuing it, and no portion of this volume was put together with this idea.[15]

Based on Newman's verbal plans, the editor drew on 'such papers as, from what was said by the Cardinal, are considered likely to have come within the compass of the contemplated volume'.[16] Among the prayers is a 'Prayer for the Faithful Departed' which was assigned in the book to be used on Good Friday.[17]

The prayer consists of the second part of the *Proficiscere* 'May the archangel Michael ... Peter ... Paul ... the Apostles ... saints ...' What is interesting is that in doing this Newman drew on part of one of the versions of the *Proficiscere* and transformed it from a prayer for the dying into a prayer for the dead. Its significance is different from the way in which he was willing to adapt and handle the *Proficiscere* in *The Dream of Gerontius*, which is a poem but not liturgy. Here is found the first example, to be repeated many times a century or more later, of material from a prayer for the dying being recast into a prayer for the departed. The excess of meaning contained within it enables the *Proficiscere* to expand its pastoral significance from use before death to use after death as well.[18] A pastoral, if not a liturgical, precedent was thus set.

The influence of *The Dream of Gerontius*

In trying to discuss the influence of *The Dream of Gerontius* we need to be aware that it is impossible accurately to quantify its impact and effect on the English community as, for example, no social surveys exist. Similarly, there is no direct evidence of the way in which people were influenced by the use of the *Proficiscere* itself within the poem. The only way its influence can be assessed is to seek evidence of its effect on those who read the poem and on liturgists who were obviously influenced by Newman's translation.

The response of both friends and the general public to the publication of *The Dream of Gerontius* was both immediate and favourable, and far wider than the Roman Catholic community. Many Protestants (and Roman Catholics who did not know Latin) were aware for the first time of the nature of some of the prayers offered when a person was about to die.

On 11 October 1865 Newman received a letter from T. W. Allies, a friend who became a Roman Catholic, saying, 'I saw Gerontius most beautifully acted lately at the Convent of Notre Dame, Liverpool, by the Students of the Training School ... I feel sure Gerontius does not stand alone: can you not give us some of his brethren?'[19] Newman replied:

> I assure you I have nothing more to produce of Gerontius. On 17th January last it came into my head to write it. I really cannot tell how, and I wrote on until it was finished, on small bits of paper. And I could no more write anything else by willing it, than I could fly.[20]

In a similar vein on 15 June, John Telford, a priest of Ryde on the Isle of Wight, wrote a letter in praise of *The Dream of Gerontius,* but complained that, although her name was mentioned, 'I should like to have seen our Dear and Blessed Lady appear ... she must have a share ... in the salvation of every predestined soul, in as much as she had her *very own* share in our Lord's Passion.'[21] It is a tribute to the Victorian postal service that the letter arrived the next day, and a tribute to

Newman that he replied, by return, on 16 June. His response was courteous, if a little testy:

> You do me too much honour, if you think I am to see in a dream everything that *has* to be seen in the *subject* dreamed about. I have said what I saw. Various spiritual writers see various aspects of it; and under their protection and pattern I have set down the dream as it came before the sleeper. It is not my fault, if the sleeper did not dream more. Perhaps something woke him. Dreams are generally fragmentary. I have nothing more to tell.[22]

Newman expressed his own gratitude and emotion when he wrote in his journal:

> The controversy which occasioned it (the *Apologia*), and then the Oxford matter and the 'Dream of Gerontius' have brought me out, and now I should be hard indeed to please, and very ungrateful to them, and to God, if I did not duly appreciate their (friends and well-wishers) thoughts of me.[23]

Reprints of *The Dream of Gerontius* were frequent, running to nearly thirty. However, any suggestion that the poem became universally known needs to be tempered with the comments of William Bennett, who was in the chorus of the first performance of Elgar's work. He wrote:

> [It is] a poem which neither he (I venture to say) [the conductor Dr Richter] nor more than half a dozen of the 350 choristers had heard of prior to the festival. Not only had they never heard it before; but even then they did not trouble to find out about it more than could be gathered from the single-voice chorus parts from which they sang.[24]

The general assumption that the publication of his poem had done much to encourage people to read it centres on one

Victorian Revival

of the more remarkable stories about the response to *The Dream of Gerontius*. It concerns General Gordon's copy of *The Dream of Gerontius*. He and Newman never met, but Gordon had been given a copy of the miniature edition to take with him on his fateful journey to Khartoum, in the Sudan, where he was killed in 1885 in a massacre of his British troops. He immediately became a national hero back home, and news of him filled the papers.

Gordon had marked his favourite passages in the poem with a pencil and underlined the word 'Gordon' in the dedication to Father Joseph. It has been suggested, although there is no evidence, that he did this the day before he was killed. Gordon gave this copy of the book to Frank Power, *The Times* correspondent (which suggests he had marked his copy earlier) who was covering the war in the Sudan. Power then died while trying to obtain relief for the beleaguered garrison. The book, however, survived him and was sent to his sister in Ireland, a Mrs Murphy, who in turn offered it to Newman for his inspection. According to Ward, on 7 April Newman wrote to Dean R. W. Church:[25]

> I have received a little book which has taken my breath away. It is the property of Mrs Murphy, who received it from Mr F. Power, her brother, and was given to him by Gordon at Khartoum. So Mr Power writes in the first page; and attests that the pencil marks, thro' the book, are Gordon's. The book is the *Dream of Gerontius*.[26]

Copies were printed with 'Gordon's markings' indicated, and Elgar received such a copy as a wedding gift. As so often happens in life, his wife already had a copy. Rowell has commented that this 'may have influenced some of the particular choices of text which Elgar used in his own oratorio',[27] but when you compare the choices of Gordon and Elgar, there does not seem to be much coincidence. Gordon did not mark the *Proficiscere*.

Edward Elgar

We can now introduce into the story an account of Elgar's use of Newman's poem for his Oratorio of the same name.[28] In terms of the biography of the *Proficiscere*, this was the vehicle which would propel it to the widest public knowledge. It was in the summer of 1898 that Elgar was asked if he would write a major new work for the 1900 Birmingham Triennial Festival. It was agreed that it would be on a religious theme and Elgar's original choice was something based on the life of St Augustine. In the early months of 1899 he was still working on the *Enigma Variations*, which was first performed in June 1899. After this Elgar made some alterations to the music, and also composed his *Sea Pictures*.

It was not until the autumn that he could seriously turn his mind to the work for Birmingham. He had been considering Newman's work for some eight years (he had had a copy of the work for about fifteen years) but 'composer's block' affected him. At New Year 1900 he wrote to a friend while in a very depressed mood regretting his choice of subject, sorry that he had accepted the commission, and even that he wished he had not followed the career of a composer. It was typical of Elgar's complex personality that he then proceeded, with enthusiasm, to write his composition.

Elgar reduced the length of the poem considerably, in particular he cut the lengthy descriptions of heaven in favour of the more dramatic dialogues between Gerontius' soul and his guardian angel. Heaven is in the sublime music. If you are not familiar with Elgar's work I can only encourage you to listen to a recording of it. No words can adequately illuminate this part of the biography, as the *Proficiscere* takes on the wings of song. As far as the use of the *Proficiscere* is concerned, Elgar dropped a number of the biblical figures from the *Libera* (which again precedes the *Proficiscere*) and which is sung by a small chorus of Assistants. The music is quiet, echoing a medieval plainsong. When the Priest starts the *Proficiscere* he sings the opening lines with slow solemnity. The words, 'Go forth' and 'Go forth in the name' are picked up with increasing power and volume by the chorus, rising to a tremendous climax of power and grace. The music fades to a quiet, ethereal tone, bringing to an end the life of Gerontius on earth. The first part of the dream is over.

But much of the work was still only in the mind and scribbled notes of Elgar, as time sped on. Both a conductor and a chorus needed ample time to learn a new score, particularly one as original and complex as *The Dream of Gerontius* turned out to be. The Festival Choir was an amateur one and it struggled as it began to receive parts of the still incomplete work. Then disaster struck when in June their brilliant chorus master, Dr Swinnerton Heap, became ill and died. Instead of finding a new chorus master, at short notice the retired chorus master, William Stockley, was recalled. He was very elderly, he had not done any conducting for a number of years, and he was said to be out of sympathy with both the theology of the work and the modernity of Elgar's music. Rehearsals, and the actual first performance, were made even more difficult by the fact that members of the choir only had single-voice chorus sheets so they could not see how their part fitted in with the other parts. The eminent conductor Dr Hans Richter only had a copy of the full score ten days before the first performance. He worked desperately hard to learn it, with the music propped up on the mantelpiece in his room, as he practised his conducting. The morale of the choir was not enhanced when Elgar attended one of the rehearsals and told everyone how bad they were.

The first performance was a disaster, caused mainly by under-rehearsal, although most of the critics distinguished between the high quality of the work and the poor quality of the performance. This was not good enough for the touchy Elgar, who wrote to a friend:

> I have worked hard for forty years &, at the last, Providence denies me a decent hearing of my work; so I submit – I

always said God was against art & I still believe it. Anything obscene or trivial is blessed in this world & has a reward ... I have allowed my heart to open once – it is now shut against every religious feeling & every soft, gentle impulse *for ever*.

It is rather sad that, in later life Elgar, who was a Roman Catholic, wholly disavowed that he had ever had a religious interest in the piece.

In spite of its bad first performance, within a few years it was being played all over Europe, translated into French and German, and widely acclaimed. It is a work which has stood the test of time, and concert halls and cathedrals were packed for a series of centenary concerts at which it was performed in 2000. It has been recorded over a dozen times under conductors such as Sargent, Barbirolli, Britten, Boult, Rattle, Hickox and Handley. Along with *Messiah* and *Creation*, it is part of the staple repertoire of every choral society. Never before have so many people heard the stirring words, made even more stirring by Elgar's inspired music, 'Go forth upon thy journey, Christian soul! Go from this world! Go in the name of God ...'

How many people hearing it have not contemplated their own death in this Christian context? Perhaps *The Dream of Gerontius* is now performing in a secular context something of the spiritual role it has always performed in the liturgy. Ward quotes the comments of a friend of Newman that the poem 'has had a strong attraction for uneducated as well as educated persons. I knew a poor stocking weaver who on his death bed made his wife read it to him repeatedly.'[29] What Ward failed to point out was the fact that, at the heart of the poem, lay the very words which for over one thousand years had served this very function for generations of Christians.

The impact of Elgar's work, and of that of the *Proficiscere*, was strengthened by world events, once again centred in France where the *Proficiscere* had been born over a thousand years earlier. This was the First World War.

Changing social attitudes

Just as prayers for the dying virtually disappeared in the Reformation, swept away on the back of prayers for the departed, so prayers for the dying seemed to reappear in the twentieth century once again on the back of prayers for the departed. As at the Reformation, the arguments centred on prayers for the dead, and not about prayers for the dying as such.

Alan Wilkinson has put the argument well when he said that the First World War was the watershed. 'In 1914 public prayer for the dead was uncommon in the Church of England; by the end of the war it had become widespread.'[30] Wilkinson argued that the reintroduction of prayers for the dead was a pastoral response to the needs of a community grieving the loss of a generation of young men: 'Bereavement was sweeping away the latent Protestantism of the English people in this matter.'[31] He summarized the change in religious beliefs which had taken place in the nineteenth century:

> [But] doctrinally, and therefore pastorally, the ministry of the Church of England to the dying and the bereaved was confused. Biblical criticism, emphasis on a social gospel, evolution, liberal views of the love of God, and a materialistic type of science had been steadily eroding the old clear-cut doctrines about heaven and hell which up to the mid-nineteenth century had been broadly held in common by the majority of Christians for centuries.[32]

If the nineteenth century laid the intellectual and cultural conditions for the revival of prayers for the dying and the dead,[33] the First World War was the cataclysmic event which brought them back into the liturgical and spiritual life of the churches. It is interesting to note that Moore, in his life of Edward Elgar, recorded that during the First World War *The Dream of Gerontius* enjoyed a revival.[34] For example, the redoubtable Dame Clara Butt recorded excerpts from the work, and sang in six performances given on consecutives days at the Queen's Hall in London. Their majesties the King and Queen attended the first performance and all proceeds were donated to the Red Cross, to bring relief to 'our boys'.

Tony Walter has also argued for the powerful influence of that War on attitudes to death and dying:

> Paradoxically it was the First World War, hell on earth, that finally killed off hell below – no field chaplain could ever so much as hint that the brave lad he was burying might be going to the wrong place, and thereafter hell disappeared off the agenda in all but the most conservative churches. And without hell, death lost any spiritual risk, and became a medical and sociological affair.[35]

If hell was no longer to be a destination, and the fears of eternal damnation ceased to linger around the deathbed, it would be easier, even in a basically Protestant environment, to reintroduce prayers for the dying. However, as we will see, the *Proficiscere* also began to fulfil new purposes in addition to those used in the *Ritual* as the excess of meaning spilled out to meet the needs of new pastoral circumstances. The twentieth-century role of prayers for the dying, and that of the *Proficiscere* in particular, became also one of commendation and affirmation of faith, rather than intercession that God would do something for the person dying. It retained a euthanastic aspect, as the prayer still authorized or allowed the dying person to 'depart' or have 'the liberty to die'. This change of use is only one of the liturgical changes to the *Proficiscere* in the twentieth century, to which we can now turn.

6
Old and New Liturgical Uses

Every so often a songwriter in a creative moment writes a song of unusual quality, which a singer discovers and decides to record. Then other singers hear it, like what they hear, and very quickly it seems that every singer is recording their own 'cover version'. Each singer approaches the song in their own way, as no two singers are alike. The orchestration of each version differs, the versions vary in length, the pace of the song varies, the way the song is sung by each singer is never the same, but the song is every time recognizable as the same song. It becomes what is called 'a standard'.

The twentieth century is the century in which the *Proficiscere* became a liturgical 'standard'. This chapter will show how it escaped from its hidden place in the Latin of the Roman Catholic *Ritual*, and became part of the liturgy and prayer life of the English churches and individual Christians.

However, there were problems. As the *Proficiscere* basked in a new acceptability, it found that the environment in which it was now living was very different from the medieval world in which it had flourished. It was a season of growth, but it had to find new ways of expressing itself. There were two areas of concern in the new environment, which particularly affected the way in which the *Proficiscere* expressed itself. The first was the change in the ways in which language was used in prayers. Prayer language had changed. The second was the use of words or concepts which some people judged to be outdated or meaningless. As far as the *Proficiscere* is concerned, this centres particularly on the use of the word 'soul', and the relevance of the biblical figures in the *Libera*.

Language old and new

One of the problems faced by all prayers in the last century, including the *Proficiscere*, was the way in which language has changed. Several writers have called for a combination of traditional forms and good contemporary language. You will have the opportunity to judge for yourself if some modern versions of the *Proficiscere* meet this requirement.

Some new styles of liturgical language have been heavily criticized, particularly by people associated with the Prayer Book Society, a mainly Anglican group. Brian Morris made the radical point and (if he is correct) one damning to all modern liturgical language, when he said, 'In its present state of development and flux the English language is simply not capable of rendering the great truths of the Christian faith in words and rhythms that are both contemporary and profound.'[1] Although this conclusion may seem extreme, he helpfully introduced the concept of 'register', adapted from the way in which an organist sets up the stops to create sound-colour. Morris said:

> Liturgy is normally considered to belong to that register of the language which is reserved for the expression of man's deepest thoughts and feelings, which use rich, powerful and often technical, abstract vocabulary, and strongly rhythmical, sometimes repetitive phraseology. Its imagery is often a form of symbolism or shorthand, comprehensible to the initiated but without much more than surface meaning to the outsider.[2]

In modern English, he argued, the 'religious register' is not strong or particularly evident, but liturgical revisers have taken an iconoclastic view and discarded much of the imagery of the past.[3] Later in this chapter we will look at a variety of modern versions of the *Proficiscere*. You will have the opportunity to judge if they have lost the 'rich, powerful ... abstract vocabulary, and strongly rhythmical, sometimes repetitive phraseology', of the longer version.

Old and New Liturgical Uses

Members of the 1993 Anglican Liturgical Commission were well aware of the problems of liturgical language:

> Our response to language is intensely subjective. Words and phrases which to one person convey a sense of majesty and awe will to another be archaic, elitist and unhelpfully obscure – if indeed they ring any bells at all – while the more simple sentences and cadences which adequately serve the needs of some worshippers will, to others, be banal and uninspiring, and devoid of that sense of mystery which, to them, is an essential in the worship of God.[4]

They then point out the importance of 'remembering' in prayer: 'If people's souls are to be fed, they need to have deep within them words committed to memory, that can surface in time of need, supremely in time of mortal illness and approaching death.'[5] This point, which is particularly relevant to the use of the *Proficiscere*, will be taken up in the next chapter when we consider the changed pastoral role of the prayer.

The Problem of using 'soul'

Although the word 'soul' is often used in a secular context, a major area of disagreement today is over the use of the word 'soul' in both theology and liturgy. What is the 'soul' in our current understanding of our humanity, and can it be separated in our thinking from our 'body'? This question has a knock-on effect for modern liturgists who wish to use the *Proficiscere*, as they must decide whether or not to use the traditional word 'soul' in the opening line. Indeed, can we use the concept of the soul at all in worship? This chapter will show how different churches have tried to solve this problem.

Should we think of ourselves in a unitary way or in a dualistic way? Much modern thinking is unitary, with the idea of a separate soul as being meaningless. Paul Badham, taking a traditional line, has argued the thesis, 'that belief in God, in the soul, and in the future life, should be seen as three interdependent beliefs, each of which relies on implicit assumptions about the validity of the two other beliefs for its own coherence'.[6] Humans, he argued, are capable of a relationship with God which is not mediated by any of the five normal senses. He thus argued for a refined form of the dualism we saw in Chapter 1, that there is a part of our humanity which engages in a personal encounter with God. He pointed out, rather cleverly, that many of the phrases used by modern writers to avoid the use of the word 'soul', such as '"the essential part of what we are", "the vital principle of our being", "the pattern of what we are" or "our moral and intellectual qualities"'[7] are the meanings given for the word 'soul' in the *Concise Oxford Dictionary*.[8] Finally, Badham made the important point that the use of the word 'soul' today does not and should not necessarily carry all the ramifications of a world view of an earlier age. You do not need to import a medieval view of the world when you use the concept of the soul today.[9] It is fair to say that Badham is in a minority among theologians, most of whom reject the concept of 'soul', believing it to be meaningless today.

This division between theologians who are generally unhappy with the word 'soul' and want to omit it, and those liturgists who wish to continue its inclusion, is well indicated in a recent review of a book on modern funerary liturgy:

Theologically, however, the book exhibits symptoms of schizophrenia. The essays concerned primarily with practice operate for the most part with the traditional combination of belief in the 'soul' and the hope of 'resurrection'. But the specialist theology chapters tend to reject 'soul' as merely 'ghost-in-the-machine' talk, incompatible with the unity of the self and its total destruction at death, and to opt for 'resurrection' language only.[10]

The current debate about the 'soul' is mentioned here, not so much to adjudicate on its merits, but more to set out the difficult environment within which the *Proficiscere* and modern liturgists are operating. The particular problem faced by liturgical writers is that they have to bridge the divide between what is judged by academics, Christian or otherwise, to be intellectually respectable and what the 'public', Christian or otherwise, finds acceptable.

The twentieth-century liturgical response has been either to continue to use the word 'soul', while aware of the conceptual misgivings held by many, or to drop the word altogether. In the latter case, instead of addressing the departing soul, the departing person is usually addressed as, '"N", go forth from this world.' This avoids any implications of (for some) unacceptable dualism, but it fails to distinguish the fact that after death the human corpse of N will remain for disposal. N is different after death than before and the difference is glossed over by such practice. Whenever N is addressed or referred to as N in other services, such as Baptism, Confirmation and Marriage, this obviously included N's human body. This is not the case when N is addressed in a funeral service.

A final comment is necessary, from a sociological perspective, on the validity and value of using the word 'soul' in contemporary liturgical versions of the *Proficiscere*, and it is one which firmly supports the use of the word 'soul'. Three recent social surveys have indicated that the word 'soul' is widely held to be meaningful by the general public. In the Great Britain response to the 1990 European Values Study, 71 per cent of the population expressed a belief in God, 64 per cent a belief in the soul, and 44 per cent a belief in life after death.[11] A similar figure for 'soul' was obtained in a random survey carried out in the UK in 2000. Of those questioned, 69 per cent indicated that they believed people had souls and 62 per cent said they believed in God. More people apparently believed in the 'soul' than they did in 'God'.[12] I am glad to say that this finding has not so far led any liturgists, who wish to discard 'soul', also to discard the use of the word 'God' in liturgies, because 'God' is even less meaningful to the population than 'soul'.

These conclusions are in line with a third survey into people's attitude to death, and life beyond death. Respondents were asked to indicate which of six possible expressions best expressed their understanding of what happened beyond death. In a random sample of 1,603 people 34.1 per cent (the largest group) chose the phrase 'our soul passes on to another world', while the phrase 'our bodies await resurrection' gained only 7.9 per cent. (The second largest group, 28.8 per cent, approved the phrase 'nothing happens, we come to the end of life'.)[13]

If the word 'soul' is of significance to the majority of the population, and best expresses their understanding of the means by which life continues beyond death, we would argue that to exclude it from liturgy indicates that liturgists are both out of touch with contemporary attitudes and, more seriously, in danger of excluding from pastoral rites religious language which still resonates with people.

We now look at how the *Proficiscere* has expressed itself in the liturgical language of different churches in the twentieth century, adopting as far as possible a chronological approach. Every church looked over its shoulder at what other churches were doing, and this process is apparent when we see how the *Proficiscere* developed.

The Church of England, Prayer Book, 1928

Liturgical revision of the Book of Common Prayer (BCP) occupied much of the twentieth century, although pressures for revision had repeatedly risen and declined ever since 1662.[14] As we saw in Chapter 4, the issue of what is said to or about the dying has become inextricably entwined with the related theological issue of the acceptability of prayers for the dead, or for the departing.[15] The two issues are united in that they both concern the future prospects of the one who is dying, or has died. While they can be kept artificially separate, both theologically and philosophically, this has rarely

Old and New Liturgical Uses 123

happened in the pastoral issues of human or liturgical life. The exclusion of the *Proficiscere* from the 1549 Prayer Book and subsequent Prayer Books indicated how the two issues collided in the thinking of the Reformers, a collision which has continued to this present day.

Although the 1928 Prayer Book did not receive parliamentary approval, it introduced an English translation of the *Proficiscere* into Church of England worship. In this it was following a 1923 version from the Episcopal Church of the USA, which was even briefer. This is the 1928 Prayer Book version:[16]

> Go forth upon thy journey from this world, O Christian soul,
> In the name of God the Father Almighty who created thee. *Amen.*
> In the name of Jesus Christ who suffered for thee. *Amen.*
> In the name of the Holy Ghost who strengtheneth thee. *Amen.*
> In communion with the blessed Saints, and aided by Angels and Archangels, and all the armies of the heavenly host. *Amen.*
> May thy portion this day be in peace, and thy dwelling in the heavenly Jerusalem. *Amen.*[17]

A comparison of this version with *The Dream of Gerontius* indicates the influence of Newman (particularly in the first line), perhaps because his version was the one better known to the revisers and the general public, rather than earlier Latin versions. It marks the first return of the *Proficiscere* to official Church of England worship since its exclusion in 1549, and is included as the final prayer in the section of commendatory prayers in the 'Visitation of the Sick', thus continuing its tradition role in the liturgy. This version has proved to be a template for other versions.

The Baptist Union of Great Britain, *Praise God*, 1980, and *Patterns and Prayers*, 1991

The Baptist Union's *Praise God*[18] contains the first liturgy to use a brief version of the *Proficiscere* as an optional commendation in the funeral service itself, rather than as a prayer for the dying. It was thus uniquely innovative. The text is as follows:

> *The Lord's Prayer and the following words of commendation may be used:*
> Depart, O Christian soul, out of this world,
> in the name of God the Father almighty who created you,
> in the name of Jesus Christ who redeemed you,
> in the name of the Holy Spirit who sanctified you.
> May your rest be this day in peace and your dwelling in the paradise of God.

This text was repeated in the 1991 *Patterns and Prayers*.[19] The Baptists, from a Free Church tradition, might be thought to oppose anything that hints at 'prayers for the departed'. Here they were including material that contains words traditionally addressed to a dying person in a funeral service, and the imagery of journey, rather than the traditional Protestant emphasis on 'this day in Paradise'. Did this represent a groundswell of change among Baptists generally, in their attitude to prayers for the departed, or only among its liturgists, or did members of the committee who prepared this service deliberately make a theological shift?[20]

I was grateful for the opportunity to discuss these points with the Revd Bernard Green, who was in 1990 both General Secretary of the Baptist Union and Chair of the Commission which compiled the 1991 book. He said he had not realized that *Praise God* and its successor were the first service books in which the *Proficiscere* had been used as a commendation in a funeral liturgy. Apparently there were no comments, either in the *Baptist Times* or within the working papers of the committee, raising any theological objections to the innovative use of the prayer in this way.[21] He said that the committee never thought of it as a prayer for the dead, although they did miss out several words such as 'angels meet'. They thought of it as an affirmation of where a loved one had gone, an affirmation of the dead for the sake of the bereaved. The prayer was affirming what they believed had already happened; it was not a prayer asking that this should be possible. The commendation was used as a comfort for mourners.[22]

This shift in understanding is helpful in identifying the way in which the *Proficiscere* can be seen by people in the twenty-first century. The prayer was included out of a desire to respond pastorally to the needs of the mourners, rather than for the dead person. Thus for at least some people, both its meaning and its purpose had changed, although during the century the words had altered very little.

The version of the *Proficiscere* used by the Baptists suggests a knowledge of the Latin original in that it eschews both Newman's 'Go forth' and his 'journey', giving a good translation of *Proficiscere anima christiana de hoc mundo*. The final sentence, however, introduces the words 'paradise of God' which is not a biblical phrase, although it echoes Jesus' words from the cross. The inclusion of the *Proficiscere* in this prayer book might suggest a measure of theological and liturgical naïvety on the part of the compilers. However, it was a liturgical precedent to be followed by the Church of England, whose liturgists could not be judged in the same light. The Baptist liturgist Paul Sheppy was not happy that the prayer used the word 'Depart' rather than Newman's 'Go forth': 'The effect is not a happy one. "Depart" in this imperative mood is redolent of the words of Simon Peter: "Depart from me, for I am a sinful man, O Lord".'[23] Perhaps Sheppy could have balanced his unhappiness with the word if he had considered other uses, such as 'Lord, now lettest thou thy servant depart in peace.' He goes on to comment: 'What is more interesting is that so Catholic a prayer should have been proposed in a book intended for those of a very different tradition.'[24]

The Church of England, *The Promise of His Glory*, 1981

So far, all the examples of the rediscovery and new use of the *Proficiscere* (outside the Roman Catholic Church) have used only the first part of the prayer. *The Promise of His Glory*[25] is the only official publication to include a version of the *Libera* part of the prayer. The book does not carry the same authorization as the Alternative Service Book (ASB) but it is 'Commended by the House of Bishops of the General Synod of the Church of England', with a personal commendation by the Archbishop of Canterbury. It is a product of the work of the Liturgical Commission, and contains a number of original and experimental liturgies. Among them is 'The Four Last Things: A Service of Preparation for the End'.[26] At the end of the service is an Appendix entitled 'The Litany for Holy Dying'. The litany begins with new material and then uses material drawn from the *Libera* in the following style:

> Deliver us, Lord, at our last hour; as you delivered Enoch and Elijah from the death which must come to all,
> R: Save and deliver us.

The litany then includes Noah, Job, Isaac, Lot, Daniel, the three young men, Esther and Susanna, but not other popular figures such as David or Peter and Paul. It also misses the opportunity of including a more balanced gender mix.

You will notice that the traditional material has been used in an innovative way. The direction and intention of the prayer has been turned round, from being focused on a dying person, to the future death of the person(s) saying the prayer, 'Deliver us, Lord, at our last hour.' Instead of being a prayer for the dying, it is now a prayer which asks that the person praying it may be saved and delivered at their own death. This shift is not out of line with other traditional Anglican liturgy. In the Book of Common Prayer's 'Commendatory Prayer for a Sick Person at the Point of Departure', quoted in Chapter 5, the prayer moves from concern for the dying person to prayers that the living too may 'seriously apply our hearts' so we may be brought to everlasting life.

This use of part of the *Libera* is another example of the way in which the traditional text of the prayer has adapted itself to offer a new expression of Christian hope. If this prayer is used as intended, at a time other than the time of death, it will speak even more powerfully when death eventually comes because it will be known and deposited in the memory of the dying person. It therefore meets a new pastoral need, aiding remembrance.

The Roman Catholic Church, *Pastoral Care of the Sick*, 1983

Reform of the Roman Liturgy was authorized by the Constitution on the Sacred Liturgy, which was promulgated on 4 December 1963, as one of the Documents of Vatican II.[27] A significant decision was made, along with other liturgies, that there should be a change from Latin to local vernacular languages. This was carried out in a two-stage process. The first was to produce a new Latin version (what is called an *editio typica*) from which all other language translations were to be made. So a new team of liturgists took their red pencils to the Latin version which, as we have seen, had served the Catholic Church for over 350 years.[28]

They kept 'Depart' etc. and the three trinitarian lines, but then cut out all nine ranks of angels together with the patriarchs, prophets, apostles and evangelists, martyrs and confessors, monks and hermits, virgins and saints of God. Mary and Joseph, who had only been added in 1919–25, survived, but with reduced attributes and at the end of the prayer.

When the liturgists turned to the *Libera* out went the mention of 'the dangers of hell and ... all evil tribulations'. From the list of Old Testament figures they cut out the references to Enoch and Elijah, to Isaac's escape from Abraham's knife, and Lot from Sodom. But what should they do with the ever-popular Thecla?

Instrumental in their decision was the work of another group of scholars at Vatican II who at the same time were preparing a report on a revised list of the saints and martyrs of the Roman Catholic Church. In a section headed 'Saints who Pose Serious Historical Problems' they included St Thecla, together with about fifty other saints who had previously been venerated with a saint's day. The authors of the report said, 'Although it cannot be stated with certainty that these saints did not exist, hagiographers are unable to find any accurate historical basis for their veneration', and then added, 'these saints are no longer listed in the calendar'.[29]

The liturgists could do nothing but follow their colleagues, so, with the stroke of a pen, the Catholic Church was able to kill off remembrance of St Thecla. This indestructible saint had survived being burned at the stake, numerous attacks of wild beasts and dangerous fish, and a gang of rapists. She could not, however, escape the reforming zeal of Vatican II, which achieved something that her contemporary adversaries had notably failed to do. The liturgists revising the *Libera* felt honour bound to exclude her from the list as the climactic figure of God's salvation. No longer would Thecla's example of faith and courage, and of God's mighty saving acts displayed through her life, be a spiritual accompaniment and support at the moment of Christian death. The *Proficiscere* emerged from the process radically reduced. No longer would a dying person be accompanied by nine ranks of angels, and the Church on earth and in heaven.

Once the standard Latin text had been approved it was then translated into English. In fact there were two English translations made in 1976 and a revision in 1982 by the International Commission on English in the Liturgy (ICEL).[30] The revised translation was as follows:

Go forth, Christian soul from this world,
In the name of God the almighty Father, who created you,

Old and New Liturgical Uses

> In the name of Jesus Christ, Son of the living God, who suffered for you,
> In the name of the Holy Spirit, who was poured out upon you,
> Go forth, faithful Christian.
> May you live in peace this day, may your home be with God in Zion.
> With Mary the Virgin Mother of God, with Joseph, and all the angels and saints.
> Welcome your servant, Lord, into the place of salvation which because of your mercy he/she rightly hoped for.
> Amen. *or* Lord save your people.
> Deliver your servant, Lord, from every distress.
> Deliver your servant, Lord, as you delivered ... [Repeated each time]
> Noah from the flood
> Abraham from Ur of the Chaldees.
> Job from his sufferings.
> Moses from the hand of Pharaoh.
> Daniel from the den of lions.
> The three young men from the fiery furnace.
> Susanna from her false accusers.
> David from the attacks of Saul and Goliath.
> Peter and Paul from prison.
> Deliver your servant, Lord, through Jesus our Saviour, who suffered death for us and gave us eternal life. Amen.

What do you think of the *Proficiscere* in its 1983 Roman Catholic guise? Has it lost something, something that is important, or is it in a form suitable for today? You may like it, or you may think it has lost something of the 'religious register' mentioned earlier. Apart from the omissions already noted, you will have noticed that the opening line eschews the influence of Newman's 'journey'. Second, the translators were well aware of the 'soul' issue. The United Kingdom version included 'soul' while the US version dropped both 'soul' and all the opening line, so that version began with the trinitarian formula. One commentator wrote:

> A problem which caused considerable discussion was what to do about *anima* [soul]. The translators of 1970 were rightly chary of suggesting a Platonist and Cartesian psychology which can make the resurrection of the body seem an irrelevant postscript. It is the whole person, constituted by body and soul, who is redeemed and saved ... In view of these problems, the 1970 translation avoided the use of 'soul' where possible ... In the 1985 *Order of Christian Funerals* it has been used wherever the logic of the prayer demanded it and sparingly on other occasions where the problems could be overcome.[31]

While this approach has a logic to it, as far as the *Proficiscere* was concerned it had lost its powerful 'soul' in one English translation.

You will have noticed that new words have been added, 'go forth faithful Christian', which is not supported by the new Latin text. This is one solution to the problem of 'soul' language (as is the use, in the *Libera*, of the words 'your servant' rather than 'the soul of your servant'). In liturgical terms 'go forth faithful Christian' echoes the opening line, rounding off the shortened first section. We have already commented on the omission of the ranks of angels, groups of biblical figures, and church figures. Their disappearance has the effect of flattening a sense of the miraculous, and cutting out any sense of a wider spiritual resource and perspective. This aspect is further emphasized by the deletion, in the English version, of an equivalent of the Latin 'holy' (*sanctus*) in relation to Jerusalem, Mary and Joseph, indicating a flattening of language and a diminishment of the religious 'register'. We might note that the English could have been improved if it had said 'for which he/she, because of your mercy, rightly hoped', instead of 'because of your mercy he/she rightly hoped for'.

The Roman Catholic Church is the only church to use the *Libera* part of the prayer, and faced the problem of how to

Old and New Liturgical Uses 131

translate it. For the word *Libera*, the UK 1983 translation uses 'deliver', which is less dramatic than Newman's 'rescue', while the 1976 US translation uses 'free'. While there are problems over the idea of the soul being 'set free' from the body, the word 'deliver' does not carry the sense of authority of 'free'.

How should the word *'Libera'* be translated in modern liturgies? Various lines of approach are possible. The first is to follow the way in which *Libera* has previously been translated.[32] In the *Vulgate*, the line in the Lord's Prayer (Matt. 6.13), *Sed libera nos a malo*, is translated in the traditional text of the prayer as 'but deliver us from evil'.[33] This is also the translation of the Revised Standard Version. Modern translations render *Libera* as 'rescue',[34] and 'deliver'.[35] Alongside these a third word, 'free', is also a possible translation of *Libera*, being used in the 1976 translation. All three words can also have different meanings in English. 'Rescue' suggests release from a danger in which a person finds him or herself; 'deliver' suggests, in addition, a safe end-point (as a parcel is safely delivered); while 'free' suggests that someone held against his or her will has been liberated. A possible image that comes to mind is of a prisoner set free when the door of the cell is opened. While this might be seen as an act of rescue, it cannot easily be described as a delivery. I would suggest that 'free' or 'set free' is the best translation for today in the context of 'the liberty to die'.

However, it is also necessary to try to understand the word in the context in which it is set. In the *Libera*'s list of mainly Old Testament figures, what is it that God is believed to be doing? An analysis of the fullest list in the *Nursia* text suggests that God is doing a number of different things. In many incidents (Noah, the three young boys, and Daniel), 'rescue' or 'deliver' might be the best translations. In the case of Elijah and Enoch, 'set free' seems a more accurate translation, while for Peter and Paul either 'rescue' or 'set free' seems appropriate.

A second line of inquiry is to try to relate what it is that is being asked in respect of the soul, and how this relates to what God was perceived to have done for the Old Testament figures in the *Libera*. As we saw in Chapter 2, in Neoplatonic thought the soul was very much understood to be a prisoner of the body. In order to be restored to God it needed to be liberated or set free. In many medieval pictures of death scenes the soul is depicted as a heart with small wings attached. It had escaped the confines of the body and was set free to fly to heaven. Of course the journey was dangerous, as it was vulnerable to attack, so safe delivery was important.

However, as we have argued in this book, the understanding of the nature of death today is different, so a translation which accords with modern understandings and needs is appropriate. In the next chapter we will suggest that the modern attitude to death is at least partly one of failure on the part of the medical services to cure (and the failure of the patient to respond); there is a need to allow a person to die. If a patient is to be allowed 'the liberty to die', then a 'setting free' or a 'liberating' from this life is a helpful pastoral context in which the prayer can be said. Thus we can see that a matter of translation can influence the way in which the Christian hope can be expressed, and pastoral concern shown.

You will note that the *Libera* ends with a new christological statement, which re-enforces the end of the prayer. In spite of this you may feel that the various omissions leave a prayer in a muted register compared with its origins. Little has been added, but it is at least somewhat closer to its original than some of the versions adopted by other churches. There is a sense of 'flattening', as both the joys of heaven and the perils of hell are diminished in the text. There is also less of a sense of the need for divine intervention, because the process through death is fairly safe and standard, without any real sense of peril. But perhaps this accurately reflects a modern experience of death. As it is the only church to include the *Libera*, the Roman Catholic Church has remained most true to the original texts.

The translation, or paraphrasing, of Latin texts into English has been a matter of considerable concern to liturgical scholars.[36] The process and the assumptions which lie behind

Old and New Liturgical Uses

an official translation are more significant than an unofficial 'paraphrase', as it cannot be open to the charge that those who prepare the text were ignorant of, or had ignored, the Latin which lay behind it. In his address to the translators of the liturgical texts, Pope Paul VI asked:

> With acumen and tireless devotion let the intent of all your efforts be that the liturgical community can be clothed in a spotless and graceful vesture of speech and 'find a beautiful mantle for the realities within'.[37] For pastoral reasons, the beauty and richness of Latin, which the Latin Church used for centuries for prayers, petitions, and thanksgivings to God, have been partially lost. Nevertheless your wise and diligent efforts should make a similar clarity of language and dignity of expression shine forth in the vernacular translations of liturgical texts.[38]

Such fine aspirations can be difficult to meet in practice.

The Church of England, *Ministry to the Sick*, 1983

The year 1983 also saw the Church of England publication of *Ministry to the Sick*,[39] as an addition to the 1980 Alternative Service Book. The 'Commendation at the Time of Death' included this version of the *Proficiscere*:

> Go forth upon your journey from this world,
> O Christian soul,
> in the name of God the Father almighty
> who created you;
> in the name of Jesus Christ
> who suffered death for you;
> in the name of the Holy Spirit, who strengthens you;
> in communion with the blessed saints,
> and aided by angels and archangels,
> and all the armies of the heavenly host.
> May your portion this day be in peace,
> and your dwelling the heavenly Jerusalem. **Amen.**[40]

It is immediately apparent that this text substantially follows the text of the 1928 Prayer Book. Modern English is used so that 'thy' and 'thee' become 'your' and 'you' etc. The most noticeable difference, and a surprising one in a time when the importance of the participation of the worshipping community was being stressed in liturgical writing, is the fact that the five 'Amens' in the body of the 1928 prayer have not been included. This denies the community a heightened sense of involvement in the liturgy, and the event it is marking.

Bishop Colin Buchanan has given a fascinating account of the processes behind the publication of the booklet.[41] There was much dissent over some aspects of the draft services. Buchanan reported that this version of the *Proficiscere*

> came in for some criticism on the Revision Committee, not only because it included the slightly romantic but arguably misleading concept of a 'journey' (and the doubtful concept of a 'soul'!), but also because its form is an optative-type[42] wish or prayer for the dying person. The critics wanted an address to him or her which would be categorical, and the Bishop of Derby, chairing the Committee, thus wrote the second form. It is full of Christian assurance, whilst still having much of the poetry of the first alternative.[43]

The Bishop of Derby's second version did not meet with approval, and was dropped. No further objection was made to the inclusion of the *Ministry to the Sick* version of the *Proficiscere* and the total votes in the three Houses of the General Synod were overwhelmingly in favour, with *Ayes* 285 and *Noes* 7.[44]

Celebrating Common Prayer, 1992

Although *Celebrating Common Prayer* (CCP) is not an official Church of England publication it is from the same stable and has a Foreword by the then Archbishop of Canterbury. It is a new version of *The Daily Office SSF* (1981) of the Society of Saint Francis, a religious community within the Church of England. It includes 'An Office of Commendation', which is an example of a new liturgy, with new purposes.[45]

It is a pity that the Introduction to *Celebrating Common Prayer* does not set out the rationale for the liturgies it contains, but it can perhaps best be understood as being complementary to the 1980 Church of England's Alternative Service Book, as there is no overlap between the two.[46] *Celebrating Common Prayer* contains a rich variety of seasonal material which feeds into the four Daily Offices. The only exception to this pattern is 'An Office of Commendation', whose distinctiveness is thus highlighted by its uniqueness in this volume.

Its title suggests a link with the traditional 'Commendation of the Soul' but the rubric which follows the title suggests a different purpose. The rubric reads: *'This service may be used on hearing the news of a death, or on the day of the funeral by those not able to be present or on any suitable occasion.'*[47] Thus three possible new uses for this liturgy are created: on news of a death, on the day of the funeral, or another time. You will note that the first two specific uses are both post-death and reflect a physical distance between the user of the liturgy and the body of the dead person, a further innovation in a death ritual. The rubric suggests that, in a mobile society in which mourners may be far away from a person at their death, and/or not able to be present at a funeral, there is a need for a new ritual. There are clear echoes here of the practice in the medieval Church of circulating names of members living and dead for commemoration.[48]

This is a new funerary rite, which reflects a desire for a sense of community, whether the Society of St Francis or among any Christian group, in a situation where members are scattered and are often not able to assemble for the funeral itself. It is a new form of commendation (although the words 'of the soul' are not included in the title) which can be used between the two usual places of commendation, at the moment of dying and at the end of the funeral service itself. *Celebrating Common Prayer* thus contains the first genuinely new funerary rite for many centuries,[49] to meet the needs of Christians in the twenty-first century, and has included in it a version of the *Proficiscere*.[50]

Apart from the opening Bible verses of the Office, the order of the material before the use of the *Proficiscere* (hymn, psalm, shared memories of the departed, canticle, intercessions which include a form of commendation), is all offered in an optional form, with each rubric including the word 'may'. The version of the *Proficiscere* used is then introduced with the mandatory 'Then is said'.[51] (The lines are numbered to assist the following comments. Words in *italics* are contained in the 1981 Daily Office.)

1 Go forth upon your journey from this world, O Christian soul; in the name of God the Father *almighty* who created you. **Amen.**
2 In the name of Jesus Christ who suffered for you. **Amen.**
3 In the name of the Holy Spirit who strengthens you. **Amen.**
4 In communion with (the blessèd Virgin Mary, Saint N. and with) all the blessèd saints;
4 *In communion with the Blessed Virgin Mary, St Francis, St Clare and with all the blessed saints,*
5 with the angels and archangels and all the heavenly host. **Amen.**
5 *and aided by Angels and Archangels, and all the armies of the heavenly host.* **Amen.**
6 May your portion this day be in peace and your dwelling in the city of God *in the heavenly Jerusalem*. **Amen.** And/or:[52]
7 N., our companion in faith and brother/sister in Christ, we entrust you to God who created you.
8 May you return to the Most High *him* who formed you from the dust of the earth,
9 May the angels and *the* saints come to meet you as you go forth from this life.
10 May Christ, who was crucified for you, take you into his Kingdom.

Old and New Liturgical Uses

11 May Christ the Good Shepherd give you a place within his flock.
12 May Christ *he* forgive you your sins and keep you among his people.
13 May you see your Redeemer face to face and delight in the vision of God for ever. **Amen.**
And/or:
14 N., may Christ give you rest in the land of the living and open for you the gates of paradise;
15 may he receive you as a citizen of the Kingdom, and grant you forgiveness of your sins: for you were his friend.

(14 *and* 15 *These lines are not found in the 1981 Order, and are taken from the Orthodox Funeral Service.*)

The prayer ends in this rather unusual form, and is followed with 'The Blessing'. It is worthy of detailed comment because of the version of the *Proficiscere* used here, and the unique nature of its use in a new service.

1   The influence of Newman, with his introduction of 'journey' into the prayer, rather than *Gellone*, which does not use it, is obvious from the first line.

4   There is the optional inclusion of the name of a saint here. CCP is very strong in its *Sanctorale*, offering a wide variety of Orthodox, Roman Catholic and Protestant 'saints' covering most days of the year.[53] It is not indicated whether the appropriate saint to be optionally included should be the one for the date of the death, the date of use of the service, or the date of the funeral itself, or the saint with whom the dead person particularly identified.[54]

7–8   These lines are unique to non-Roman Catholic liturgy, being heavily influenced by the English translation of the Latin *Ordo Unctionis*.[55] Line 7 draws on the brother/sisterhood experienced within a community life, or that of a church community, or common humanity. Line 8 links a 'return' motif, which is not particularly biblical (apart from Jesus returning to the Father) with the bodily creation of Genesis. However, it may be that this is intended to echo the return of the Prodigal Son to his father, although that was in the context of life and not death.

12–15 If parts two and three are both used there are two requests for the forgiveness of sins, which suggests a weakness in drafting rather than a considered repetition of the request. The inclusion of these words also raises the issue of seeking forgiveness of sins for those who have died, which has traditionally been unacceptable to post-Reformation churches. Also, it is unusual to see the word 'paradise' without its customary capital letter.[56]

Generally, the main area of comment on this prayer concerns the problem over its concept of time. This is partly caused by moving the prayer from its traditional place as a prayer for the dying, when the idea of setting out (on a journey) from this world is clear and appropriate in temporal terms. Once it is said after death it creates problems both temporal and cosmological. As we mentioned above, the Church of England had found the subject of prayers for the departed to be one of considerable theological controversy. Phrases such as 'Go forth upon your journey' (line 1), 'May you return to the Most High' (line 8), and 'come to meet you' (line 9) can all suggest a continuing 'time' or 'delay' before the benefits of heaven are received. Perhaps the most surprising use of tense, the past tense, is found in the final line, 'for you were his friend'. Is this phrase, copied from the Orthodox material, another example of infelicitous drafting, a comment on a relationship which only reflects life on earth, or (and this is an unlikely intention) does it indicate in some way the ceasing of a relationship of friendship with Jesus at death?[57]

These significant theological issues make it a little surprising that *Celebrating Common Prayer* carries the warm endorsement of the conservative-evangelical (then) Archbishop of Canterbury, George Carey, who says in his Foreword, 'this book will help us to know that we are sharing fully in the Church's prayer'.[58]

Brother Tristram SSF offered an insight into the workings of the Liturgical Commission (1995–97) in relation to the attitude of evangelicals by saying:

> When we were trying to establish a common mind on prayer and the departed, it became clear that we, including most of the evangelicals present, had an assumption that prayer around a dying person was much less a feature of life than it had been heretofore, often for reasons of geographical distance; and that such prayers as would previously have been said around the deathbed were not inconsistent with being recited later as the pray-ers share in the life of prayer. The chronological distance became more of a problem with evangelicals the further it got from the time of death, but the closer the proximity of prayer to the time of death seemed less of a problem.'[59]

This comment offers an explanation of the possible use of the *Proficiscere* both before and after death in the Church of England funeral services, detailed below. As will be seen, this liturgy was substantially copied by the Methodist Church, but without the *Proficiscere*.

The Church of England, the Funeral Service for Princess Diana, 1997

Mention must be made of the Funeral Service for Diana, Princess of Wales, held at Westminster Abbey on 6 September 1997. Because she was formerly a member of the Royal Family the service was a Church of England service.[60] It was conducted for one of the world's most famous women, and was watched on television 'by nearly three-quarters of the adult population of the United Kingdom and by a worldwide audience of 2.5 billion'.[61] Diana was 'let-go' by an adoring public, as an original modern English version of part of the *Proficiscere* was said by the Dean of Westminster standing by the catafalque, not as a prayer for the dying, but as a Commendation of the Dead:

> Let us commend our sister Diana to the mercy of God, our Maker and Redeemer.
>
> Diana, our companion in faith and sister in Christ, we entrust you to God.
> Go forth from this world in the love of the Father, who created you;
> In the mercy of Jesus Christ, who died for you;
> In the power of the Holy Spirit, who strengthens you.
> At one with all the faithful, living and departed,
> may you rest in peace and rise in glory,
> where grief and misery are banished
> and light and joy evermore abide. **Amen.**[62]

Thus the words of the old Latin prayers for the dying, popularized in English by Cardinal Newman, were recast into a Commendation of the Dead, and were publicly heard coming from the Church of England by vast numbers of the world's population, a very public demonstration of that church's liturgical changes.

The Methodist Church, *Methodist Worship Book*, 1999

In 1990 the Methodist Conference authorized a Liturgical Sub-Committee to produce a new service book. The Committee prepared preliminary drafts of (among others) the funeral services. The first draft of one service, an 'Order of Commendation', was heavily influenced, both in purpose and in content, by the Commendation in *Celebrating Common*

Old and New Liturgical Uses

Prayer (CCP). The version of the *Proficiscere* used in the Methodist draft was identical to lines 1–6 in *CCP*, except that it omitted 'In communion with (the blessèd Virgin Mary, Saint N. and with) all the blessèd saints'.[63]

It was clear that placing this prayer in a service to be used after death, rather than at the point of death, changed the way in which it had traditionally been used and understood, both liturgically and theologically. Here the Methodist Church faced the same theological issues as the Church of England. It remained a commendatory prayer but, as it was said after death rather than before, it was capable of being interpreted as being addressed to the deceased person or to their soul. It thus became for some Methodists a prayer for the departed, evoking criticism from those of a more evangelical persuasion, who rejected such prayer.

When the Committee met to consider comments on the draft service, and the reflections of its own members, there were objections (particularly from the Methodist Church in Ireland), but also from evangelical Methodists in England, saying that the prayer was a prayer for the departed and unacceptable to Methodist doctrine. All responses to the draft services were presented to the Committee anonymously. The following two comments represent the strength of some of the criticisms:

> Prayers for the dead! I am aware that this practice has crept into Methodism from non-Protestant traditions in recent decades. I still cannot see any ground for it in either scripture or reason. Words addressed to the deceased … [The *Proficiscere*]. Really! This is both silly and abhorrent, smacking as it does of spiritism and the occult. It must be excised.

> The opening phrase … is one which will cause grave offence to the evangelical constituency, to the extent that I feel that most of us will find it totally impossible to use it … How can we speak to the dead? Did not the soul leave the body when

the person died? Or is the soul to stay in the body until, at the whim of relatives, minister, undertaker, and the crematorium booking bursar, the moment finally comes for the minister to release the soul? What an extraordinary manner of proceedings.[64]

The Committee proved to be less concerned about these theological viewpoints than it did about being accused of liturgical innovation, or perhaps ignorance, by using a prayer intended for use before death in a post-death service. It responded more favourably to comments such as, 'It is of course not a prayer at all, but a valediction to a dying person. Its proper place is at the deathbed, just before or at the point of departure; by the time of a funeral the Christian soul has already gone forth upon the journey.'[65]

Although it was pointed out that the highly regarded *Celebrating Common Prayer* had used it in this way, it was decided, on a split vote, to remove the prayer from the Commendation, but to add it to 'Prayer with the Dying' (not then drafted), so that the prayer could be included in the service book. It was argued that it could still be used by ministers at funerals, or on other occasions, if they wished to do so. By restoring the *Proficiscere* to its traditional position, as a prayer for the dying, the Committee demonstrated liturgical conservatism, and avoided criticism from evangelicals, but it still offered the *Proficiscere* as a funeral text in a handy form.[66] This decision was made before *Common Worship* included the *Proficiscere* as a funeral prayer.

When the draft order of service of 'Prayer with the Dying' was submitted to the Committee the *Proficiscere* was amended further to the following:

Go forth upon your journey, Christian soul,
in the name of God the Father who created you;
In the name of Jesus Christ who suffered for you;
In the name of the Holy Spirit who strengthens you;.
In communion with the blessèd saints,

Old and New Liturgical Uses

with angels and archangels and with all the heavenly host.
May you rest in peace and may the City of God
be your eternal dwelling. *Amen.*[67]

On a personal note, I do regret that at the time the Committee was discussing the wording of the prayer I was not aware of the Latin origins behind the Newman version. My research into its origins began later. If I had, I would have argued for omitting 'journey' but retaining, 'from this world'. The concept of 'journey' might be felt to introduce a non-Protestant suggestion of a purgatorial interval, rather than permission to be released from the body. The prayer was accepted without dissent when the *Methodist Worship Book* was approved by the 1998 Conference.

The Church of England, *Common Worship*, 2000

As part of its preliminary work towards *Common Worship*, the Liturgical Commission of the Church of England produced draft funeral liturgies in 1997, which included versions of the *Proficiscere*.[68] They were based on, or heavily influenced by, Newman and the 1928 Prayer Book rather than *Gellone*.

The text of this draft is worth quoting in full because of the way in which *Proficiscere* material and other material was interwoven.

> Go forth from this world:
> in the love of God the Father who created you,
> in the mercy of Jesus Christ who redeemed you,
> in the power of the Holy Spirit who strengthens you.
> May the heavenly host sustain you
> and the company of heaven enfold you.
> In communion with all the faithful,
> may you dwell this day in peace. **Amen.**[69]
> *and/or*

May the angels lead you into paradise;
may the martyrs come to welcome you
and take you into the holy city,
the new and eternal Jerusalem.
May choirs of angels welcome you
and lead you to the bosom of Abraham;
and where Lazarus is poor no longer
may you find eternal rest.
May saints and angels lead you on,
Escorting you where Christ has gone.
Now he has called you, come to him
Who sits above the seraphim.
Come to the peace of Abraham
And to the supper of the Lamb:
Come to the glory of the blessed,
And to perpetual light and rest.[70]
and/or
N, go forth upon your journey from this world,
in the name of God the Father almighty who created you;
in the name of Jesus Christ who suffered death for you;
in the name of the Holy Spirit who strengthens you;
in communion with the blessed saints,
and aided by angels and archangels,
and all the armies of the heavenly host.
May your portion this day be in peace,
and your dwelling the heavenly Jerusalem. **Amen.**[71]

In 1998 the Liturgical Commission published three further booklets of responses from the parishes which had used the new material.[72] In the comments on the 'Funeral Service' the Commission said that an alteration would be made to insert a name, changing 'Go forth from this world' to 'N, go forth', as it was not clear who is being addressed.[73] The Commission rejected a suggestion that using the *Proficiscere* as a commendation in the Funeral Service was not the right place because it was too late.[74]

Old and New Liturgical Uses

Two points of weakness in the text may be suggested. The first is the double use of 'heaven' in 'heavenly host' and in the next line 'company of heaven' when other, more varied images might have been used. The other is the problem of the word 'portion' in the 1983 and later versions which is not a particularly felicitous word. Other liturgists have avoided the use of it. You will note there is no 'soul'.

When *Common Worship* was published in 2000, the two alternative versions of the *Proficiscere* were brought together with '*or*' between them. However, the longer ending of the first version in the draft service (from '*and/or* May the angels lead you into paradise ... and to perpetual light and rest') was omitted.

Two types of authorization were used to overcome the theological problem caused by some people's concern over what might be considered prayers for the dying. 'Ministry at the time of Death',[75] which contains 'everything controversial' was not 'authorized pursuant to Canon B 2 of the Canons of the Church of England for use until further resolution of the General Synod', but was 'commended by the House of Bishops of the General Synod pursuant to Canon B 2 of the Canons of the Church of England and are published with the agreement of the House'.[76]

Some other Anglican liturgies

Although they strictly lie outside the scope of this book, we should note some of the funerary liturgies of parts of the Anglican Communion other than England. Versions of the *Proficiscere* are found in the 1985 *Book of Alternative Services of the Anglican Church of Canada*;[77] and the Scottish Episcopal Church's *Revised Funeral Rites 1987*,[78] which handles the 'soul' problem by using the rather cringe-making 'dear child of God'.

Special mention must be made of the 1989 New Zealand Prayer Book because it offers a novel version of the *Proficiscere* in its 'Prayer at the Time of Death', which has influenced other liturgical books:

> Go forth N (*Christian soul*), on your journey from this world,
> in the love of God the Father who created you,
> in the mercy of Jesus the Redeemer who suffered for you,
> in the power of the Holy Spirit who keeps you in life eternal.
> **May you dwell this day in peace,**
> **and rest in the presence of God. Amen.**[79]

As is apparent, the first innovation here is to offer the option of either using the dying person's name or to refer to them as 'Christian soul'. The other innovation is the change of the triple 'in the name' to three different attributes of the persons of the Trinity, 'love', 'mercy' and 'power'. By losing the power of repetition in the original versions, this innovation has changed a strong sense of authority for sending forth in the name of the Trinity, to what might be judged to be a weaker addition of further attributes to the three persons of the Trinity. As has been seen, this version was influential on the Church of England as it revised its liturgies.

Miscellaneous collections of prayers

We saw in Chapter 4 that the *Proficiscere* survived after the Reformation partly because it moved outside the liturgical books of the churches into books for private devotion. Something similar has happened in recent years, as people seek spiritual sustenance outside the liturgies of the Church. In recent years there has been a stream of versions of the *Proficiscere* included in anthologies of prayer, prayer cards on sale at church bookstalls, or devotional books with prayer material in them. Because they carry no official authorization, these often carry the author's or compiler's own version of the prayer, as writers put their own interpretation on original

Old and New Liturgical Uses 147

texts. Frequently they offer no acknowledgement of source (although Newman's influence of 'journey' is evident).

The fact that the *Proficiscere* appears in so many places outside the formal liturgy indicates that it is performing a new pastoral function, expressing Christian hope outside the liturgies of the Church for individuals in their private devotions. The prayer has once again become accessible to people who may not otherwise partake in the liturgical rituals of the Church. Operating outside the confines of 'Prayers for the Dying', it can become familiar and comforting in circumstances far removed from a group of people meeting around the bed of a dying person. If people are familiar with it before having heard or read it at a time of death, it functions as a spiritual resource for 'remembrance', both at the time of reading and at the moment of death.

Among many examples of the presence of the *Proficiscere* are the following. Norman Autton offers an original version in *Watch with the Sick*.[80] He is scrupulously careful about acknowledging the source of every prayer in this book, with the sole exception of this one. Does it indicate that it is his own composition from a half-remembered source? He begins with new opening lines of the prayer, before the *Proficiscere* starts, not found in any other material for the dying, but echoing familiar material. The use of the word 'depart' without the word 'journey' suggests a non-Newman source, but the unique reference to the 'guardian angel', which is found in *The Dream of Gerontius* (although not in the *Proficiscere* within it), does suggest the influence of Newman, who was attracted to the idea of guardian angels.

The second half of the prayer, with its repetition of the word 'May', is recast into a petitionary pattern rather than the usual performative pattern. 'May thy guardian angel succour and defend thee; May the prayers of the blessed saints help thee' etc. The line 'May the Redeemer look upon thee in pardon and mercy' is original to this prayer. The final line is an amalgam of the 1928 Prayer Book and perhaps a partly remembered text of *The Dream of Gerontius*. All this suggests that this version is based on perhaps half-remembered phrases, with Autton's own original contributions.

Bill Kirkpatrick used a version, based on the 1928 Prayer Book, in the prayer resources section in his pastoral guidebook, appropriately called *Going Forth*.[81] In it he has used 'Holy Spirit' rather than 'Holy Ghost'; he has added the 'Blessed Virgin Mary' to the 1928 version, and has added the title 'Mother of God'.

A more unusual version appears in an anthology selected and edited by three theological luminaries, George Every, Richard Harries and Kallistos Ware. This version is an unusual mixture of translations. In the second line they add, 'In the peace of him in whom thou hast believed', a line which echoes an early variant, *migrare in pace*. Other lines come from other parts of the 'Commendation of the Soul', and the traditional opening line is repeated at the end, perhaps influenced by the Roman Catholic translation of 1972.

These three examples indicate that writers who use versions of the prayer outside official liturgical books exercise a greater sense of freedom in adapting original material. They illustrate the prayer's ability continually to 'reinvent' itself to meet new pastoral circumstances. In this third example, it appears in an anthology of readings for the Christian Year, in the November section under the heading 'Death and the Communion of Saints'. It may be very appropriate, but it is far removed from its original pastoral intention.

Finally, J. D. Crichton was concerned that lay people played their part in preparing people for death.[82] This task was enabled by the publication of *In Sure and Certain Hope*, a pastoral book for lay people.[83] It is a collection of prayers, rather than a liturgy, and it contains both the *Libera* and the *Proficiscere* in the 1983 English version. It is interesting to note that their traditional order has been reversed, following the pattern first adopted by Thomas Becon in *The Sicke Manne's Salve*, and later by Newman in *The Dream of Gerontius*. It is indicated that the *Proficiscere* is to be said when the moment of death seems near.[84] On a pastoral note, it is also worthy of comment that the Roman Catholic Church, which has not traditionally been in the forefront of lay involvement, is the only church to have produced a funerary book specifically for the use of lay people.

Conclusion

Liturgists and compilers of books of prayers have provided the *Proficiscere* with many new venues to speak its words of Christian hope to an ever-wider public. In late twentieth-century and recent liturgies it is used in its traditional place as a prayer for the dying, as a prayer contemplating one's own death, as part of a Commendation on hearing of a death, or when the user cannot attend the funeral, and as a prayer at the funeral itself. The *Proficiscere*'s excess of meaning has continued to allow its words and phrases to influence the ways in which death is interpreted today. There seems little reason to doubt that the prayer is better known today than it has been for many centuries. It is a remarkable 'late flowering' in the biography of the prayer. But why has it become more popular? And how does it speak in new ways to Christians today? It is to these questions that we now turn in our last chapter.

7
The Liberty to Die

The title of this chapter, which you will have realized is a constant theme in this biography, is taken from a poem, 'The heart asks pleasure first', by the American poet Emily Dickinson (1830–86).

The heart asks pleasure first,
And then, excuse from pain;
And then, those little anodynes
That deaden suffering;

And then, to go to sleep;
And then, if it should be
The will of its Inquisitor,
The liberty to die.[1]

Prologue

I was called to the hospital to visit an elderly woman church member who was close to death. Her family told me that Dorothy was just 'hanging on'. Arriving at her bedside I saw that she had been laid on her side, with her legs drawn up in a foetal position – the same for both birth and death. Her shrivelled body was dwarfed by a diaphanous nightdress with the name of the hospital prominently stamped on it. She was breathing irregularly, with an oxygen mask over her face, her sunken eyes were shut, and she was clearly close to death. I said her name several times as I greeted her, with no response. There was similarly no flicker of response from her face as I spoke to her, while holding her hand or stroking her head.

I sat with her in silence for a while and then took her hand again and started to say the words of the *Proficiscere*, 'Go forth, Christian soul, upon your journey from this world.' As soon as I started to say these words, her hand suddenly gripped mine tightly and held on until I had finished the prayer. There was still no movement or reaction on her face. All her response had been through her hand in mine. She then relaxed her grip and continued to lie still. Not long after I had left the hospital the family rang to tell me that she had died.

This experience confirmed something within me that I had long suspected. Near to the point of death some people need and value permission to 'let go'. They need to be granted the liberty to die. I could not interpret Dorothy's tight grip on my hand during the prayer, and her release of it at the end, as a desire to hold on to this life; it was her only way of saying that the words spoke of her deepest spiritual wish and desire. She wanted to depart and was holding on to God as she journeyed, not clinging to me to stay behind. There was no longer any need to struggle to stay alive, and the *Proficiscere* allowed her to offer up her life into God's hands.

This chapter will argue that some of the purposes to which the prayer was put in the twentieth century have changed, as a result of changing attitudes to death, and as a pastoral response to newly felt needs. The *Proficiscere* has changed from a deeply religious medieval blessing and assurance of safe passage, to a modern offering 'in the name of God' of the liberty to die. It is a 'setting free' from the pressures of modern medical and social expectations about death. Once again this chapter will demonstrate how the excess of meaning in the *Proficiscere* has enabled it to be used in a new liturgical understanding of the traditional 'Commendation of the Soul'.

First this chapter will summarize the main changes that have taken place in the way in which death is interpreted today. Then it will show an original way in which it is possible to demonstrate that the words of the prayer are pastorally effective, using a modern method of analysing prayer. Finally it will reflect on the important role that the *Proficiscere* has in helping a person to have the liberty to die, opening up new pastoral opportunities.

Changing attitudes to death

In every chapter in this book we have argued that, while death is always death, at different times in history the way in which death is *interpreted* has affected the way it is handled and treated. To meet these changes the Church has provided liturgies and pastoral opportunities, and we have looked at how one of these, the *Proficiscere*, has played a central part. We saw how the early Middle Ages produced the prayer as part of a response to a new fear of death and its consequences. Then we saw how the Reformation, with its new interpretation of death, decreed that all this was unnecessary. It was only at the end of the nineteenth century and early twentieth century that another change in the interpretation of death enabled the *Proficiscere* to return. But its words are now speaking to an understanding of death very different from the understandings in the eighth, sixteenth or nineteenth centuries. How can we best understand what is happening today?

Tony Walter, who has almost cornered the market in death studies, is a helpful guide to the changes which have taken place in the last century in attitudes to death. Walter argues that modern death has been subjected to changing interpretive approaches, which have together led to what he called 'The dying of death', by which he means the end of interpreting death as we have done traditionally The first interpretive change is that death has been rationalized. Commenting on the Consumers' Association book, *What to Do When Someone Dies*, he commented:

> This tells you nothing about what you should do to prepare the soul for the next life, nothing even about the emotions you may feel, but it is entirely about the forms that have to be filled in, the bureaucratic procedures that have to be gone through in order legally to dispose of the body.[2]

The Liberty to Die

Deaths he argued were now primarily interpreted as statistics (with average life expectancies and annual death rates), and even the grief processes experienced by individuals have been analysed, categorized, and treated as 'normal' or 'abnormal'.[3] Second, and more importantly, Walter argued that death has become medicalized: 'Death has ceased to be a spiritual passage, and has became a natural process overseen by doctors.'[4] He drew attention to the way in which death has been further medicalized by the removal of the deathbed from the home to the hospital, where two-thirds of deaths now take place.[5] However, in discussing the medical aspect of death, Walter did not explore the sense of failure, particularly a sense of failure felt by the dying person, which can accompany death. This theme was well expressed by Laungani Pittu when he said:

> In Western societies the spectacular advances in the medical sciences have raised hopes in people of longevity. Such advances have given rise to the belief that death can be put off, postponed, held in check, or even conquered permanently. Modern medicine, by regarding death as a medical failure, may have unwittingly perpetuated this image. The belief in longevity allows one to distance oneself from one's own death and those of one's loved ones.[6]

You can now complete, if you want to, a health survey on the internet which will calculate an estimated age that you should reach before you die. I won't tell you mine, but it seems very, very old! Will I feel cheated or a failure if on my deathbed I realize that I will not reach my calculated final age? Pittu argued that a person's self-understanding that their death is a failure can permeate a hospital ward and affect those who visit the dying person. Consciously or unconsciously, the dying person feels she or he must keep struggling on, fighting death. To die is to admit that they have failed. They will be judged to have failed the doctors, their family, themselves, and perhaps their faith, if they let themselves die.

Third, Walter argued that ever since the Reformation, and particularly in the twentieth century, the religious interpretation of death declined, as secular models have developed. For example, funerals have moved from a forward-looking, eschatological, religious perspective, to a backward-looking, secular celebration of the life of the deceased. The sermon on Christian hope of resurrection has been overshadowed, or replaced, by a carefully crafted eulogy on a person's life. Funeral rhetoric has changed from eschatology to history, from a pastoral concern for the deceased to a pastoral concern for the bereaved. If this is the situation, and you may recognize some uncomfortable truths here, what insights can be gained into the pastoral value of the *Proficiscere* in this new situation? Can it still be an effective prayer?

The 'effectiveness' of the *Proficiscere*

How do we evaluate the effectiveness of a prayer? Of course in an ultimate sense we cannot. All objective attempts to argue that prayers are effective, or answered (whatever that means), fall before the awesome mystery that is God. Subjectively, we can say that we 'like' a prayer, perhaps because it makes us feel 'good', or it is effective because what we asked for subsequently happened. But these are methods of judgement which are at best subjective, effective only in our own personal interpretation. Is there any more objective method of analysis which might open up new ways of judging the question of the pastoral effectiveness of a prayer, and the *Proficiscere* in particular?

The linguist David Crystal has made a significant contribution in the field of the linguistic analysis of liturgy. He pointed out that in recent years there has been a major shift in linguistic studies from formal analysis of the structure of language to the functions that language performs. He wrote:

> [And] throughout the various domains of linguistic enquiry there developed a concern to see language not solely in

terms of sounds, words and structures, but in terms of the *social situations* in which language was used. The focus switched from the forms of language to the functions language performed in society – and thus to the characteristics of those who use language and of the setting in which linguistic activity took place.[7]

Crystal looked at the way in which words 'do things' and the settings in which 'language performed' rather than the traditional way of looking at what words mean.

Crystal detailed a number of functions that liturgical language performs, which are full of insight. Some of them are particularly relevant to an assessment of the pastoral significance and effectiveness of the *Proficiscere*.

1 Informative

One function of liturgical language is the communication of ideas so that information is accurately exchanged from one person to another. To what extent is the *Proficiscere* informative?

When the words of the *Proficiscere* are spoken, they are informing the person on whose behalf they are addressed, and others present, that the speaker judges that the sick person is approaching the end of her or his life. Its use conveys a very different message from a prayer which informs the sick person that the minister, and attendant community, wish for healing and recovery in this life. It is thus a 'letting-go' prayer, which can inform the dying person that in the judgement of the minister the dying person can let go of life. It is 'permission to leave' and offers, in the name of God, the liberty to die. The *Proficiscere* also pastorally informs its hearers, living and dying, that all the spiritual resources of God, and the Church on earth and in heaven, are available to 'authorize' and assist at the time of death. In addition, the *Libera* is a method of informing the dying person that the community of faith is asking God to extend to the dying person the liberating power revealed by God in the lives of the figures in the *Libera*.

This informative function is less apparent in modern versions, particularly as most do not include the *Libera*. The greatest difference in the informative function of the language comes in the use of the modern *Proficiscere*, when it is not used in any form of 'Prayer for the Dying', but as a commendation at the end of the Funeral Service, as death has already taken place. Here it loses its main informative function, as it only informs the living that the dead person is being commended to God.

2 *Identifying*

A second function of language is to identify, to be a signal or to indicate the social identity of the participants. Just as a doctor will pronounce a significant judgement in respect of a medical condition, and will be recognized as being authoritative, so the words of a minister will identify who she or he is, and the status of the addressee. Thus the language of the *Proficiscere* identifies the significant participants in the liturgy as being the minister (or someone acting out this authoritative role) and the dying person. If the liturgy includes 'Amens' to be said by other participants around the dying person, these words identify their part in the liturgy in affirming what is being said and done. The social identities of the participants are clear.

3 *Expressive*

This function of language enables an expression of affective feelings within the individual. As Crystal said, speaking about the Mass, 'To see the liturgy as a drama in which all actively participate ... motivates a heightened awareness and excitement which can imbue everything that is said with a powerful emotive force.'[8] The recitation of the words of the *Proficiscere* before the moment of death is clearly a deeply emotional moment, deep feelings are aroused, and the words carry expressive and emotive weight. In the midst of fear, pain or a sense of failure, the words of the *Proficiscere* convey Christian assurance and peace. Although the dying person may feel that he or she is in great danger and faces terrors or doubts, the words themselves speak of the comfort of 'superior forces' ranged on the side of the dying person. They express the feelings of all present that the dying person is being committed to a God who is present and active. The words enable all of them to feel the power and assurance of God's grace. A historical knowledge of the prayer will enable them to feel in a positive way that they are taking part in events which have been hallowed and sanctioned by use at the deaths of many previous dying Christians. If the prayer has been said previously for parents or grandparents as they approached their death, there is a powerful sense of continuity (just as people often return to the same firm of funeral directors who 'did' a parent even though the personnel have changed). If the prayer was said at a parent's death you are more likely to want it at your own.

4 Performative

The performative function of language is of particular significance to the study of the *Proficiscere*, so we will look at it at greater length than the other categories outlined by Crystal. The concept of 'performative utterances' was originally introduced by J. L. Austin.[9] He was reacting to the previous dominance of the verification principle, made popular by A. J. Ayer,[10] which maintained that language consisted of statements that were either true or false. Austin argued that people might write or say things which were not intended to be statements or report facts, but to *influence* people one way or another. Like Crystal, he was exploring a different use of language.

Austin's work has now been swept up into, and developed, under the general title of 'speech–action theory'. This is the theory of how language is used so that it 'works', rather than what it means. It is the study of communicative intention, what you intend to *happen* when you communicate, and how this intention is recognized or expressed.

Speech–action theory also looks at language which is self-involving. In other words it looks at how the person who utters it is 'tied' to what is said. This means that performative utterances have an operative intent, they are said so that something happens. For example, 'I baptize you, John' is an example of how language 'works'. Something 'happens' when these words are spoken, apart from any physical acts. However, if the words spoken are to 'work' they must be uttered in the appropriate circumstances, such as a ceremony of baptism, and not at a birthday party. Austin said that to be a performative utterance the words must be said in, what he calls, felicitous circumstances. These are particularly relevant to the *Proficiscere*.

Several rules apply to a felicitous circumstance. First, the words must be spoken in the midst of a conventional procedure, which is accepted to exist. For example, the performative utterance 'I declare you to be husband and wife' requires among other things the convention that this is a way in which a couple can become married partners. Second, 'the circumstances in which we purport to invoke this procedure must be appropriate for its invocation'.[11] This means that there needs to be present a person with authority to perform a marriage, two people able to marry each other and intending to do so, and two witnesses, otherwise the infelicity of inappropriate circumstances will produce a kind of mismatch. Third, a performative utterance is insincere 'if you use one of these formulae when you do not have the requisite thoughts or feelings or intentions'.[12] Words said at the wedding rehearsal do not 'marry' the couple because these 'requisite thoughts or feelings or intentions' do not apply at that time of rehearsal even if the witnesses are present.

Finally, Austin wrote about performative utterances carrying a kind of 'force' or force potential. They are more than statements of fact. When utterances are made it is necessary to ask not only what they mean, but also what is the force of the utterance. The force is carried not just by the words, which could be ambiguous in simple written form, but by the content and context. Austin said:

The Liberty to Die

There are a great many devices that can be used for making clear, even at the primitive level, what act it is we are performing when we say something – the tone of voice, cadence, gesture – and above all we can rely upon the nature of the circumstances, the context in which the utterance is issued.[13]

How illuminating is the concept of the performative utterance to the study and understanding of the effect of *Proficiscere* in modern liturgies?

The opening words of the *Proficiscere*, 'Depart, Christian soul, from this world', clearly exhibit the internal criteria laid down by Austin. In terms of a strict verification approach the words are meaningless as they are not capable of being proved true or false, but they are intended to bring influence to bear on the person to whom they are addressed. As a person lies dying, holding on to the edge of life, the words carry the communicative intention of encouraging and offering the person the liberty to die with the authoritative injunction, 'Depart'. Austin said that the word 'hereby' can often be used to indicate the performative nature of the words. This word is often the operative word in a legal document, 'I hereby declare' etc. The word 'hereby' is silently echoed in the opening words of the prayer.

This is not to suggest that this is a request that the soul of the dying person 'may' be allowed to depart to heaven. When the *Proficiscere* is pronounced over a dying person something is being said, but something is also being done by the words themselves. The departure of the soul is being allowed and authorized, and it is certainly being given the liberty to go. The performative nature of the words means that something happens.

The force of the opening line is re-enforced by the following lines which begin with the words 'In the name of ...', repeated many times.[14] Austin said, in an entirely secular context, that a performative utterance often carries with it a signature of authority. He wrote:

of a document reading 'You are hereby authorized' to do so-and-so. These are undoubtedly performative words, and in fact a signature is often required in order to show who it is that is doing the act of warning, or authorizing, or whatever it may be.[15]

The 'signature of authority' in the *Proficiscere* is none less than that of the Trinity, and all the powers of heaven and earth. The opening injunction 'Depart' is echoed each time the words 'In the name of ...' are repeated, whether or not the word 'Depart' is repeated each time. It is when we consider the circumstances in which the *Proficiscere* could be used that the insights offered by Austin are particularly helpful in explaining its popularity in modern liturgy. It will be remembered that three criteria were outlined as being necessary for a statement to be a performative utterance.

First, there must be a conventional procedure within which the utterance is made. The Church has always had problems, pastorally and liturgically, about the appropriate time when prayers should change from prayers of healing and recovery to prayers in preparation for dying. At various stages of liturgical development these prayers have been included in either one section of a prayer book or in two, to indicate the pastoral intention. As we saw in Chapter 2, part of the innovative nature of the *Proficiscere* was that it was written to affect the process during which preparation is made for a person to die. Prayers of hope that the person would recover, the prayers of healing, became separated from the ritual of prayers for the dying.

When a priest started the service for the Commendation of the Soul, the person who was dying and those around the person would not be in any doubt that they were entering a familiar procedure during which various steps were carried out which would end with the death of the person concerned. Gathering around the bed of the dying person, the familiar recitation of psalms and prayers, according to the pattern of the particular rite being used, would be a recognized ritual, conventional to all who took part. If the person thought to be dying was feeling far better than doctors, family or colleagues initially judged, it is unlikely that the ritual would proceed and the performative utterance of the *Proficiscere* would not take place.

Second, the words should not be said in infelicitous circumstances or they would not be a performative utterance. To use the words at an inappropriate moment, such as saying them as a dismissal at the end of an act of worship, or to say them over a strong, fit young person with a slight infection, would be infelicitous, and would not carry the force, nor could they carry the intention, even if they were in some way 'intended', perhaps as a way of getting someone to die against his or her will.

Third, the *Proficiscere* is said at a time of personal intensity and is not said lightly or thoughtlessly. The person for whom it is said is believed to be close to the point of death. The priest or minister would use, in Austin's words, the correct and most appropriate voice, cadence and gesture as a means of conveying the fact that the words were performative utterances. Few of the texts of the *Proficiscere* carry any indication of gestures which might be used. As we mentioned, some of the medieval manuscripts included the points at which the sign of the cross is made, others indicate where the dying person and/or the community surrounding the dying person make the response, 'Amen'. The very word 'Amen', meaning 'let it be so', can be seen to indicate an acknowledgement that performative words have been used and that this use is recognized by the hearers.

This rather lengthy section on the performative language of the *Proficiscere* is a reflection on how a modern discipline can cast light on the familiar, opening up new understandings about what is happening when we pray. After this examination of performative language, we will look at the remaining functions of language described by Crystal more briefly.

5 Historical

Some language, Crystal said, has the purpose of recording and preserving the past: 'Liturgical language frequently looks backwards, in its concern to display continuity with a doctrinal or devotional tradition.'[16] We can see this most clearly in the narrative part of the Prayer of Thanksgiving at Holy Communion when we remind ourselves of, and give thanks to God for, the great saving acts of history, especially in Jesus Christ. The *Proficiscere*, particularly in its medieval form, has at its heart a look back at part of the history of salvation as a means of assurance to the dying person that they are sharing in this historical pattern. This is particularly expressed in the long list of biblical figures in the *Libera*. The historical orientation provides a frame of reference within which the interpretation of the person's death can be understood. Although the context is that of remembrance that God 'set free' the named historical figures from situations of mortal danger, the implication is that God will do the same for the dying person. This is made explicit in the repeated refrain, 'Set free the soul of this your servant as you set free ...' In this way the historical figures are linked to the central performative act of the prayer. Salvation history is used to buttress and support the performative power of the prayer.

6 Aesthetic

Crystal said that some liturgy can have an aesthetic value: 'Spoken or written language can be enjoyed purely as a formal display, as in the use of poetic rhythms.'[17] He made the point about the aesthetic value of pace and repetition ('The Lord be with you.' 'And also with you.') or the constant repetition of some modern choruses. In other traditions there is the example of the recitation by the congregation of a litany of the names of the saints. The full form of the *Proficiscere* contains two groups of repetitions which can be said to add to its aesthetic appeal. In the first part of the prayer there is the repetition of 'In the name of ...', and in the *Libera* there is the frequently repeated, 'Set free the soul of this your servant as you set free ...'. Writing about prayers naming the saints, Crystal made the important point, lost when the prayer is shortened, that 'ignorance of the identity of some of the saints invoked would not affect the dramatic impact conveyed by the prayer's pace and rhythm'.[18]

In the early 1970s I was minister of Burley Methodist Church in Leeds – a church that had a Remembrance Sunday tradition which illustrates this point. Before the two-minute silence, the minister solemnly read out a long list of men named on the church's two war memorials, who had died in the World Wars. I can still remember some of the names: 'Albert Atkinson, Frank Buxton, Willie Cawtheray ... Jack Thompson, Richard Toms, Ernest Wilcock', because they have an aesthetic quality about them. As a new minister, interested in change, I asked if anyone in the church still remembered any of the people we commemorated in this way because, if they did not, we should think about stopping the practice. No one I asked said that they could still remember any of those named. In a sense the names were meaningless as names, as no relationship still existed. But when I suggested at a church council that perhaps the time had come to stop the tradition, my proposal was firmly and unanimously resisted. The tradition still continues at that church 35 years later, and 60 after the Second World War. One of Burley's members, Mollie Falkiner, said to me only recently, 'There has never been any discussion or suggestion of stopping the practice. Personally I would be very much against stopping ... I believe that we should honour the sacrifice they made if only by hearing their names read out. To me they are "saints" of Burley, along with many people who have served in other ways.'

The naming of the 'saints' still carried meaning for members of the congregation although they did not know them. Many years after the names had ceased to have personal significance as people, they were still familiar 'anchors' who fixed the liturgy of remembrance in human reality. The annual ritual of reading the names performed both an *aesthetic* and a *historical* function, in the same way as the naming of the biblical figures in the *Proficiscere*.

7 Social

There are significant social aspects in the language when words are said, by one or more persons, for another person who is dying. Two of them are relevant to a study of the *Proficiscere*. First, the use of the prayer in its original place in the liturgy is a social activity which binds together all those taking part. People who pray together around the bed of a dying person are uniquely united by the prayers. The community of faith on earth, even if only represented by two people, is drawn into the presence of the community of faith in heaven. If a number of people are present, there is an enhancement of their connectedness, because they are drawn together in a common task of eschatological proportions, assisting a person to journey to the life of eternity.

A second insight into the social function of the prayer is drawn from the fact that, as we have seen, in some modern liturgies it can be used both for the dying and later as a commendation at the funeral. Don Pickard pointed out to me that when the *Proficiscere* is used again at a funeral it rehearses for that wider community what was said, generally with a smaller group, at the moment of dying. This both draws them back to 'share in' that particular death, when it was said, and forward to their own death when it might be said again. It thus provides an integrative social function binding the dead and the living.

We have now seen seven ways in which Crystal's and Austin's methods of linguistic analysis provide a number of valuable insights into what is happening through the language of the prayer. This method stops short, of course, at the point of any ultimate analysis as to the efficacy of this or any other prayer, but it offers insights not previously open to us as to why the *Proficiscere* has carried in the liturgy over many years, and still does carry, a powerful pastoral and theological message of Christian hope. This analysis may give clues to one of the reasons for the prayer's longevity.

Offering the liberty to die

As we have seen in this biography of the *Proficiscere*, there have been changes in understanding the nature of death, from an early medieval one, through a Reformation response to a modern one. Different attitudes to death produced different responses to the need, or lack of need, for the prayer. Some of the scholars who have opened up to us the biography of the prayer have attempted to express what can only be called 'timeless' expressions of its pastoral role. One scholar, Canon A.-G. Martimort, may sound old fashioned, but if his words are read sympathetically they echo something that we may have lost to our detriment today. He said of the dying person:

> As he listens to the Church's prayer about his death-bed, the Christian understands that he is about to experience his last Easter, more beautiful than all that have gone before; it is to bring him final deliverance from all attachments that prevent his seeing God. He goes forth in the night of faith, leaving all, like the patriarch Abraham, so as to enjoy at last the Promise made to our forefathers.[19]

For a Catholic, Martimort displayed an almost Protestant theology when he added, 'If the body must still wait for the resurrection, the soul is called to see God at once.'[20] Gone in his theology is any hint of a doctrine of purgatory.

Damien Sicard acknowledged that sociocultural changes had affected the habits of contemporary society. The majority of people did not experience death surrounded by members of the family, theirs is a more isolated and individual death. He also added that the language of angels and saints, and the vast array of biblical images, were out of keeping with people who no longer associate death with the company of the redeemed. He may be right, but perhaps we have lost something precious to the faith if we can no longer hold to an element of this understanding? If the biography of the *Proficiscere* is not rehearsed, is it surprising that death is no longer associated with the company of the redeemed?

Sicard acknowledged that death takes place in a very different world today, in which death is still a taboo subject, but summoned up a wonderful, almost medieval picture which, he thought, the *Proficiscere* produced:

> An immense cortège is thus summoned for a final journey that is to be made in the festive atmosphere proper to the individual's 'passing over' and to the assembly over which the Triune God presides amid the angels and saints.[21]

He pointed out that the use of the *Proficiscere* 'presuppose(s) a prior knowledge of the Bible and a prior experience of Christian community'.[22] Perhaps Sicard was displaying an understanding of the prayer which is too intellectual. A dying person may know little of the way in which some of the servants of God were delivered, but the rolling, repetitive phrases of God's saving acts can carry within them a salvific effect and evoke a salvific response even though the dying person knows little of the details of what God has done. The important affirmation is that this is how God saves, even though the dying person may not know the details.

Perhaps Martimort's and Sicard's comments did not differentiate sufficiently between the medieval and the modern context of death. In Chapter 2 it was argued that, in the medieval context in which it was created and developed, the *Proficiscere* met a particular need because death was being interpreted in a new way. It provided help with the agony of death, and an 'envelope' in which the vulnerable soul could be carried through the perils of dying and death, including the unwelcome attention of devils, so that it could be delivered safely in heaven. The power and strength of the performative aspects of the prayer carried the soul safely through death and beyond.

Many biographies, as they reach the final pages, reflect on the impact their subject had during their lifetime, and on the impact they might have had if circumstances had been different. As this biography of the *Proficiscere* draws to a close, I want to suggest that a renewed use of the prayer, in the current century, offers the Christian Church an opportunity to enable people to reflect on their death in a Christian context, but in a different way. Over the years the Church has produced many pastoral guidebooks and handbooks for priests and ministers. What seems remarkable, at least at first sight, is the lack of material on the words and action at the moment of death. Time and again the books deal with sickness, facing death, pastoral care of the dying persons and their families, and pastoral support after death. However, when it comes to words about the moment of death, when a prayer for the dying would be appropriate, the books are strangely silent.

An honourable exception to this failure is *Letting Go*, which speaks of the appropriateness of commendatory prayers, for the benefit of both the dying person and the relatives. The authors, Ian Ainsworth-Smith and Peter Speck, offered (unacknowledged) a brief version of the *Proficiscere*.[23] Perhaps the reason why there is so little pastoral material for the moment of death is that the Church (apart from the Roman Catholic Church) had not, until the very end of the twentieth century, had any adequate liturgical material for prayers for the dying. The lack of liturgical material is reflected in the lack of pastoral material.

Perhaps there is a lack of pastoral material for two reasons. First, as we have indicated, there is considerable ambivalence, both within and without the Christian community, about what happens after death. Second, meaningful imagery about life after death is sparse. How did you react to Sicard's imagery of the 'immense cortège' and 'the assembly over which the Triune God presides amid the angels and saints'? Too much heavenly imagery today is limited to stories about the 'pearly gates' and 'sitting on clouds playing a harp'. Even those who are firm believers about life beyond death remain either agnostic or tight-lipped about what the prospects will be like. Appropriate or meaningful visual images are hard to come by.

In Chapter 3 we suggested that the earliest texts of the *Proficiscere* could have been influenced by the apocalyptic visions of death recorded in the *Apocalyse of Paul* and other writers of visions. These visions offered a language about what had been 'seen' beyond the veil of death, which could then provide the subject of discourse for prayers to be offered for those who are about to die. The visionary material about what lies beyond death provided a plausible picture for prayers this side of death.

Liturgists who use the *Proficiscere* today are working in a very different world. Visions about the glory of heaven and the terrors of hell are not generally part of the world view outlined by Walter and experienced today. In Chapter 6 it was seen that, when the *Proficiscere* had been reintroduced into the liturgy of churches other than the Roman Catholic Church, it was in a very attenuated form. In order to be plausible, the language has to speak of what lies beyond death in terms that are acceptable and meaningful today. 'Angels and archangels' are just about acceptable, but 'thrones' and 'heavenly virtues' may not help. Perhaps part of the, understandable, failure of the modern Church is that it has not been able to present a plausible vision of what lies beyond death. There is no clear and powerful 'vision' acceptable to the modern culture which offers anything that can be reflected in meaningful prayer before death.

In view of this, a new pastoral understanding of the Christian significance of death, and use of the *Proficiscere* in the twenty-first century, can help to reinterpret dying as the liberty to die into God without going into too many details. A liturgy containing the words of the *Proficiscere* can reinterpret death in a hopeful Christian light, remove some of the fear, and offer the dying person, if not a powerful vision of heaven, then at least a sense that they die with the permission of a loving God who supports and welcomes them.

Such a clear shift in theological thinking about the role of the *Proficiscere* as part of the 'Commendation of the Dying' can be found in the writings of J. D. Crichton. He said that the Roman Catholic *Order of Christian Funerals* was aware of the difficulty of assisting the dying, and he urged both clergy and laity to do all they could to help the person who was dying. The aim should be to help a person to overcome the natural fear of death by arousing their hope in the power of the resurrection of Christ through whom they will enter into eternal life. Dying people should be led to accept their own death in imitation of the suffering and dying of Christ.[24] A sense of assisting an exit from this world, rather than providing a means of protection or a blueprint of what is to come in the next, is clear in what Crichton wrote.

Another theologian who has commented pastorally on 'Prayers for the Dying' is Charles Gusmer. He is one of the few writers who has attempted to distinguish medieval and modern understandings of death and thus of a changed purpose for the prayer of Commendation, although he was anxious to suggest that the modern Church still supports the traditional understanding.[25] However, his comments reflect the twentieth-century view that the prayer meets a current pastoral need, rather than the medieval concern for the perilous journey after death. Gusmer reflected a modern understanding of the prayer as the liberty to die when he said, 'It may be necessary to reassure the dying Christian that it is all right to let go and die.'[26] He also raised an original point, asking why 'assisting the dying' had 'never been explicitly enumerated as a corporal or spiritual work of mercy'.[27] Perhaps the hospice movement is partly fulfilling this role, although only a minority of people die in its care. Gusmer's final comment, when he commended the use of Commendation of the Dying, reflected the potential gap between the provision of liturgy and its actual use:

> If the Church has restored *viaticum* as a sacrament for the dying with a canonical insistence on its ministration and a ritual format all its own, perhaps a similar priority should be assigned to the use of the rite of Commendation of the Dying whenever possible.[28]

A church may produce the finest liturgy, but if it remains unused on the pages of a service book and is not liberated through use, it is of little value. No one can force the clergy to use the services which include the *Proficiscere*, but its presence in so many of the modern prayer books is at least the first stage in its wider use.

When the *Proficiscere* is used, a person is at the very cusp of the divide between life and death. Any service of 'Prayer for the Dying' is unique when compared with other services. In all other services the person leading the service has a substantial measure of control over the major elements and the timing of the service. Of course, a server may stumble, a bride may arrive late, or the wine might unfortunately be spilled, but the person leading the service retains control over the basic elements of the parts of the service. She or he controls the timing. 'Prayers with the Dying' are unique in that the person leading them has no control over a vital element – when is the person going to die? Death may come too soon, before the climax of the prayers, or more often the dying person may still be alive some time after it is finished, giving the conduct of the service a pastoral frisson which is unique. The service retains within it an uncertainty which relies on the pastoral skill, experience (and fortune?) of the person leading the service. Of course the prayer has not failed to be performative just because a person continues to live for further hours or indeed days.

The *Proficiscere* also assists in the answer to the crucial question, 'What can you say when a person is about to die?' It contains words which commend the dying person to God, however their state is understood. It is said for the dying person, it is also said for the dead person, and it is said for and to their soul, whether we think of the 'person' and the 'soul' as one and the same, or two parts of the same.

We can now return to the statement, in the Introduction, that the *Proficiscere* is a 'euthanastic' prayer. Following the ideas of Austin and Crystal earlier in this chapter, it is clear that the prayer can be interpreted as a means of euthanasia, in the correct sense of the word, one of the means towards a good death.

The moral and legal objection to medical euthanasia is that

it is action that takes life away or hastens death.[29] It could not seriously be argued that the use of the *Proficiscere* achieves, illegally through words, what is sometimes achieved, equally illegally, through medicine. But it is a well-recognized medical fact that some people exercise some control over their death by 'hanging on' until a particular event. There are many stories of people who hold on until a loved one has arrived from abroad to be at their bedside. A Scottish friend of mine, John Symon, held out until Hogmanay, and I have always been surprised by how many devoted Methodists die on 24 May, Wesley Day! Once the significant date or arrival has taken place they 'let go' and die. In other words, some people seem to exercise a measure of control over the timing of their death. The *Proficiscere* can offer other people the moment to cease hanging on.

In the context of this discussion, it is helpful to draw a distinction between 'letting-go' and 'giving up' as death approaches. W. M. Clements has written:

> Letting go is different from *giving up*, which implies a passive resignation to fate and a withdrawal of the inner self from others and even from reflective self-awareness. *Letting go* is an active process of trust, an opening up of the self to one's inability to control the future, an active giving over of the self to the care of One beyond human finitude. It is a blessing of personal dependence on others for a while, and on God for ever. If life's delicate balance between control and dependence, trust and mistrust, should ever so gently tilt towards letting go at any point during the dying process, then surely the grace of God has been present. Pastoral care may enable this to happen, but faith is a gift.[30]

If a dying person, whether or not prepared by faith for death, is able to hear within their being the words of the *Proficiscere*, 'Go forth, Christian soul, from this world, in the name of God the Father ...' they will be able more easily to experience that 'ever so gentle tilt towards letting go', and find they have been given, by God's grace, the liberty to die into him.

The use of the *Proficiscere* does not take life away, nor does it hasten death, in the way in which medication can, but it does allow, permit or authorize a person, who has some control over their rate of dying, to move into death with assurance and peace. In particular it is a means by which a minister, or other person with pastoral sensitivity, can indicate to a dying person the time is approaching, and assist them in their moment of death. Accounts of the use of the *Proficiscere* in a pastoral situation are rare. Fr James Currie, who was private secretary to Cardinal Basil Hume, recounted how he anointed the Cardinal after a decline in his condition and prayed using the modern Roman Catholic English version of the *Proficiscere*. Currie wrote:

> As we prayed, he died. He was a man ready to die: impatient to see God. It was as if he lay in a boat and we gently gave that boat a nudge and it sailed into the presence of God.[31]

This account confirms a changed understanding or interpretation of the role of the *Proficiscere* today, compared to medieval times. The prayer was not said to protect the vulnerable soul, it was said to help the Cardinal, so that 'Go forth' was a performative act that granted him the liberty to die.

In a more secular context, a newspaper article spoke movingly about a father's words and actions in permitting his daughter, who was desperately ill with variant Creutzfeldt-Jacob disease, to die. He whispered in her ear, after she had fought death for three days and nights: '"Rachel sweetheart, I love you, goodnight, God bless, let yourself go now, I'll always love you, until the day I die." And she was gone.'[32] Rachel's father, by his words, had offered her the liberty to die. It was an impromptu and heart-rending substitute for the words of the *Proficiscere*.

Thus, in today's understanding of death, the *Proficiscere* is not only permission to let go, it is the specific help through which the letting-go can be achieved, in a better way than it would be without its use. 'Go forth, Christian soul, on your journey from this world' is the gentle nudging of the boat, to use Fr Currie's phrase, or 'a gentle tilt towards letting go', which allows a person the liberty to die. Through the rhetoric of the words of the *Proficiscere* a person is eased through the dying moments and death itself, and it can be an alternative to the frequent modern obliteration of consciousness by the medical use of powerful drugs.

Of course a person will still die whether or not the *Proficiscere* is said, as will a person who receives no medical attention in the hours before death. But just as a natural medical death can be eased by the appropriate administration of drugs, so a 'spiritual release' can be eased by the use of the *Proficiscere*.

It would also be an incorrect conclusion to assess the *Proficiscere* as a prayer which sees the soul as 'good' and the body as 'bad'. Its euthanastic intent is to enable the inevitable change of state (however human embodiment is envisioned), which takes place at death, to come about in an appropriate, gracious and orderly context. The *Proficiscere* sees the moment of death itself as a 'triumph' or as a 'success'. Another soul is being assisted through the difficult transition between this life and the next by being given the liberty to die.

If the imagery is switched from death to birth, the role of the *Proficiscere* can be understood as the spiritual equivalent of the secular injunctions of a midwife in a hospital delivery room. As the moment of delivery comes, a woman struggles to give birth. She is labouring to separate from her body a new independent life, in the form of her baby. As the time approaches, the midwife, who is the person of authority in the situation, encourages her with the regular invocation, 'Push, push.' It is the moment of permission from the midwife that the struggle and pain are right at that moment. They are authoritative words of encouragement and exhortation to the body of the woman to 'let go' the new life form within and united to her. 'Push, push' are words to the mother and through her to the baby, to 'come forth, into this world'.[33]

The *Proficiscere* can therefore be understood, when it is placed in a pre-death and moment-of-death context, as a spiritual invocation and a performative utterance, at life's end. Its use helps a 'push, push' as the body of the dying person struggles to 'push the soul out of the body', which is mortal and decaying, into that place which is eternal and everlasting where the soul (however it is understood) can forever dwell in God.

In this chapter we have shown how disciplines such as linguistics and sociology open up new insights into how the *Proficiscere* can effectively perform its function in a new age. We have seen how it can say and do something different in the twenty-first century than it did in medieval times, because the way in which death is interpreted has changed. Although the words may be the same or similar, the situation to which they are addressed affects the way they are understood. The *Proficiscere* is able to do this because, during its life, it has exhibited an excess of meaning enabling it to speak to very different generations, and offer to each, in their own terms, 'the liberty to die'. The *Proficiscere*, although it is 1,200 years old, still has a most valuable role to play in Christian death. The biography of its life and influence has not drawn to a close.

Final word

My final word can only be a very personal one. After many years of study and research, many hundreds of miles travelled, and many thousands of words written, my love for the words of the *Proficiscere* has grown ever stronger. The subject of this biography still holds for me as its first biographer an awesome and powerful resonance of Christian hope, which reaches out and grips my soul (or my being, whichever concept you want) as I contemplate the certainty of death.

Tucked in with my Will, among my personal papers, is a handy copy of the *Proficiscere*. Those closest to me know that, if it is God's will, it is my wish before dying to hear, as a prayer, the full *Nursia* text, *Proficiscere, anima christiana, de hoc mundo*, 'Go forth, Christian soul, from this world', with lots of Amens. I want to go forth in the name of the Trinity, all nine ranks of angels and all the ranks of the Church, from bishops to faithful widows (especially faithful widows). And through the words of the *Libera* I want to relive the saving power of God, 'Set free the soul of this your servant', as revealed through everyone, from Noah, Moses and Elijah to Daniel, Susanna, Peter and Paul. And I definitely want the blessed Thecla to be there with me at the end as well.

May I finally have the strength to be able to respond, with voice or heart, to the promise of the heavenly city Jerusalem, 'AMEN'.

Notes

1 *The* Proficere, *'Depart, Christian Soul'*

1 'Vale in Christo. Pax tecum. Amen' is found in several manuscripts.
2 *Pseudo-Dionysius: The Complete Works*, The Classics of Western Spirituality, trans. C. Luibheid, New York, Paulist Press, 1987, p. 145.
3 The words in brackets from verse 36 were omitted by Dionysius.
4 Paul Rorem, *Pseudo-Dionysius: A Commentary on the Texts and an Introduction to Their Influence*, New York and Oxford, Oxford University Press, 1993, p. 51.
5 Jacques Le Goff, *The Birth of Purgatory*, trans. A Goldhammer, London, Scolar Press, 1981, p. 103. It is worth noting that, while more extensive prayers for the dead developed in the later medieval period, the later texts of the *Proficiscere* were not affected by the growth of the doctrine of purgatory.
6 This is, perhaps, an echo of Philippians 2.8.
7 For fuller details, see Wesley Carr, *Angels and Principalities*, Cambridge, Cambridge University Press, 1981.
8 Alexander Souter, *A Glossary of Later Latin to 600 A.D.*, Oxford, Clarendon Press, 1949, p. 130.
9 *Pseudo-Dionysius: Complete Works*, p. 248.
10 *Pseudo-Dionysius: Complete Works*, p. 217
11 Benedicta Ward, 'The Relationship between Hermits and Communities in the West' in Benedicta Ward (ed.), *Signs and Wonders*, Aldershot, Variorum, 1992, pp. 54–63.
12 'Deinde secundum genus est anachoritarum, id est eremitarum, horum qui non conversationis fervore novicio, sed monasterii probatione diuturna.' Latin text and translation in *RB 1980. The Rule of St. Benedict in Latin and English with Notes*, ed. Timothy Fry, Collegeville, Minn., The Liturgical Press, 1980, pp. 168–9.
13 A. Savage and N. Watson (eds), *Anchorite Spirituality: Ancrene Wisse and Associated Works*, New York, Paulist Press, 1991, pp. 15–16. However, not all writers see the matter in such a clear-cut way. See, for

example, P. Doyère, who indicates no differences between the two in the later Middles Ages. 'Ermites du Haut Moyen Age' in *Dictionnaire de Spiritualité Ascétique et Mystique*, Paris, Beauchesne, 1960, vol. 4, part 1, pp. 957–8.

14 'Idem de virginibus. 2 Non ordinatur virgo; nam praeceptum Domini non habemus; voluntatis enim est haec certaminis gloria, non ad criminandum matrimonium, sed ad vacandum pietati.' Franciscus X. Funk (ed.), *Didascalia et Constitutiones Apostolorum*, vol. I, Paderborn, Schoeningh, 1895, p. 529. And see further, 'Virgins' in William Smith and Samuel Cheetham (eds), *A Dictionary of Christian Antiquities*, London, John Murray, 1880, vol. II, cols. 2019–22.

15 J. K. Elliott (ed.), *The Apocryphal New Testament*, Oxford, Clarendon Press, 1993, pp. 357–9.

16 Elliott, *The Apocryphal New Testament*, pp. 364–74.

17 Albert Mirgeler, *Mutations of Western Christianity*, trans. E. Quinn, London, Burns & Oates, 1964, p. 47.

18 Mirgeler, *Mutations of Western Christianity*, p. 48.

19 On the centrality of the miraculous in the medieval world, see Benedicta Ward, *Miracles and the Medieval Mind*, Aldershot, Wildwood, 1987, in particular pp. 20–32.

20 David Knowles, in Mirgeler, *Mutations of Western Christianity*, p. vii.

2 From Birth to Maturity

1 Bernard Moreton, *The Eighth-Century Gelasian Sacramentary*, Oxford, Oxford University Press, 1976.

2 Moreton, *The Eighth-Century Gelasian*, p. 168.

3 Although, see the ambiguous nature of this feast in Moreton, *The Eighth-Century Gelasian*, p. 15.

4 Moreton, *The Eighth-Century Gelasian*, pp. 15–16.

5 Moreton, *The Eighth-Century Gelasian*, p. 187.

6 For fuller details, see Cyrille Vogel, *Medieval Liturgy: An Introduction to the Sources*, trans. and rev. W. Storey and N. Rasmussen, Washington, The Pastoral Press, 1986, p. 71.

7 'The heading of the mass-set given for the feast of the finding of the Cross is particularly outstanding because of the attention given to it both in script and in colouring; Lowe is therefore inclined to find the origin of the manuscript in the monastery of the Holy Cross at Meaux.' Moreton, *The Eighth-Century Gelasian*, p. 188.

8 Moreton, *The Eighth-Century Gelasian*, p. 186.

9 While palaeographic evidence is important, it is better evidence of where a document was copied rather than evidence of where the text within it was originally created.

10 Moreton, *The Eighth-Century Gelasian*, p. 173.
11 Eric Palazzo, *A History of Liturgical Books: From the Beginning to the Thirteenth Century*, trans. Madeleine Beaumont, Collegeville, Minn., The Liturgical Press, 1998, pp. 47–8.
12 Moreton, *The Eighth-Century Gelasian*, p. 15.
13 Paul Bradshaw, *The Search for the Origins of Christian Worship: Sources and Methods of the Study of Early Liturgy*, London, SPCK, 1992, p. ix.
14 John M. Wallace-Hadrill, *The Frankish Church*, Oxford History of the Christian Church, Oxford, Clarendon Press, 1983; Anton Wessels, *Europe: Was It Ever Really Christian? The Interaction between Gospel and Culture*, London, SCM Press, 1994; Michael S. Driscoll, 'Penitential Practice' in Lizette Larson-Miller (ed.), *Medieval Liturgy: A Book of Essays*, New York, Garland, 1997, pp. 121–63; James C. Russell, *The Germanization of Early Medieval Christianity*, New York, Oxford, Oxford University Press, 1994; Pierre Riché, 'Spirituality in Celtic and Germanic Society' in B. McGinn and J. Meyendorff (eds), *Christian Spirituality: Origins to the Twelfth Century*, vol. 16 of *World Spirituality: An Encyclopaedic History of the Religious Quest*, London, Routledge, 1986, pp. 163–76.
15 Wallace-Hadrill, *The Frankish Church*. The author does not refer specifically to the *Proficiscere*, and there are only two references as such to *Gellone*, on pp. 178 and 212. There are no references to *Rheinau*.
16 Wallace-Hadrill, *The Frankish Church*, p. 144.
17 Wessels, *Europe*, p. 57.
18 Wallace-Hadrill, *The Frankish Church*, p. 148.
19 Wallace-Hadrill, *The Frankish Church*, p. 154.
20 Although, against this, see the views of Baumstark in Chapter 3.
21 Wallace-Hadrill, *The Frankish Church*, p. 147. While it needs to be acknowledged that Wallace-Hadrill was writing about a period up to one hundred years before the earliest extant copy of the *Proficiscere*, his picture of the *mélange* of interrelated missionary outreaches and activities in the area in which the *Proficiscere* was born illustrates the creative cultural context in the area.
22 Wallace-Hadrill, *The Frankish Church*, p. 149.
23 Wessels, *Europe*, p. 95.
24 Wessels, *Europe*, p. 154.
25 Driscoll, 'Penitential Practice', p. 131.
26 Riché, 'Spirituality', p. 163.
27 Riché, 'Spirituality', p. 163.
28 Russell, *The Germanization of Christianity*, p. 162.
29 Riché, 'Spirituality', p. 172.
30 Riché, 'Spirituality', p. 172.

Notes

31 Michel Andrieu (ed.), *Les Ordines Romani Haut Moyen Age*, Louvain, *Spicilegium Sacrum Louvaniense*, 1956.

32 Damien Sicard, *La liturgie de la mort dans l'église latine des origines à la réforme carolingienne*, *Liturgiewissenschaftliche Quellen und Forschungen*, 63, Münster, Aschendorff, 1978, p. 3. 'Mox ut eum videris ad exitum propinquare, communicandus est de sacrificio sancto, etiamsi comedisset (comedisse) ipso dei, quia communio ei defensor et adiutor in resurrectione iustorum. Ipsa enim resuscitabit eum. Post communionem percepta (praecepta) legenda sunt passionis dominicae ante corpus infirmi seu presbiteri seu diaconi, quousque egrediatur anima de corpore.' Frederick S. Paxton, *Christianizing Death: The Creation of the Ritual Process in Early Medieval Europe*, Ithica and London, Cornell University Press, 1990, p. 39.

33 Paxton, *Christianizing Death*, p. 93.

34 Paxton, *Christianizing Death*, p. 93.

35 Kenneth Stevenson has noted in both the work of Van Gennep and others the way in which ritual studies have thrown light on the origins of liturgies, and is aware of their use in the field of Christian initiation. He writes about the 'deep structures' within the marriage services of the early medieval West, but he does not refer to Paxton's work on funerary rites published the year before his chapter, which substantially develops this point. Kenneth W. Stevenson, 'The Pastoral Offices' in Kenneth W. Stevenson and Bryan Spinks (eds), *The Identity of Anglican Worship*, London, Mowbray, 1991, p. 104.

36 Paxton, *Christianizing Death*, p. 116.

37 Paxton, *Christianizing Death*, p. 78.

38 *Sancti Caesarii Arelatensis opera omnia*, ed. G. Morin, vol 2, *Opera varia*, Maretioli, 1942, p. 127. 'Liceat ei transire portas infernorum et vias tenebrarum maneatque in mansionibus sanctorum.' Paxton, *Christianizing Death*, p. 54.

39 Paxton, *Christianizing Death*, p. 100.

40 See 'Journeying' and 'Commendatory Letters' in William Smith and Samuel Cheetham (eds), *A Dictionary of Christian Antiquity*, London, John Murray, 1875, vol. 1, pp. 891 and 407.

3 Discovering the Ancestors

1 Butler, *Dictionary of National Biography*, 1912–21, Oxford, Oxford University Press, 1927, p. 47.

2 This would be the *Rituale Romanum* then currently in use in the Roman Catholic Church in England, which was increasingly of interest to Church of England clergy and others responding to the influence of the Oxford Movement.

3 Many of the people who helped me have died before this book was published, but Father Unsworth died long before I began!

4 Edmund Bishop, *Liturgica Historica*, Oxford, Clarendon Press, 1918, pp. 182–92.

5 Damien Sicard later discovered a manuscript which filled this gap.

6 Louis Gougaud, 'Étude sur les "Ordines commendationis animae"', *Ephemerides liturgicae*, 49, 1935, pp. 1–27.

7 Gougaud, 'Étude', 12. The work he refers to is Ludwig Fischer, 'Commendatio animae' in *Lexikon für Theologie und Kirche*, ed. Martin Buchberger, Freiberg, 1930, vol. 2, cols 16–17.

8 Gougaud, 'Étude', pp. 26–7.

9 Gougaud, 'Étude', p. 25.

10 Damien Sicard, *La liturgie de la mort dans l'église latine des origines à la réforme carolingienne*, Liturgiewissenschaftliche Quellen und Forschungen 63, Münster. Aschendorff, 1978.

11 J. K. Elliott, *The Apocryphal New Testament*, Oxford, Clarendon Press, 1993, p. 616.

12 Damien Sicard, 'Preparation for Death and Prayer for the Dying' in *Temple of the Holy Spirit*, trans. M. J. O'Connell, New York, Pueblo, 1983, p. 243.

13 As Rorem, who has written the standard work on Dionysius, says, 'They were actually written some five hundred years later, although we do not know precisely when or where ... We do not know its birthday, its native land, or its author. The personal identity of the writer is still a mystery, and he is known only and awkwardly as Pseudo-Dionysius, or Dionysius the Pseudo-Areopagite.' Paul Rorem, *Pseudo-Dionysius*, New York and Oxford, Oxford University Press, 1993, p. 3. Rorem usually refers to the writer as Dionysius, and this book follows his example.

14 John M. Wallace-Hadrill, *The Frankish Church*, Oxford History of the Christian Church, Oxford, Clarendon Press, 1983, p. 226.

15 Jacques Paul Migne (ed.), *Patrologiae cursus completus, Series Latina*, Paris, Garnier Fratres, 1844–1904, p. 122, cols 1029–194.

16 Judith Herrin, *The Formation of Christendom*, Oxford, Blackwell, 1987, p. 394.

17 Herrin, *The Formation of Christendom*, p. 394.

18 Rorem, *Pseudo-Dionysius*, p. 5.

19 Bishop, *Liturgica Historica*, p. 191. The book in which he published his writings was Edmund le Blant, *Étude sur les Sarcophages chrétiens de la ville d'Arles*, Paris, 1878.

20 'Coupe de Podgoritza' in *Dictionnaire d'archéologie chrétienne et de liturgie (DACL)*, ed. Fernand Cabrol and Henri Leclercq, vol. 3, Paris, Libraire Letouzey et Ané, 1907–53, Part 2, col. 3010.

21 See, for example, a mid-twentieth-century follower, Werner

Notes 181

Keller, *The Bible as History: Archaeology Confirms the Book of Books*, trans. William Neil, London, Hodder & Stoughton, 1956.

22 F. van der Meer and Christine Mohrmann, *Atlas of the Early Christian World*, trans. and ed. Mary F. Hedlund and H. H. Rowley, London, Nelson, 1958, pp. 53–5.

23 Gougaud, 'Étude', p. 26.

24 Thierry Ruinart, *Passio S Philippi, Acta primorum martyrum sincera et selecta*, Paris, F. Muguet, 1689, p. 452: 'qui servasti Noë et Abrahae divitias obtulisti, qui liberasti Isaac, et parasti pro eo victimam; qui cum Jacob exercitatus es palaestra dulcedinis, et eduxisti Loth ex Sodomis de terra maledicta; qui visus es Moysi, et Josu Nave prudentem fecisti; qui cum Joseph iter habere dignatus es, et eduxisti populum ejus de terra Aegypti; ad terram repromissionis adducens; qui auxilio fuisti tribus pueris in camino, quos sancto majestatis tuae rore perfusos flamma non attigit; qui leonum ora clausisti, vitam Daniëli et cibum tribuens; qui Jonam nec maris profundo, nec morsu ceti crudelis exceptum laedi passus es aut perire; qui Judith armasti, qui liberasti Susannam a judicibus injustis; qui Hester gloriam dedisti, qui Aman perire jussisti; qui eduxisti nos de tenebris ad lumen aeternum.'

25 The translation here is taken from Sicard, 'Preparation for Death', p. 244.

26 Damien Sicard, 'Christian Death' in *The Church at Prayer, Volume III: The Sacraments*, ed. A. G. Martimort, trans. M. J. O'Connell, London, Geoffrey Chapman, 1987, p. 233.

27 The full text of the prayers can be found in *DACL*, vol. 12, Part 2, cols 2332–4.

28 Sicard, 'Preparation for Death', p. 244.

29 Fernand Cabrol, *Liturgical Prayer: Its History and Spirit*, trans. a Benedictine of Stanbrook, London, Burns, Oates & Washbourne, 1922, p. 118.

30 Ruinart, *Acta primorum*, p. 441.

31 Bede, *A History of the English Church and People*, trans. and intro. Leo Sherley-Price, rev. R. E. Latham, London, Penguin, 1955, pp. 289–94.

32 Wetti was offered the help of Samson, who had resisted temptation for most of his life, but Samson never appears in the *Proficiscere*.

33 David A. Trail, *Walahfrid Strabo's Visio Wettini: Text, Translation and Commentary*, Bern and Frankfurt/M, Lang, 1974.

34 Anton Baumstark, 'Untersuchungen' in Anton Baumstark and Kunibert Mohlberg, *Die älteste erreichbare Gestalt des Liber Sacramentorum anni circuli der römischen Kirche*. Liturgiegeschichtliche Quellen, 11/12, Münster, Aschendorffsche Verlag, 1927, pp. 146–8.

35 For a modern study, which dates the manuscript between 820 and the 840s, see Michelle P. Brown, *The Book of Cerne*, London, The British Library; Toronto, University of Toronto Press, 1996, p. 164.

36 'Peccauimus domine Peccauimus parce peccatis nostris et salua nos qui gubernasti noe super undas dilui exaudi nos et ionam diabiso uerbo reuocasti libera nos qui petro mergenti manum porrexisti auxiliare nobis christe fili dei ficisti mirabilia domine cum patribus nostris et nostris propitiare temporibus emite manum tuam de alto libera nos christe audi nos christe audi nos christe audi nos cyrie elezion.' *The Stowe Missal*, vol. II, ed. G. F. Warner, Henry Bradshaw Society, vol. XXXII, London, Henry Bradshaw Society, 1915, p. 3.

37 Esther de Waal, *Celtic Light: A Tradition Rediscovered*, London, Fount, 1991, pp. 113–14.

38 *Stowe Missal*, pp. xxiii–xxxvii.

39 *Félire Óengusso Céli Dé, The Martyrology of Oengus the Culdee*, ed. Whitley Stokes, Henry Bradshaw Society, vol. XXIX, London, Henry Bradshaw Society, 1905.

40 De Waal, *Celtic Light*, p.114.

41 Tom O'Loughlin, *Celtic Theology: Humanity, World and God in Early Irish Writings*, New York, Continuum, 2000, p. 88, but in *Journeys on the Edges: The Celtic Tradition*, London, Darton, Longman & Todd, 2000, p. 144, he dates it as early ninth century.

42 Tom O'Loughlin, letter, 30 September 2000.

43 *The Book of Aedeluard the Bishop, commonly called The Book of Cerne*, ed. A. B. Kuypers, Cambridge, Cambridge University Press, 1902, p. xxx.

44 *The Book of Saints*, compiled by the Benedictine Monks of St Augustine's Abbey, Ramsgate, London, A. & C. Black, 1934, p. 253.

45 *Butler's Lives of the Saints: New Full Edition*, vol. 10, October, rev. Peter Doyle, Tunbridge Wells, Burns & Oates; Collegeville, Minn., The Liturgical Press, 1996, p. 102.

46 Colm Luibheid, *Pseudo-Dionysius: The Complete Works*, New York, Paulist Press, 1987, p. 285.

4 Extinction and New Species

1 See, for example, Charles Nevinson (ed.), *Later Writings of Bishop Hooper*, Cambridge, Cambridge University Press, 1852, vol. II, p. 31.

2 See, for example, Aubrey Townsend (ed.), *The Writings of John Bradford*, Cambridge, Cambridge University Press, 1853, vol. II, p. 279.

3 For a useful study of their writings, see Philip E. Hughes, *The Theology of the English Reformers*, London, Hodder & Stoughton, 1965, pp. 47–75.

Notes

4 Horton Davies, *Worship and Theology in England: From Cranmer to Baxter and Fox, 1534–1690,* Grand Rapids, Eerdmans, 1970, p. 18.

5 Christopher Haigh, *English Reformations,* Oxford, Clarendon Press, 1993, p. 66.

6 Claudia Carlen, *The Papal Encyclicals 1878–1903,* Wilmington NC, McGrath, 1981, p. 208.

7 F. M. Comper (ed.), *The Book of the Craft of Dying,* London and New York, Longmans, 1917, p. 48. A copy of this book, from which Comper made her translation, is held in the British Museum. She gives its reference as C. 11, c.8.

8 Quoted in Nancy L. Beaty, *The Craft of Dying,* New Haven and London, Yale University Press, 1970, p. 127.

9 Beaty, *The Craft of Dying,* p. 129.

10 John Ayre (ed.), *Prayers and Other Pieces of Thomas Beacon,* Cambridge, Cambridge University Press, 1844, p. 179.

11 The only other writer to reverse the order of the parts of the prayer was Cardinal Newman.

12 The abbreviated form adumbrates some of the twentieth-century versions to be examined in Chapter 6.

13 Ayre, *Prayers,* p. 188.

14 Beaty, *The Craft of Dying,* p. 130.

15 Beaty, *The Craft of Dying,* pp. 173–4.

16 St Edmund Campion (1540–81), a Jesuit, was executed for conspiracy against the Crown. In 1970 he was canonized as one of the Forty English and Welsh Martyrs who were put to death between 1535 and 1680.

17 Beaty, *The Craft of Dying,* n183. The quotation is taken from Denis Meadows, *Elizabethan Quintet,* London, Longmans, Green, 1956, pp. 173–5. Meadows' full text reads: 'At the very end Father Persons made a sign and whispered a request to someone, lay brother infirmarian, student, or his *socius* (priest assistant). From among the scanty personal belongings which a Jesuit can call his own, more or less, there was brought him his most precious possession, the rope with which Edmund Campion had been hanged at Tyburn on the stormy morning of December 1, twenty-nine years earlier. Father Persons kissed the rope and had it put round his own neck as the ministering priest read the prayers of the dying, which begin, *Proficiscere, anima Christiana* ...' (p. 175).

18 John Cosin, *A Collection of Private Devotions,* ed. P. G. Stanwood, Oxford, Clarendon Press, 1967, pp. 279–80.

19 Jeremy Taylor, *The Rule and Exercises of Holy Dying* in *The Whole Works of the Right Rev. Jeremy Taylor,* ed. Reginald Heber, vol. IV, London, Ogle Duncan, 1822, p. 555.

20 This is Manual 15 in J. D. Blom, *The Post Tridentine English*

Primer, Catholic Records Society Publications Monograph Series, vol. 3, 1982.
21 *A Manual of Prayer*, 1614, Preface, no page number.
22 *A Manual of Prayer*, pp. 357–8.
23 J. D. Crichton, *Worship in a Hidden Church*, Dublin, Columbus Press, 1988, p. 43.
24 F. E. Brightman, *The English Rite*, vol. 2, London, Rivingtons, 1921, pp. 839–41.

5 Victorian Revival

1 *Prayers for the Dead: For the Use of Members of the Church of England*, London, James Toovey, 1845.
2 *Prayers for the Dead*, p. 72.
3 It is also worth noting that, in spite of the popularity of *The Dream of Gerontius*, it does not seem to have inspired in Victorian spirituality a rediscovery of the doctrine of purgatory.
4 John Henry Newman, *Apologia pro vita sua*, London, Longman, Green, Longman, Roberts and Green, 1864. In the *Apologia* Newman sets out, in autobiographical style, the growth and development of his spiritual and religious life. The postscript to it is dated 4 June 1864, which sets the completion of it very much in the context of the mood which led to the writing of *The Dream of Gerontius* seven months later.
5 The full text is to be found in *Meditations and Devotions of the late Cardinal Newman*, ed. William P. Neville, London, Longmans, Green & Co., 1893, pp. 607–9.
6 *The Letters & Diaries of John Henry Newman*, vol. XXI, ed. C. S. Dessain and E. E. Kelly, London, Nelson, 1971, p. 364.
7 Elizabeth Jay, 'Newman's Mid-Victorian Dream' in David Nicholls and Fergus Kerr (eds), *John Henry Newman: Reason, Rhetoric and Romanticism*, Bristol, The Bristol Press, 1991, pp. 219–20.
8 This was an attempt by Newman and others to allow Roman Catholics to attend Oxford University. However, on 13 December 1864 the Roman Catholic Bishops of England passed resolutions in favour of an absolute prohibition on Oxford being used for the education of Roman Catholics.
9 Wilfred Ward, *The Life of John Henry Cardinal Newman*, London, Longmans, Green & Co., 1912, pp. 76–7.
10 Jay, 'Newman's Mid-Victorian Dream', p. 216. Although Newman was composing apparently in something of a frenzy this did not stop him continuing his correspondence with a wide variety of people, including continuing correspondence about a petition to the Propaganda in Rome against the decision of the English Bishops. See, for

example, *Letters & Diaries*, vol. XXI, pp. 388–407, for his correspondence over the same period.

11 Rowell adds to this point, 'The "friends around the bed" are literally there in Newman's room at the Oratory in Birmingham, where his Anglican friends' pictures were pasted up on the screen which separated the bed-space.' Letter, 7 September 1999.

12 Geoffrey Rowell, *Hell and the Victorians*, Oxford, Clarendon Press, 1974, p. 159.

13 Jay, 'Newman's Mid-Victorian Dream', pp. 221–2, quoting from *Apologia*, ed. M. J. Svaglic, Oxford, Oxford University Press, 1967, p. 137.

14 It will be remembered that Becon in *The Sicke Mannes Salve* was the only other writer to reverse the order.

15 *Meditations and Devotions*, p. vii.

16 *Meditations and Devotions*, p. vi.

17 *Meditations and Devotions*, p. 294.

18 As will be seen in Chapter 6, this is a pattern adopted in *Common Worship*.

19 *Letters & Diaries*, vol. XXI, p. 534.

20 *Letters & Diaries*, vol. XXI, p. 72.

21 *Letters & Diaries*, vol. XXI, p. 498, n2.

22 *Letters & Diaries*, vol. XXI, p. 498.

23 Henry Tristram (ed.), *John Henry Newman: Autobiographical Writings*, London, Sheed & Ward, 1956, p. 264.

24 William Bennett, *The Monthly Musical Record*, February 1933, reproduced in G. Hodgkins (ed.), *The Best of Me: A Gerontius Centenary Companion*, Rickmansworth, Elgar Enterprises, 1999, pp. 137–8.

25 On checking in *Letters & Diaries*, vol. XXXI, which covers this period, it is surprising to find that there is no mention of this letter. There is a letter of the same date, 7 April 1885, in which he wrote to Mrs Murphy thanking her for showing her the volume and returning it to her, but none to Dean Church.

26 In the typically romantic style of some of Newman's early biographers, Henri Bremond says, 'It was perhaps the last thing Gordon read before his heroic death.' Henri Bremond, *The Mystery of Newman*, trans. H. C. Corrance, London, Williams and Norgate, 1907, p. 86, n2.

27 Geoffrey Rowell, letter, 7 September 1999.

28 The following account of Elgar's struggles is taken from Hodgkins, *The Best of Me*.

29 Ward, *Life*, vol. II, pp. 356–7.

30 Alan Wilkinson, *The Church of England and the First World War*, London, SPCK, 1978, p. 176.

31 Wilkinson, *The Church of England*, p. 178.
32 Wilkinson, *The Church of England*, p. 175.
33 Because this chapter has to avoid any attempt to become an intellectual history of the nineteenth century, it is not possible to detail the impact of the thinking of Darwin, Marx and Freud.
34 J. N. Moore, *Edward Elgar: A Creative Life*, Oxford, Oxford University Press, 1984, pp. 674–82, 705.
35 Tony Walter, *The Revival of Death*, London and New York, Routledge, 1994, p. 15. The contribution of Walter will be explored further in Chapter 7.

6 Old and New Liturgical Uses

1 Brian Morris, 'Introduction' in Brian Morris (ed.), *Ritual Murder: Essays on Liturgical Reform*, Manchester, Carcanet Press, 1980, p. 8.
2 Morris, 'Liturgy and Literature' in *Ritual Murder*, p. 61.
3 Morris does not make the point, but this is the opposite position of those who have responsibility for historic church property; their policy is increasingly oriented towards the conservative preservation of the past rather than innovation.
4 Phyllis James, Michael Perham and David Stancliffe, 'Image, Memory and Text' in Michael Perham (ed.), *The Renewal of Common Prayer: Unity and Diversity in Church of England Worship*, London, SPCK, 1993, p. 27.
5 Perham, *Renewal of Common Prayer*, p. 35. Substantially the same point was made by Kenneth Stevenson in the Introduction: 'People need also, at times of stress or illness, to be able to draw on a reservoir of material that lies deep within their soul', p. 4. It is interesting to note that these are apparently the only two references to 'soul' in the book.
6 Paul Badham, 'God, the Soul, and the Future Life' in S. T. Davis, *Death and Afterlife*, London, MacMillan, 1989, p. 36.
7 Badham, 'God, the Soul, and the Future Life', p. 47.
8 It is unfortunate that Badham does not indicate the sources for the phrases he uses, as it leads to a speculation that a circular process is taking place if the *Concise Oxford Dictionary* has drawn its definitions for the soul from the same sources.
9 Other writers have attempted to avoid dualism. Paul Sheppy introduced two new uses of the words *bios*, 'that which the self organises in order to be a living being', and *zoe*, 'the God-ward orientation of *bios*'. Paul Sheppy, 'Towards a Theology of Transition' in Peter C. Jupp and Tony Rogers (eds), *Interpreting Death: Christian Theology and Pastoral Practice*, London, Cassell, 1997, pp. 44–5.
10 John Austin Baker, review of Peter C. Jupp and Tony Rogers (eds),

Notes

Interpreting Death: Christian Theology and Pastoral Practice in *Mortality*, vol. 4, no. 2, July 1999, Oxford, Carfax, p. 205.

11 For an analysis and discussion of this survey, see Grace Davie, *Religion in Modern Europe*, Oxford, Oxford University Press, 2000, pp. 5–13.

12 Quadrant, the Christian Research Association, quoting research by Opinion Research Business for the BBC in *Free Church Chronicle*, November 2000, vol. LIII, no. 2, p. 10.

13 Douglas Davies and Alistair Shaw, *Reusing Old Graves: A Report on Popular British Attitudes*, Crayford, Kent, Shaw & Sons, 1995, pp. 92–3.

14 See R. C. D. Jasper, *The Development of the Anglican Liturgy 1662–1980*, London, SPCK, 1989, pp. 358, 359. It is unfortunate that Jasper ends his study in 1980 so this excludes the reintroduction of the *Proficiscere* in the 1983 *Ministry to the Sick* services. Jasper only makes a passing reference to the 1983 services and offers no real analysis or comment.

15 See, for example, *Prayer and the Departed: A Report of the Archbishops' Commission on Christian Doctrine*, London, SPCK, 1971; *The Commemoration of Saints and Heroes of the Faith in the Anglican Communion: The Report of a Commission appointed by the Archbishop of Canterbury*, London, SPCK, 1957; and Jasper, *The Development of the Anglican Liturgy*, pp. 319–321.

16 On the Parliamentary battles over the 1928 Prayer Book, see Jasper, *Development of the Anglican Liturgy*, pp. 113–42. The Episcopal version starts, 'Depart, O Christian Soul out of this world' and does not include the line, 'In communion with the blessed saints'.

17 *Book of Common Prayer with the Additions and Deviations Proposed in 1928*, London, Oxford University Press, 1928, p. 416.

18 *Praise God*, London, Baptist Union of Great Britain and Ireland, 1980. The prayer was repeated in *Patterns and Prayers for Christian Worship: A Guidebook for Worship Leaders*, Baptist Union of Great Britain, Oxford, Oxford University Press, 1991, p. 150, reproduced by permission of the Baptist Union of Great Britain.

19 *Patterns and Prayers*, p. 150.

20 For an initial discussion, see John Lampard, 'Funeral Liturgies of the Free Churches' in Peter C. Jupp and Tony Rogers (eds), *Interpreting Death: Christian Theology and Pastoral Practice*, London, Cassell, 1997, pp. 185–7.

21 It should be pointed out that worship books such as *Praise God* and *Patterns and Prayers* do not carry the same authorization or even 'norm' which the worship books of many other churches carry. They can be used, adapted or ignored by ministers, so objections are likely to be more muted than in, for example, the Church of England.

22 Conversation, 5 November 1999.
23 Paul P. J. Sheppy, *Death Liturgy and Ritual*, vol. II, *A Commentary on Liturgical Texts*, Aldershot, Ashgate, 2004, p. 126.
24 Sheppy, *Death Liturgy and Ritual*, p. 126.
25 *The Promise of His Glory: Services and Prayers for the Season from All Saints to Candlemas*, London, Church House Publishing/Mowbray, 1991.
26 *The Promise of His Glory*, pp. 102–11. This text is taken from David Silk (ed.), *Prayers for Use at the Alternative Services*, London, Mowbray, 1980, rev. edn, 1986.
27 There are a number of volumes setting out the Documents: see for example, Walter M. Abbott (ed.), *The Documents of Vatican II*, London, Geoffrey Chapman, 1966; and the fuller, *Documents on the Liturgy, 1963–1979, Conciliar, Papal, and Curial Texts*, Collegeville, The Liturgical Press, 1982.
28 *Ordo Unctionis infirmorum eorumque pastoralis curae*, Rome, Editio Typica, Typis Polyglottis Vaticanis, 1972.
29 *Norms Governing Liturgical Calendars*, Liturgy Documentary Series vol. 6, Washington DC, US Conference of Catholic Bishops Publishing, p. 75. And see D. H. Farmer (ed.), *The Oxford Dictionary of Saints*, Oxford, Clarendon Press, 1978, p. 369.
30 *The Rites of the Catholic Church: As Revised by Decree of the Second Vatican Council and Published by Authority of Pope Paul VI*, New York, Pueblo Publishing Co., 1976; *Pastoral Care of the Sick: Rites of Anointing and Viaticum*, Dublin, Veritas Publications; London, Geoffrey Chapman, 1983. The English translation of the Prayer of Commendation of the Dying from *Pastoral Care of the Sick* © 1982, International Committee on English in the Liturgy, Inc. All rights reserved.
31 Michael Hodgetts, 'Revising the Order of Christian Funerals' in, F. C. Finn and J. M. Schellman (eds), *Shaping English Liturgy*, Washington DC, The Pastoral Press, 1990, pp. 208–9. It is not clear why Hodgetts refers to '1970', perhaps he meant '1970s'.
32 '*Libero-are*: liberate, free, acquit, discharge', *Dictionary of Ecclesiastical Latin*, Peabody, Mass., Hendrickson, 1995; '*Libero*: to set free, liberate, deliver, release', *Cassell's Latin Dictionary*, London, Cassell, 1948.
33 The Lukan version (Luke 11.2–4) does not contain the line.
34 NRSV.
35 REB and the English Language Liturgical Commission (ELLC), *Praying Together*, Norwich, Canterbury Press, 1988, p. 1. This is a revision of *Prayers We Have in Common*, ICET, 1975.
36 For a detailed discussion in relation to funerals, see Michael

Notes   189

Hodgetts, 'Revising the Order of Christian Funerals'; and for an English contribution, see Mark T. Elvins, *Towards a People's Liturgy: The Importance of Language*, Hereford, Gracewing, Fowler Wright Books, 1994.

37 This is a quotation from Jerome, *Interpret. Chron. Euseb. Pamph.*, Praef.: *PL* 27, 36.

38 *Documents on the Liturgy, 1963–1979*, p. 273.

39 *Ministry to the Sick: Authorised Alternative Services*, Cambridge, Cambridge University Press, 1983. Note: as with *The Alternative Service Book*, this service book is jointly published with William Clowes (Publishers), Oxford University Press and SPCK.

40 *Ministry to the Sick*, p. 39, © The Central Board of Finance, 1983, The Archbishops' Council 1999, reproduced by permission.

41 Colin Buchanan, *Latest Liturgical Revision in the Church of England 1978–1984*, Bramcote, Grove Books, 1984. He acknowledges in the Introduction, 'As before, I have been up to my neck in the middle of the events recorded – and only rarely as an impartial observer!' p. 2.

42 'Optative' is defined by the *Shorter Oxford English Dictionary* as 'having the function of expressing wish or desire'.

43 Colin Buchanan and David Wheaton, *Liturgy for the Sick: The New Church of England Services*, Bramcote, Grove Books, 1983, pp. 25–6.

44 Buchanan, *Latest Liturgical Revision*, p. 31.

45 *Celebrating Common Prayer: A Version of the Daily Office SSF (CCP)*, London, Mowbray, 1992.

46 This was confirmed by the Preface in the 1981 predecessor of the 1992 version, which stated, 'The basis of this revision, therefore, is to supplement *The Alternative Service Book 1980* rather than to supplant, and to provide enriching optional material', p. 6.

47 *CCP*, p. 494. The SSF 1981 version refers to 'news of the death of a brother or sister', p. 317.

48 Frederick Paxton, *Christianizing Death: The Creation of the Ritual Process in Early Medieval Europe*, Ithica and New York, Cornell University Press, 1990, p. 100.

49 The other new funerary rite, which also developed in the twentieth century, is the service for the burial of ashes after a cremation: see *Common Worship: Pastoral Offices*, London, Church House Publishing, 2000, pp. 323–30, and *Methodist Worship Book*, Peterborough, Methodist Publishing House, 1999, pp. 497–500, both of which contain separate services. Earlier books had only suggested possible readings and prayers, but not a separate liturgy.

50 *CCP*, pp. 495–6. Copyright material reproduced with permission.

51 *CCP*, p. 495.

52 The next seven lines are not part of the *Proficiscere* but are

included here as an example of the way in which 'new' material is woven into the traditional text of the *Proficiscere*.

53 See CCP, pp. 329–40, and 431–90.

54 It is apparent from the 1981 Order that the saints there are St Francis and St Clare.

55 See the modern Roman Catholic service already detailed.

56 In a letter dated 29 July 1999, Brother Tristram SSF, who edited both *The Daily Office SSF* and *CCP*, commented: 'Paradise was included here in direct reference to Luke 23:43, though ... it should have been with an upper-case P.'

57 Brother Tristram (letter, 29 July 1999) says that the phrase is taken from the Orthodox Funeral Service, and acknowledges that if he were rewriting this prayer again he would rephrase it, 'for you are his friend'.

58 CCP, p. viii. Did he read 'An Office of Commendation' before he commended the book?

59 Letter from Brother Tristram, 29 July 1999.

60 It is a matter of debate as to whether or not this was a funeral service or a memorial service, as it patently did not follow the form of any recognized Anglican rite for a funeral. Furthermore, I have been informed, on a non-attributable basis, that a full Church of England funeral service was held privately before the coffin was buried at Althrop.

61 Ian Bradley, *God Save the Queen*, London, Darton, Longman & Todd, 2002, p. 156, but he does not quote his source.

62 The Dean of Westminster, the Revd Dr Wesley Carr (who granted permission to reproduce this version), was asked for confirmation of the sources he used in composing this prayer. He replied (letter dated 15 September 1997): 'The version used in the service was largely my own but built upon that which I believe was found originally in the *New Zealand Prayer Book*. That is a simplified version of the old familiar "go forth upon thy journey, Christian soul." I suspect, therefore, that I may merit a footnote!' However, I was present at an informal discussion group (August 2000) which included the Revd Dr Donald Gray, a former Canon of Westminster Abbey, when he seemed to hint that he was the author of the revised prayer!

63 *Funerals and Related Services*, Peterborough, Methodist Publishing House, 1994.

64 *Comments on Funeral and Related Rites* (sic), Papers presented to the Liturgical Sub-Committee, December 1994, 3 and 5.

65 *Further Comments on Funeral and Related Services (from November 1995)*. Papers presented to the Liturgical Sub-Committee, 3.

66 Although the *Methodist Worship Book* is approved by the

Notes

Methodist Conference, ministers are not required to use it. The book represents a standard or a norm for the conduct of the liturgy.

67 *Methodist Worship Book*, p. 431, copyright permission granted by the Trustees for Methodist Church Purposes.

68 *The Funeral Service with Services before and after the Funeral, Prayers and Other Resources*, 1997. Such is the provisional nature of this document that it carries none of the usual publication details.

69 This prayer, with the addition of 'N' at the beginning became one of the two standard versions offered in *Common Worship* (see below).

70 The section 'May the angels lead you' ... 'perpetual light and rest', was omitted from *Common Worship* when it was finally approved.

71 The later part was the second standard version used in *Common Worship*; see below. Extracts from *Common Worship: Pastoral Services* are copyright © The Archbishops' Council 2000; extracts from *The Funeral Services before and after the Funeral, prayers and other resources* (draft) are copyright © The Central Board of Finance of the Church of England 1997, The Archbishops' Council 1999, and are reproduced by permission.

72 *Pastoral Rites: Responses from the Experimental Parishes*, General Synod, Liturgical Commission, GSMisc 531, 1998.

73 *Pastoral Rites*, Part 1, p. 7.

74 *Pastoral Rites*, Part 1, p. 9.

75 *Common Worship: Pastoral Services*, pp. 216–35. The prayers themselves are on p. 229.

76 *Common Worship: Pastoral Services*, pp. 403–4.

77 *The Book of Alternative Services of the Anglican Church of Canada*, Toronto, Anglican Book Centre, 1985, p. 564.

78 *Revised Funeral Rites, 1987*, Edinburgh, General Synod of the Scottish Episcopal Church, 1987.

79 Copyright material taken from *A New Zealand Prayer Book – He Karikia Mihinare O Aotearoa*, Aukland, William Collins, 1989, p. 815, is used with permission.

80 Norman Autton (comp.), *Watch with the Sick*, London, SPCK, 1976, first published as *A Manual of Prayers and Readings with the Sick*, rev. and enlarged with new title, London, SPCK, 1970, p. 92.

81 Bill Kirkpatrick, *Going Forth: A Practical and Spiritual Approach to Dying and Death*, London, Darton, Longman & Todd, 1997, p. 118.

82 J. D. Crichton, *Christian Celebration*, London, Chapman, 1973, p. 189.

83 *In Sure and Certain Hope: Rites and Prayers from the Order of Christian Funerals for the Use of Lay Leaders*, London, Geoffrey Chapman, 1999.

84 *In Sure and Certain Hope*, p. 43.

7 The Liberty to Die

1 *The Oxford Book of American Verse: Chosen and with an Introduction* by F. O. Matthiessen, New York, Oxford University Press, 1950, pp. 414–15. In at least one published version of this poem the last line reads, 'The privilege to die'. This phrase, although very different from that quoted, expresses equally powerfully an underlying theological assumption of this book. For Christians, death and the experience of what lies beyond it is a profound privilege of grace.

2 Tony Walter, *The Revival of Death*, London and New York, Routledge, 1994, p. 11.

3 Walter, *The Revival of Death*, p. 10.

4 Walter, *The Revival of Death*, p. 12.

5 Walter, *The Revival of Death*, p. 13.

6 Laungani Pittu in Colin Murray Parkes, Laungani Pittu and Bill Young (eds), *Death and Bereavement across Cultures*, London, Routledge, 1997, p. 219.

7 David Crystal, 'Liturgical Language in a Sociolinguistic Perspective' in D. Jasper and R. C. D. Jasper (eds), *Language and the Worship of the Church*, London, Macmillan, 1990, p. 121.

8 Crystal, 'Sociolinguistic Perspective', p. 131.

9 J. L. Austin, *Philosophical Papers*, Oxford, Clarendon Press, 1961, pp. 220–39.

10 See A. J. Ayer, *Language, Truth and Logic*, London, Gollancz, 1936.

11 Austin, *Philosophical Papers*, p. 224.

12 Austin, *Philosophical Papers*, p. 226.

13 Austin, *Philosophical Papers*, p. 231.

14 This is not the case with some of the modern versions, which either reduce the number of repetitions or use alternative words.

15 Austin, *Philosophical Papers*, p. 229.

16 Crystal, 'Sociolinguistic Perspective', p. 132. This is not to deny the powerful eschatological looking-forward also contained in liturgy, and in the *Proficiscere*.

17 Crystal, 'Sociolinguistic Perspective', p. 125.

18 Crystal, 'Sociolinguistic Perspective', p. 135.

19 Martimort, *'In Remembrance of Me'*, trans. A. Dean, London, Challoner Publications, 1958, p. 172.

20 Martimort, *'In Remembrance of Me'*, p. 173.

21 Damien Sicard, 'Christian Death', in *The Church at Prayer: An Introduction to the Liturgy, Volume III, The Sacraments*, ed. A. G. Martimort, trans. M. O'Connell, London, Geoffrey Chapman, 1987, p. 233.

22 Sicard, 'Christian Death', p. 235.

Notes

23 Ian Ainsworth-Smith and Peter Speck, *Letting Go: Caring for the Dying and the Bereaved*, London, SPCK, 1982, pp. 73–4.

24 J. D. Crichton, *Christian Celebration: The Mass, The Sacraments, The Prayer of the Church*, London, Geoffrey Chapman, 1973, 2nd edn, 1980, p. 188.

25 Charles W. Gusmer, *And You Visited Me: Sacramental Ministry to the Sick and the Dying*, New York, Pueblo, 1984, pp. 119, 124.

26 Gusmer, *And You Visited Me*, p. 125.

27 Gusmer, *And You Visited Me*, p. 124.

28 Gusmer, *And You Visited Me*, p. 125.

29 John Hinton, *Dying*, London, Penguin, 1967, pp. 139–46, although dated, sets out the moral grounds clearly.

30 W. M. Clements, 'Pastoral Care of the Dying' in Rodney J. Hunter (ed.), *Dictionary of Pastoral Care and Counselling*, Nashville, Abingdon Press, 1990, p. 323.

31 Fr James Curry, 'Cardinal Hume in the Face of Death' in *Priest and People*, vol. 14, November 2000, p. 409.

32 Emma Brockes, 'To the Last Breath' in *Guardian*, 15 January 2002.

33 It can only be a matter of comment that there have not traditionally been comparable Christian prayers offered at the time of birth. Could it be that until recently the moment of birth has been an exclusively female area of activity and most liturgy has, traditionally, been a male preserve? The study of modern feminist birthing rituals, with the possibility of discovering a 'Come forth' equivalent of the *Proficiscere's* 'Go forth', is outside the scope of this book.

Bibliography

Liturgical texts and prayer books

NOTE: A full list of medieval manuscripts containing versions of the *Proficiscere* can be obtained from the author, johnlampard@jlampard.freeserve.co.uk

Alternative Service Book 1980, London, Hodder & Stoughton, 1980.
Andrieu, M. (ed.), *Les Ordines Romani Haut Moyen Age*, Louvain, Spicilegium Sacrum Lovaniense, 1956.
Ars Moriendi (editio princeps c. 1450), a reproduction of the copy in the British Museum, ed. W. H. Rylands, with introduction by G. Bullen, London, Holbein Society/Wymans, 1881.
Becon, T. *Prayers and Other Pieces of Thomas Beacon*, ed. J. Ayre, Cambridge, Cambridge University Press, 1844.
The Book of Aedeluard the Bishop, commonly called The Book of Cerne, ed. A. B. Kuypers, Cambridge, Cambridge University Press, 1902.
The Book of Alternative Services of the Anglican Church of Canada, Toronto, Anglican Book Centre, 1985.
Book of Common Prayer, London, Eyre & Spottiswoode, 1662.
Book of Common Prayer with the Additions and Deviations proposed in 1928, London, Oxford University Press, 1928.
Celebrating Common Prayer: A Version of the Daily Office SSF, London, Mowbray, 1992.
Common Worship, London, Church House Publishing, 2000.
Common Worship: Pastoral Services, London, Church House Publishing, 2000.
Cosin, J., *A Collection of Private Devotions*, ed. P. G. Stanwood, Oxford, Clarendon Press, 1967.
Félire Óengusso Céli Dé, The Martyrology of Oengus the Culdee, ed. W. Stokes, Henry Bradshaw Society, vol. XXIX, London, Henry Bradshaw Society, 1905.

Bibliography

Funeral of Diana, Princess of Wales, printed for the Dean and Chapter of Westminster Abbey by Barnard and Westwood Ltd, 1997.

The Funeral Service with Services before and after the Funeral, Prayers and Other Resources, 1997.

Funeral Services of the Christian Churches in England, Norwich, Canterbury Press, 1986.

Funerals and Related Services, Peterborough, Methodist Publishing House, 1994.

Horae Diurnae, Breviarii Romani, Rome, Marietti, 1925.

In Sure and Certain Hope: Rites and Prayers from the Order of Christian Funerals for the Use of Lay Leaders, London, Geoffrey Chapman, 1999.

Liber Sacramentorum Gellonensis, Corpus Christianorum, Series Latina, CLIX, ed. A. Dumas, Turnhout, Brepols, 1981.

Methodist Worship Book, Peterborough, Methodist Publishing House, 1999.

Ministry to the Sick, Authorised Alternative Services, Cambridge, Cambridge University Press, 1983.

A New Zealand Prayer Book – He Karikia Mihinare O Aotearoa, Aukland, William Collins, 1989.

Ordo Unctionis infirmorum eorumque pastoralis curae, Rome, Editio Typica, Typis Polyglottis Vaticanis, 1972.

Orders of Christian Funerals (Study Edition), London, Geoffrey Chapman, 1991.

Pastoral Care of the Sick: Rites of Anointing and Viaticum, Dublin, Veritas Publications; London, Geoffrey Chapman, 1983.

Patterns and Prayers for Christian Worship: A Guidebook for Worship Leaders, Baptist Union of Great Britain, Oxford, Oxford University Press, 1991.

Praise God, London, Baptist Union of Great Britain and Ireland, 1980.

Prayers for the Dead: For the Use of Members of the Church of England, London, James Toovey, 1845.

Prayers for Use at the Alternative Services, ed. D. Silk, London, Mowbray, 1980, rev. 1986.

Praying Together, Norwich, Canterbury Press, 1988.

The Promise of His Glory: Services and Prayers for the Season from All Saints to Candlemas, London, Church House Publishing/Mowbray, 1991.

Revised Funeral Rites 1987, Edinburgh, General Synod of the Scottish Episcopal Church, 1987.

The Rites of the Catholic Church: As Revised by Decree of the Second Vatican Council and Published by Authority of Pope Paul VI, New York, Pueblo, 1976.

Rituale Romanum; Pauli V Pont. Max. Iussu Editum, Antverpiae (Antwerp), Ex Officina Plantiniana, Apud Balthasarem Moretum, & Viduam Joannis Moreti, & Io. Meursium, 1624.

Ruinart, T. (ed.), Passio S. Philippi, Acta primorum martyrum sincera et selecta. Paris, Muguet, 1689.

Sacramentarium Rhenaugiense (Handschrift Rh 30 der Zentralbibliothek Zürich), ed. A. Hänggi and A. Schönherr, Switzerland, Universitätsverlag Freiburg, 1970.

The Small Ritual, Being Extracts from the Rituale Romanum in Latin & in English, London, Burns & Oates, 1964.

The Stowe Missal, vol. II, ed. G. F. Warner, Henry Bradshaw Society, vol. XXXII, London, Henry Bradshaw Society, 1915.

Watch with the Sick, comp. N. Autton (revised and enlarged with new title, London, SPCK, 1976), first published as *A Manual of Prayers and Readings with the Sick*, London, SPCK, 1970.

Secondary material

Abbott, W. M. (ed.), *The Documents of Vatican II*, London, Geoffrey Chapman, 1966.

Abercrombie, N., *The Life and Work of Edmund Bishop*, London, Longmans, 1959.

Ainsworth-Smith, I. and Speck, P., *Letting Go: Caring for the Dying and the Bereaved*, London, SPCK, 1982.

Austin, J. L., *Philosophical Papers*, Oxford, Clarendon Press, 1961.

Ayer, A. J., *Language, Truth and Logic*, London, Gollancz, 1936.

Badham, P., *Christian Beliefs about Life after Death*, London, SPCK, 1978.

Baumstark, A., *Liturgie Compareé*, Belgium, Éditions de Chevetogne, 1953; ET (third edn rev. B. Botte, 1953), trans. F. L. Cross, *Comparative Liturgy*, London, A. R. Mowbray, 1958.

Baumstark, A. and Mohlberg, K., *Die älteste erreichbare Gestalt des Liber Sacramentorum anni circuli der römischen Kirche*, Liturgiegeschichtliche Quellen, 11/12, Münster, Aschendorffsche Verlag, 1927.

Beaty, N. L., *The Craft of Dying: A Study in the Literary Tradition of the Ars Moriendi in England*, New Haven and London, Yale University Press, 1970.

Bede, *A History of the English Church and People*, trans. and intro. L. Sherley-Price, rev. R. E. Latham, London, Penguin, 1955.

Bishop, E., 'Spanish Symptoms' in *Journal of Theological Studies*, vol.

VIII (1906/07), Oxford, Clarendon Press, 1907.
——, *Liturgica Historica*, Oxford, Clarendon Press, 1918.
The Book of Saints, compiled by the Benedictine Monks of St Augustine's Abbey, Ramsgate, London, A. & C. Black, 1934.
Blunt, J. H., *The Annotated Book of Common Prayer: Forming a Concise Commentary on the Devotional System of the Church of England* (compendious edn), London, Rivingtons, 1888.
Bouyer, L., *Newman: His Life and Spirituality*, London, Burns & Oates, 1958.
Bowker, J., *The Meanings of Death*, London, Cambridge University Press, 1991.
Bradford, J., *The Writings of John Bradford*, ed. A. Townsend, Cambridge, Cambridge University Press, 1853.
Bradley, I., *God Save the Queen*, London, Darton, Longman & Todd, 2002.
Bradshaw, P., *The Search for the Origins of Christian Worship: Sources and Methods of Study of Early Liturgy*, London, SPCK, 1992.
Bradshaw, P. and Spinks, B. (eds), *Liturgy in Dialogue*, London, SPCK, 1993.
Bremond, H., *The Mystery of Newman*, trans. H. C. Corrance, London, Williams and Norgate, 1907.
Brightman, F. E., *The English Rite: Being a Synopsis of the Sources and Revisions of the Book of Common Prayer with an Introduction and an Appendix*, 2nd edn, London, Rivingtons, 1921.
Brown, M. P., *The Book of Cerne*, London, The British Library; Toronto, University of Toronto Press, 1996.
Brown, P., *The Cult of the Saints*, London, SCM Press, 1981.
Buchanan, C., *Latest Liturgical Revision in the Church of England 1978–1984*, Bramcote, Grove Books, 1984.
Buchanan, C. and Wheaton, D., *Liturgy for the Sick: The New Church of England Services*, Bramcote, Grove Books, 1983.
Bugnini, A. and Braga, C. (eds), *The Constitution of the Sacred Liturgy: A Commentary on the Constitution and on the Institution of the Sacred Liturgy*, trans. V. P. Mallon, New York, Benziger Brothers, 1965.
Butler's Lives of the Saints: New Full Edition, vol. 10, October, rev. P. Doyle, Tunbridge Wells, Burns & Oates; Collegeville, Minn., The Liturgical Press, 1996.

Cabrol, F., *Liturgical Prayer: Its History and Spirit*, trans. a Benedictine of Stanbrook, London, Burns, Oates and Washbourne, 1922.
Caldecott, S. (ed.), *Beyond the Prosaic: Renewing the Liturgical Movement*, Edinburgh, T & T Clark, 1998.

Carlen, C. (ed.), *The Papal Encyclicals 1878-1903*, Wilmington, NC, McGrath, 1981.
Carr, W., *Angels and Principalities*, Cambridge, Cambridge University Press, 1981.
Charlesworth, J. H. (ed.), *The Old Testament Pseudepigrapha*, vol. I, *Apocalyptic Literature and Testaments*, London, Darton, Longman & Todd, 1983.
The Commemoration of Saints and Heroes of the Faith in the Anglican Communion: The Report of a Commission appointed by the Archbishop of Canterbury, London, SPCK, 1957.
Comper, F. M. M. (ed.), *The Book of the Craft of Dying, and Other Early English Tracts Concerning Death: Taken from Manuscripts and Printed Books in the British Museum and Bodleian Libraries: Now first done into Modern Spelling*, London, New York, Longmans, Green & Co., 1917.
Crichton, J. D., *Christian Celebration, The Mass, The Sacraments, The Prayer of the Church*, London, Geoffrey Chapman, 1973 (2nd edn, 1980).
——, *Worship in a Hidden Church*, Dublin, Columbus Press, 1988.
——, *Lights in Darkness, Forerunners of the Liturgical Movement*, Dublin, The Columba Press, 1996.
Crystal, D., *Linguistics, Language and Religion*, London, Burns & Oates, 1965.
——, 'Liturgical Language in a Sociolinguistic Perspective' in D. Jasper and R. C. D. Jasper (eds), *Language and the Worship of the Church*, London, Macmillan, 1990.
Cuming, G. J., *A History of Anglican Liturgy*, London, Macmillan, St Martin's Press, 1969.

Davie, G., *Religion in Modern Europe*, Oxford, Oxford University Press, 2000.
Davies, D. J. and Shaw, A., *Reusing Old Graves: A Report on Popular British Attitudes*, Crayford, Kent, Shaw & Sons, 1995.
Davies H., *Worship and Theology in England: From Cranmer to Baxter and Fox, 1534-1690*, Grand Rapids, Eerdmans, 1970.
Davies, J. G., 'Deacons, Deaconesses and the Minor Orders in the Patristic Period', *Journal of Ecclesiastical History*, vol. XIV, 1963.
Davis, S. T., *Death and Afterlife*, London, MacMillan, 1989.
Dessain, S. C. and Kelly, E. J. (eds), *The Letters and Diaries of John Henry Newman*, London, Nelson, 1971.
Dictionary of Pastoral Care and Counselling, ed. R. J. Hunter, Nashville, Abingdon Press, 1990.
Dictionnaire d'Archéologie Chrétienne et de Liturgie, ed. F. Cabrol and

Bibliography

H. LeClercq, Paris, Libraire Letouzey et Ané, 1907-53.
Dictionnaire de Spiritualité Ascétique et Mystique, Paris, Beauchesne, 1960.
The Documents of Vatican II, ed. W. M. Abbott, London, Geoffrey Chapman, 1966.
Documents on the Liturgy, 1963-1979: Conciliar, Papal, and Curial Texts, Collegeville, The Liturgical Press, 1982.

Elliott, J. K. (ed.), *The Apocryphal New Testament*, Oxford, Clarendon Press, 1993.
Elvins, M. T., *Towards a People's Liturgy: The Importance of Language*, Hereford, Gracewing, Fowler Wright Books, 1994.
Every, G., Harries, R. and Ware, K. (eds), *The Time of the Spirit: Readings through the Christian Year*, Crestwood, NY, St Vladimir's Seminary Press, 1984.

Farmer, D. H. (ed.), *The Oxford Dictionary of Saints*, Oxford, Clarendon Press, 1978.
Fenwick, J. R. K. and Spinks, B. D., *Worship in Transition: The Twentieth Century Liturgical Movement*, Edinburgh, T & T Clark, 1995.
Finn, F. C. and Schellman, J. M. (eds), *Shaping English Liturgy*, Washington DC, The Pastoral Press, 1990.
Funk, F. X. (ed.), *Didascalia et Constitutiones Apostolorum*, Paderborn, Schoeningh, 1895.

Gougaud, L., 'Etude sur "les Ordines commendationis animae"', *Ephemerides liturgicae*, vol. 49, 1935.
Gusmer, C. W., *And You Visited Me: Sacramental Ministry to the Sick and the Dying*, New York, Pueblo, 1984.

Haigh, C., *English Reformations: Religion, Politics, and Society under the Tudors*, Oxford, Clarendon Press, 1993.
Herrin, J., *The Formation of Christendom*, Oxford, Blackwell, 1987.
Hinton, J., *Dying*, London, Penguin, 1967.
Hodgkins, G. (ed.), *The Best of Me: A Gerontius Centenary Companion*, Rickmansworth, Herts, Elgar Enterprises, 1999.
Hooper, J., *Later Writings of Bishop Hooper*, ed. C. Nevinson, Cambridge, Cambridge University Press, 1852.
Howard-Johnson, J. and Hayward, P. A. (eds), *The Cult of Saints in Later Antiquity and the Early Middle Ages*, Oxford, Oxford University Press, 1999.
Hughes, P. E., *The Theology of the English Reformers*, London, Hodder & Stoughton, 1965.

Jasper, R. C. D., *Prayer Book Revision in England 1800–1900*, London, SPCK, 1954.
——, *The Development of the Anglican Liturgy 1662–1980*, London, SPCK, 1989.
Jasper, D. and Jasper, R. C. D. (eds), *Language and the Worship of the Church*, Basingstoke, Macmillan, 1990.
Jupp, P. C. and Rogers, T. (eds), *Interpreting Death: Christian Theology and Pastoral Practice*, London, Cassell, 1997.

Keller, W., *The Bible as History: Archaeology Confirms the Book of Books*, trans. W. Neil, London, Hodder & Stoughton, 1956.
Kirkpatrick, B., *Going Forth: A Practical and Spiritual Approach to Dying and Death*, London, Darton, Longman & Todd, 1997.

Larson-Miller, L. (ed.), *Medieval Liturgy: A Book of Essays*, New York, Garland, 1997.
Le Goff, J., *The Birth of Purgatory*, trans. A. Goldhammer, London, Scolar Press, 1984.
Liturgiam Authenticam: On the Use of Vernacular Languages in the Publication of the Books of the Roman Liturgy, Rome, Congregation for Divine Worship and the Discipline of the Sacraments, 2001.
The Liturgical Portions of the Apostolic Constitutions: A Text for Students, trans., ed., ann. and intro. W. J. Grisbrooke, Alcuin/GROW Liturgical Study 13–14 (Grove Liturgical Study 61), Bramcote, Grove, 1990.
Luibheid, C. (trans.), *Pseudo-Dionysius: The Compete Works*, The Classics of Western Spirituality, New York, Paulist Press, 1987.

Maine, B., *Elgar: His Life and Works*, Portway, Bath, Cedric Chivers, 1933.
Martène, M., *De antiquis ecclesiae ritibus*, vols 1–3, Rouen, Behourt, 1700–02.
Martimort, A.-G., *In Remembrance of Me*, trans. A. Dean, London, Challoner Publications, 1958.
——, 'Prayer for the Sick and Sacramental Anointing' in A. G. Martimort (ed.), *The Church at Prayer: An Introduction to the Liturgy, Vol. III, The Sacraments*, the authorized translation of *L'Eglise en Prière: Les Sacraments*, Paris-Tournai, Desclée, 1984, trans. M. J. O'Connell, London, Geoffrey Chapman, 1987.
Martin, D. and Mullen, P. (eds), *No Alternative: The Prayer Book Controversy*, Oxford, Blackwell, 1981.
Meadows, D., *Elizabethan Quintet*, London, Longmans, Green, 1956.

Bibliography

van der Meer, F. and Mohrmann, C., *Atlas of the Early Christian World*, trans. and ed. M. F. Hedlund and H. H. Rowley, London, Nelson, 1958.

Migne, J. P. (ed.), *Patrologiae cursus completus, Series Latina*, Paris, Garnier Fratres, 1844–1904.

Mirgeler, A., *Mutations of Western Christianity*, trans. E. Quinn, from *Rückblick auf das abendländische Christentum*, Mainz, Matthias Grünewald, 1961; London, Burns & Oates, 1964.

Moore, J. N., *Edward Elgar: A Creative Life*, Oxford, Oxford University Press, 1984.

Moreton, B., *The Eighth-Century Gelasian Sacramentary*, Oxford, Oxford University Press, 1976.

Morris, B. (ed.), *Ritual Murder: Essays on Liturgical Reform*, Manchester, Carcanet Press; London, Darton, Longman & Todd, 1980.

Mursell, G., *English Spirituality: From Earliest Times to 1700*, London, SPCK; Louisville, KY, Westminster John Knox Press, 2001.

Myres, W. M., *The Book of Common Prayer compared 1549–1886*, London, Griffith, Farran, Okeden & Welsh, 1887.

Newman, J. H., *Apologia pro vita sua: Being a Reply to a Pamphlet entitled, 'What, then, does Dr Newman Mean?'*, London, Longman, Green, Longman, Roberts and Green, 1864.

——, *The Dream of Gerontius*, London, Burns & Oates, 1865.

——, *Meditations and Devotions*, London, Longmans, Green & Co., 1893.

——, *Verses on Various Occasions*, London, Burns, Oates & Co., 1868.

Nicholls, D. and Kerr, F. (eds), *John Henry Newman: Reason, Rhetoric and Romanticism*, Bristol, The Bristol Press, 1991.

Norms Governing Liturgical Calendars, Liturgical Documentary Series vol. 6, Washington DC, US Conference of Catholic Bishops Publishing.

Nunn, H. P. V., *Christian Inscriptions – Texts for Students*, London, SPCK, 1920.

O'Connor, M. C., *The Art of Dying Well: The Development of the Ars Moriendi*, New York, Columbia University Press, 1942.

O'Loughlin, T., *Celtic Theology, Humanity, World and God in Early Irish Writings*, New York, Continuum, 2000.

——, *Journeys on the Edges: The Celtic Tradition*, London, Darton, Longman & Todd, 2000.

Oxford Book of American Verse: Chosen and with an Introduction, comp. F. O. Matthiessen, New York, Oxford University Press, 1950.

Palazzo, E., *A History of Liturgical Books: From the Beginning to the Thirteenth Century*, trans. M. Beaumont, Collegeville, Minn., The Liturgical Press, 1998.

Parkes, C. M., Pittu, L. and Young, B. (eds), *Death and Bereavement across Cultures*, London, Routledge, 1997.

Pastoral Rites: Responses from the Experimental Parishes, General Synod, Liturgical Commission, GSMisc 531, London, Church House Publishing, 1998.

Paxton, F. S., *Christianizing Death: The Creation of the Ritual Process in Early Medieval Europe*, Ithica and New York, Cornell University Press, 1990.

Perham, M. (ed.), *The Renewal of Common Prayer: Unity and Diversity in Church of England Worship*, London, SPCK, 1993.

Prayer and the Departed: A Report of the Archbishops' Commission on Christian Doctrine, London, SPCK, 1971.

RB 1980, The Rule of St. Benedict in Latin and English with Notes, ed. T. Fry, Collegeville, Minn., The Liturgical Press, 1980.

Riché, P., 'Spirituality in Celtic and Germanic Society', trans. D. Tamburello in B. McGinn and J. Meyendorff, *Christian Spirituality: Origins to the Twelfth Century*, Vol. 16 of *World Spirituality: An Encyclopaedic History of the Religious Quest*, London, Routledge, 1986.

Rorem, P., *Pseudo-Dionysius: A Commentary on the Texts and an Introduction to their Influence*, New York and Oxford, Oxford University Press, 1993.

Rowell, G., *Hell and the Victorians*, Oxford, Clarendon Press, 1974.

——, *The Liturgy of Christian Burial*, London, Alcuin Club/SPCK, 1977.

——, 'The Dream of Gerontius' in *The Ampleforth Journal*, vol. 73, ii, 1968.

Russell, J. C., *The Germanization of Early Medieval Christianity*, New York and Oxford, Oxford University Press, 1994.

Rutherford, R. and Barr, T., *The Death of a Christian: The Order of Christian Funerals*, rev. edn, Collegeville, Minn., The Liturgical Press, 1990.

Savage, A. and Watson, N. (eds), *Anchorite Spirituality: Ancrene Wisse and Associated Works*, New York, Paulist Press, 1991.

Sheppy, P. P. J., *Death Liturgy and Ritual*, vol. II, *A Commentary on Liturgical Texts*, Aldershot, Ashgate, 2004.

Sicard, D., *La liturgie de la mort dans l'église latine des origines à la réforme carolingienne*, Liturgiewissenschaftliche Quellen und

Forschungen, 63, Münster, Aschendorff, 1978.

———, 'Préparation à la Mort et prière pour les agonisants' in *La maladie et la mort du chrétien dans la liturgie, Conférences Saint-Serge, XXI, 1974*, Bibliotheca EL, Subsida 1; Rome, Edizioni liturgiche, 1975; ET, 'Preparation for Death and Prayer for the Dying' in *Temple of the Holy Spirit: Sickness and Death of the Christian in the Liturgy*, trans. M. J. O'Connell, New York, Pueblo, 1983.

———, '*La Mort du Crétien*' in R. Cabié, et al., *L'Eglise en Prière, Les Sacraments*, ed. A. G. Martimort et al., Paris-Tournai, Desclée, 1984; ET, 'Christian Death' in *The Church at Prayer: An Introduction to the Liturgy, Volume III, The Sacraments*, ed. A. G. Martimort, trans. M. J. O'Connell, London, Geoffrey Chapman, 1987.

Souter, A., *A Glossary of Later Latin to 600 AD*, Oxford, Clarendon Press, 1949.

Stevenson, K. and Spinks, B., *The Identity of Anglican Worship*, London, Mowbray, 1991.

Stevenson, K. (ed.), *Liturgy Reshaped*, London, SPCK, 1982.

Taylor, J., *The Rule and Exercises of Holy Dying* in *The Whole Works of the Right Rev. Jeremy Taylor*, ed. R. Heber, London, Ogle Duncan, 1822.

Trail, D. A., *Walahfrid Strabo's Visio Wettini, Text, Translation and Commentary*, Bern and Frankfurt/M, Lang, 1974.

Tristram, H. (ed.), *John Henry Newman: Autobiographical Writings*, London, Sheed & Ward, 1956.

Van Gennep, A., *The Rites of Passage*, Chicago, Chicago University Press, 1960.

Vidler, A. R., *A Variety of Catholic Modernists*, Cambridge, Cambridge University Press, 1970.

Vogel, C. *Medieval Liturgy: An Introduction to the Sources*, trans. and rev. W. Storey and N. Rasmussen, Washington, The Pastoral Press, 1986.

de Waal, E., *Celtic Light: A Tradition Rediscovered*, London, Fount, 1991.

Wallace-Hadrill, J. M., *The Frankish Church*, Oxford History of the Christian Church, Oxford, Clarendon Press, 1983.

Walter, J. A., *Funerals and How to Improve Them*, London, Hodder & Stoughton, 1990.

———, *The Revival of Death*, London and New York, Routledge, 1994.

Ward, B., *Miracles and the Medieval Mind*, Aldershot, Wildwood, 1987.

———, *Signs and Wonders*, Aldershot, Variorum, 1992.

Ward, W., *The Life of John Henry Cardinal Newman*, London, Longmans, Green & Co., 1912.
Wessels, A., *Europe: Was it Ever Really Christian? The Interaction Between Gospel and Culture*, trans. J. Bowden, London, SCM Press, 1994, from J. *Kerstening en Ontferstening van Europa. Wisselwerking tussen Evangelie en Cultuur*, Baarn, Uitgeverij Ten Have, 1994.
Wilkinson, A., *The Church of England and the First World War*, London, SPCK, 1978.

Index

Ainsworth-Smith, Ian, 167
Arezzo, Sacramentary of, 49
Ars Moriendi (The Art of Dying), 14, 80, 89–90, 99, 108
Art and Craft to Know Well to Die, The, 90
Austin, J. L., 157–161, 164, 170
Autton, Norman, 147–8

Badham, Paul, 119–120
Baptist Union of Great Britain, 124
Baumstark, Anton, 38, 68–9
Becon, Thomas, 91, 93, 148
Bede, The Venerable, 67
Benedict of Nursia, 13, 33, 38, 45
Bibliotheca Vallicelliana, viii, xi, 1
Bibliothèque Mazarine, viii, 31
Bibliothèque Nationale, viii, xviii
Bishop, Edmund, 53–4, 56, 60–1

Blant, Edmund le, 60
Boniface, St., 38, 76
Book of Common Prayer, see Prayer Books
Bradshaw, Paul, 35
Burley Methodist Church, Leeds, 163

Carr, Wesley, xxi
Catacombs of Priscilla, viii, 62
Catholic Church, xviii, 2, 12, 46, 51, 85, 127–8, see also Roman Catholic Church
Caxton, William, 90
Celebrating Common Prayer (1992), 134–5, 138, 142
Collection of Private Devotions (1627), 93
Cerne, Book of, 68, 74–5
Church of England, xviii, xix, xxi, 84–5, 94, 96, 99, 103, 115, 122–3, 125–6, 133–5, 138–41, 143, 145–6
Clements, W. M., 171

Commendation of the Soul, xviii, 1, 44, 48–9, 54, 73, 80, 85, 87, 94, 96, 99, 106–7, 135, 148, 151, 160
Common Worship (2000), 142–3, 145
Cosin, John, 93
Crichton, J. D., 96, 148, 168–9
Crystal, David, 154–7, 161–2, 164, 170

Death, changing attitudes to, xix, xxiv–xxvi, 30, 36, 40, 42–6, 50–1, 80–5, 90–1, 97, 116, 121–2, 132, 152–4, 165–74
de Waal, Esther, 69, 73
Diana, Princess, xxi, 139–40
Dionysius, 5–6, 9, 12, 58–60, 77
Dream of Gerontius, The, xx, xxiv–v, 99–104, 108–11, 113–15, 123, 147–8
Driscoll, Michael, 40

Eighth-century Gelasian, *see* Frankish Gelasian
Elgar, Edward, xx, xxi, xxiv, xxv, 98, 110–15
Euplus, St., 63, 66
Euthanasia, euthanastic prayer, xxvi, 5, 116, 170, 173

Falkiner, Mollie, 163

First Booke of Christian Exercise, 93
Fischer, Ludwig, 54
Frankish Church, xvii, 8, 14, 30–46, 59, 68–9, 74
Frankish Gelasian Sacramentaries, 32–5, 53, 56, 68, 73

Gelasian Sacramentary, *see* Frankish Gelasian Sacramentaries
Gellone, Sacramentary of, xviii, 6, 22–3, 32–9, 42, 46, 49, 53, 59, 63, 69, 73–4, 143
Gougaud, Dom Louis, 54, 56, 63, 68, 74
Gordon, General, 111
Green, Bernard, 124–5
Gregory I, Pope, 33–4, 43
Gusmer, Charles, 169
Gy, P.-M., viii, 54–6

Herrin, Judith, 59–60
Hume, Cardinal Basil, 172

Irish monks, 37

Jay, Elizabeth, 101–3

Kirkpatrick, Bill, 148
Knowles, David, 28,

Luther, Martin, 79, 85

Martène, Edmund, 31, 53

Index

Martimort, A. G., 66, 165–6
Methodist Church, ix, xxiv, 139–42, 163
Methodist Worship Book (1999), xxiv, 140–3
Ministry to the Sick (1983), 133–4
Mirgeler, Albert, 27–8, 36
Moreton, Bernard, viii, 32–6

Newman, Cardinal J. H, xvi, xx, xxi, xxv, 5, 89, 98–112, 114, 123, 125, 129, 131, 137, 140, 143, 147–8
New Zealand, Prayer Book (1989), 145
Nursia, Sacramentary of, xiii–xv, xxv, 1, 4, 8, 20, 28, 46–9, 56, 62, 131, 174

Oengus, Maryrology of, 68–74
O'Loughlin, Tom, viii, 73–4
Oscott College, Birmingham, viii, xix, 94–5
L'Ottobonianus 312, 43

Palazzo, Eric, 35
Parsons (Persons), Robert, 93
Pastoral Care of the Sick (1983), 127
Patterns and Prayers (1991), 124
Paul, Apocalypse of, 57–8
Paul and Thecla, Acts of, 23

Páxton, Frederick, 42–5, 48
Peregrinatus, 37–9
Pickard, Don, ix, 164
Podgoritza, Cup of, 61
Promise of His Glory, The (1981), 126
Praise God (1980), 124
Prayer Book, (1549), 93
Prayer Book, (1662), 98, 126
Prayer Book, (1928), 122, 134, 143, 147–8
Pseudo-Cyprianus, 63–6
Pseudo-Dionysius, *see* Dionysius
Purgatory, 7–8, 82, 106, 143, 165

Rheinau, Sacramentary of, 6, 13, 23, 34, 39, 42, 46, 48–9, 53, 56, 68, 73–4, 76–7
Riché, Pierre, 40–1
Ritual (Rituale Romanum) (1614), 49, 50, 53, 80, 85–7, 94–6, 99–100, 116
Ritual (Rituale Romanum) (1925), 88–9, 96
Roman Catholic Church, 26, 51, 85–7, 89, 96, 103, 126–8, 130, 132, 149, 167–8
Rorem, Paul, 60,
Rowell, Geoffrey, ix, 102, 104, 111
Ruinart, T, 67
Rule and Exercises of Holy Dying, The (1651), 94

Russell, James, 41

Sarum Missal, xviii
Severus, St., 63–6
Sheppy, Paul, ix, 54, 125
Sicard, Damian, 54–6, 64–6, 165–7
Sick Mannes Salve, The (1561), 91–2
Soul, problem of using, 119–23
Speck, Peter, 167
Stowe Missal, 68
Sure and Certain Hope, In (1999), 96, 148
Symon, John, 171,

Taylor, Jeremy, 94
Thecla of Kitzingen, 76–7
Thecla, St., 23–6, 57, 64–5, 76, 128, 175

Tristram SSF, Brother, viii, 139

Unsworth, Father, 53

Vatican II, 12, 55, 86–7, 127–8
Vatican Library, Rome, 43
Viaticum, the, 5, 48, 169
Vogel, Cyrille, 34

Wallace-Hadrill, John, 36–8
Walter, Tony, 116, 152–4, 168
Ward, Wilfred, 101–2, 111, 114
Wessels, Anton, 37–9
Wetti, 68
Wilkinson, Alan, 115

www.ingramcontent.com/pod-product-compliance
Lightning Source LLC
Chambersburg PA
CBHW070249230426
43664CB00014B/2466